HOW TO

BE A FRIEND

TO A FRIEND

WHO'S SICK

HOW TO
BE A FRIEND
TO A FRIEND
WHO'S SICK

LETTY COTTIN POGREBIN

PublicAffairs
New York

Published in the United States by PublicAffairs™,
a Member of the Perseus Books Group

PublicAffairs books are available at special discounts for bulk purchases in the
U.S. by corporations, institutions, and other organizations. For more information,
please contact the Special Markets Department at the Perseus Books Group, 2300
Chestnut Street, Suite 200, Philadelphia, PA 19103, call (800) 810-4145, ext. 5000,
or e-mail special.markets@perseusbooks.com.

Book Design by Pauline Brown

Library of Congress Cataloging-in-Publication Data

Pogrebin, Letty Cottin.
  How to be a friend to a friend who's sick / Letty Cottin Pogrebin.—First edition.
     pages   cm
  Includes bibliographical references and index.
  ISBN 978-1-61039-283-9 (hardcover)—978-1-61039-284-6 (e-book) 1. Care of
the sick—Psychological aspects. 2. Caregivers. 3. Helping behavior. 4. Diseases—
Psychological aspects. I. Title.
  R726.5.P62 2013
  610—dc23

                                                           2012049749

First Edition

10 9 8 7 6 5 4 3 2 1

*To all those who shared
their stories and their secrets,
and to Dr. Larry Norton*

If I can stop one heart from breaking,
I shall not live in vain;
If I can ease one life the aching,
Or cool one pain,
Or help one fainting robin
Unto his nest again,
I shall not live in vain.

—EMILY DICKINSON

CONTENTS

WHO AM I AND WHY THIS BOOK

I'M NOT A DOCTOR, SOCIAL WORKER, PSYCHOLOGIST, religious leader, or grief counselor—so who am I to write this book? Very simply, I'm someone who has—whoops, who *had*—cancer. I'm also a woman with lots of friends and a writer who became fascinated by the disconnect between how people treat sick people and how sick people wish to be treated. To illuminate this phenomenon I started with my firsthand experience, buttressed it with some research, and conducted nearly eighty in-depth interviews with other sick people, many of them my fellow patients at the Memorial Sloan-Kettering Cancer Center. I've distilled everything into a book that I know can make you a better friend to a friend who's sick. Before the movie begins, let's cut to the chase. Here's what you're going to learn in these pages: empathy translated into action equals kindness. It's a foolproof formula; all you need is the appropriate vehicle for your best impulses and the commitment to stick it out over the long haul. I'm sure you already know how to "be friends" when it means catching up over lunch, sitting side by side at a ball game, or texting each other about a movie. But when a pal or loved one falters physically or mentally—when they're hobbled or hurting, when your role in the relationship is no longer easy or obvious, when your interests and exchanges are not entirely reciprocal, and your once-easy conversation tips jarringly toward matters of crisis and pain—you may have to find new ways of being together, new means for you to be helpful, and new words to keep things real.

My sensitivity to these issues was sharply honed when I observed my friends' responses to me after I was diagnosed. But the most valuable lessons in this book came from my fellow patients who comprise the majority of those I interviewed for this book. Though strangers to one another, we shared a commonality of crisis that inspired mutual revelation, a situational intimacy that somehow entitled me to ask astonishingly personal questions and get remarkably candid answers. Like seatmates on a long plane trip, we had nothing to lose by opening up to each other and letting the truth leak out—a truth with no consequences because we knew it could be recorked when we parted company, never to see one another again.

Entering other people's truth, I learned that illness is friendship's proving ground, the uncharted territory where one's actions may be the least sure-footed but also the most indelible; that illness tests old friendships, gives rise to new ones, changes the dynamics of a relationship, causes a shift in the power balance, a reversal of roles, and assorted weird behaviors; that in the presence of a sick friend, fragile folks can get unhinged and Type A personalities turn manic in order to compensate for their impotence; and that hale fellows can become insufferably paternalistic, and shy people suddenly wax sanctimonious.

Other patterns took shape in these testimonies: not all sick people want the same amount or kind of attention. Women and men tend to "do" friendship and illness differently. A joke amusing to one patient can be offensive to another. A squeeze of the hand can feel comforting when one friend does it, patronizing when the hand belongs to someone else. Emotions stirred by illness can be overwhelming, a friend's symptoms alienating, medical jargon intimidating. Someone else's health crisis can trigger memories of our own past ordeals or those of a person we loved. It's not uncommon for people to freeze or panic in the company of misery, botch gestures that were meant to ease, attempt to problem-solve when we have no idea what we're talking about, say the wrong thing, talk too much, fidget in the sick room, sit too close to the patient or stand too far away. Some of us don't visit our sick friends at all. Others visit, overstay, and make things worse. Some bring an inappropriate gift or arrive empty handed, only to be mortified when they find the sickroom stuffed with bouquets and balloons.

The stories I collected from others helped me understand my own reactions and fueled my determination to be a better friend to my ailing friends. Among other lessons, I learned that it's not enough to be a good-hearted person if you're oblivious to the pain in someone's eyes; that friendship can nourish, help, and heal but also disappoint and suffocate. With every interview I marveled at how thin and permeable is the membrane between good intentions and bad behavior, how human it is to be both strong and vulnerable, and how people process the sickness, stress, and sorrow of their friends in many different ways.

My interviewees' generosity, their willingness to spend time talking to me, to revisit painful memories and share their often hard-won advice has been the making of this book. But fair warning: some of their tips may seem platitudinous or self-evident to you (or maybe just to me). I've included them nonetheless because they were repeated often enough to suggest that they're not so obvious or intuitive to everyone else. If 5 or 10 percent of the advice makes you wince, I beg your indulgence on behalf of those readers who need a little extra help being helpful.

Likewise, some advice will be irrelevant to what's happening in your life at the moment. You may not have any relatives with prostate cancer, friends who are slipping into dementia, or whose kids are terminally ill. Remember that this book does not have to be read from cover to cover; it can be dipped into as needed. You can skim the chapter titles, hone in on what you need to know right now, and set the book aside for future reference when those other awful situations eventually crop up. And trust me, they will.

This book couldn't have been written a generation ago when many sick people—especially those with cancer, invisible diseases like diabetes or heart disease, and mental disorders—were as closeted as many gay people were at that time and as reluctant to divulge their condition for fear of being penalized or stigmatized for it. In the case of ailments and infirmities, the zeitgeist changed radically with the passage of the Americans with Disabilities Act in 1990 and the explosion of tell-all talk shows, Internet medical sites, and online chat rooms tailored to specific afflictions.

Also crucial to the changing environment is the fact that so many well-known people have gone public with their diseases (most on their own initiative, though some involuntarily). Think Elizabeth Edwards, Ann Romney, Sheryl Crow, Christina Applegate, and Betty Ford (breast cancer); Kitty Dukakis, Dennis Quaid, Bob Dylan, Lindsay Lohan (addiction); Michael J. Fox, Muhammad Ali, Billy Graham, Johnny Cash (Parkinson's); Michael Douglas (throat cancer); Steve Jobs (pancreatic cancer); Barbara Walters and Rosie O'Donnell (heart disease); Princess Diana (eating disorder); Sheryl Crow (brain tumor); Glen Campbell, Loretta Young, Iris Murdoch, Ronald Reagan or, rather, Nancy on his behalf (Alzheimer's); Dick Clark, Gerald Ford, Della Reese, Ted Williams, and Clarence Clemons of the E Street Band (stroke); Catherine Zeta-Jones, Kurt Cobain, Britney Spears, Mariette Hartley (bipolar disorder); Harry Belafonte, Robert De Niro, Colin Powell, John Kerry, and Rudy Giuliani (prostate cancer); Lance Armstrong (testicular cancer); Earvin "Magic" Johnson, Rock Hudson, Anthony Perkins, former Playboy Playmate Rebekka Armstrong, and New York State Senator Thomas Duane (HIV or AIDS); Richard Pryor, Montel Williams, Joan Didion (multiple sclerosis); Neil Young, Elton John, Margot Hemingway, and Danny Glover (epilepsy); Drew Barrymore, Elton John, Steven Tyler, Ben Affleck, Texas Governor Ann Richards, Stephen King, Anthony Hopkins, and, again, Betty Ford (alcoholism), to name just a few.

Although we might decry "sick celebrity" stories as carrion for pop culture vultures, the mainstreaming of headliners' illnesses produces the salutary by-product of a more informed public. Ordinary people struggling with similar issues feel less isolated and more normalized for having a problem that Diana, De Niro, or Didion shares, and the rest of us know a lot more than we otherwise would about the causes, symptoms, and treatment of various ailments and diseases.

If I had to get cancer, I couldn't have picked a better era in which to do it. Not only did the web provide copious answers to my most arcane questions, but I never had to hide what I had. (In some cases health insurance discrimination and workplace bias *do* require people to conceal their conditions, but that's another story.) As soon as I was diagnosed, I "outed" myself. Unashamed, I was open to advice and able to connect with other women in the same boat. Best of all, I felt free to share my ups and downs with my friends, fellow patients, and now with you.

MY SUMMER
OF BLISS

JUNE 9, 2009. MY AWESOMELY BIG BIRTHDAY wasn't as bad as I'd expected. Taking stock of my life and circumstances, my main sensation was astonishment at having reached this age at all, much less in good health and fine fettle. Seventy! Incredible! Surreal! Formidable! A number I never thought I'd see. My mother died at fifty-three. I had already outlived her by seventeen years. I thought I had dodged the bullet. I thought I was home free.

My well-being was nothing short of intoxicating. I had more energy than women half my age. I could still walk miles at a fast clip without puffing, get by on five hours sleep, or pull an all-nighter to meet a deadline without paying for it the next day by drag-assing around. Though deeply dismayed by world events—that summer it was the economic downturn, the Israeli invasion of Gaza, the reelection of Iranian president Mahmoud Ahmadinejad, to name a few calamities—I was utterly content with my own little patch of reality, my marriage, family, work, and friendships. No, wait—at the risk of sounding like a complete cornball, what I felt in June 2009 was much bigger and more buoyant than contentment: it was euphoria.

As a birthday gift to myself, I started a journal in which I hoped to snare a few drive-by epiphanies about aging, chronicle my daily activities, and secretly crow about how amazed I was to find myself happy at seventy. (Secretly because I'm too superstitious to tempt the Evil Eye by crowing out loud about anything good.) As poets know, the smooth topography of pleasure is harder to render with originality or precision than the craggy landscape of sorrow, but I wanted to try to put into words how it felt to have finally made peace with my years.

Seventy, quite simply, was my best birthday since I turned ten (ahh! double numbers, at last!). It was even better than my twentieth, when I celebrated my liberation from my teens by moving into my first single-girl apartment in Greenwich Village. After turning twenty-one and the thrill of casting my first-ever vote for John F. Kennedy in the 1960 presidential election, none of my birthdays seemed worth celebrating because each brought me one year closer to the age my mother died. But it was the decade upticks that really sent me reeling.

Thirty was the first shocker. As a refugee from the "Never trust anyone over thirty" generation (Abbie Hoffman, the high priest of rebellious youth, was a Brandeis classmate of mine and a fellow cheer-leader), finding myself on the uncool side of the divide was deeply disorienting. Forty unsettled me because I felt as if half my life was gone and I hadn't accomplished enough. Fifty triggered time tremors so seismic I felt compelled to make sense of them in a memoir entitled Getting Over Getting Older (which, in fact, I hadn't). Sixty piled on the existential stress plus physical depredations that accumulated daily. But seventy was different. Seventy was sublime. On June 9 the universe shifted on its axis and my half-full glass became a bottomless jug. To borrow one of Johnny Mercer's lyrics, I began to "Accentuate the posi-tive, eliminate the negative, and latch onto the affirmative." Though still obsessing over the swift passage of time, still feeling compelled to make each day count, still worried about what might go wrong (an occupational hazard for Jews of my generation) and which of my loved ones might die (a fear common to those who've lost a parent in childhood), I also found myself reveling in the glory of the good stuff. Suddenly, the name of the game was gratitude. My default verbs were "savor" and "celebrate." I was alive and well at seventy! Who'd have thunk it?

One weekend in July, my husband, Bert, and I and our immediate family—a lucky thirteen altogether—gathered on Shelter Island to celebrate my birthday. After a beautiful dinner at sunset, all of us seated at a long picnic table overlooking the glistening harbor, we adjourned to the house. I sat back and allowed myself to be feted and fussed over by my husband, son, daughters, sons-in-law, and grandchildren, who all plied me with original poetry, skits, speeches, and songs while I did nothing but embrace the bliss.

My journal's woefully inadequate attempt to wrestle that evening's pleasure into prose includes this banality that at the time struck me with the force of an Aha! moment: "I realized tonight in the midst of being lavishly celebrated that what entitles me to enjoy the blessings of this precious family is the fact that I've used up seventy years of my time on earth by amassing loved ones, life, and memories. That's the trade-off: gain life, lose time. The past is our reward for spending down our future. To this, my grandkids would no doubt say, 'Well, duh!' but its obviousness doesn't make the thought less profound. At ten and at twenty, I had years ahead of me but none of this lived bliss."

At seventy I was too busy counting my blessings to count my years. Instead of doing my usual number on myself and ruminating on the relatively short time I have left—sixteen-point-five years, according to the actuarial tables for the average seventy-year-old white American female—I focused on how much can happen in that period of time. You can grow a large tree in sixteen years, start an internet company and make or lose a fortune, create a whole person from nothing—Justin Bieber, for example, or my six grandchildren, none of whom existed sixteen years ago. In sixteen years you can change deeply entrenched national habits and cultural perceptions—for instance about homosexuality or smoking. In sixteen years an America that never had a female Secretary of State can see three different women in that office.

Sixteen years was time enough for me, a confirmed Luddite weaned on the typewriter and the turntable, to adjust to computers, cassettes, floppies, CD-ROMs, VCRs, VHS, and DVDs. In sixteen years I've conquered inventions that initially seemed indecipherable and daunting, among them Google, Facebook, iTunes, iPhoto, Hulu, Pandora, and Netflix.

When I looked back to where I was in life at age fifty-four, it seemed a very long time ago, and this persuaded me that the next sixteen years can be similarly commodious, abundant, and fully packed.

A journal entry in late August seems especially poignant given how oblivious I was to what would happen to me a month later:

> This summer has been the most contemplative, inner-directed time of my life. After decades of activism and hyperproductivity, my contentment and quietude require no product but their own reward. I can't explain why I feel so serenely happy. Perhaps it's because I have the luxury of being able to say that I don't want anything more from life than what I already have. I just want more of the same. Possessed of this new, bone-deep calm, I watch the lake ripple and shimmer like the folds of a satin skirt and follow the sun until it sinks behind the rim of the mountain and pigments of coral, aqua, and gold dapple the evening sky. I sit and think and feel and cherish. Mostly cherish.
>
> In the book I'm reading, Lost in Translation, Eva Hoffman precisely captures my feelings: "I have stumbled into the very center of plenitude," she writes, "and I hold myself still with fulfillment, before the knowledge of my knowledge escapes me."

That's where I spent every day of the summer of 2009—at "the very center of plenitude." Then I got diagnosed.

EVERYTHING I KNOW
I LEARNED IN THE WAITING ROOM

A woman enlarges all that is given to her,
Give her groceries, she'll make you a meal.
Give her a house, she'll make you a home.
Give her your sperm, she'll give you a baby.
Give her your crap, she'll give you a ton of shit.
Give her cancer, she'll give you a book.

ANONYMOUS WROTE THE FIRST FIVE LINES; I added the sixth because getting cancer put me in treatment, which put me in the waiting room at the Memorial Sloan-Kettering Cancer Center (MSK) every day for six weeks, which put me in proximity with many other patients, who allowed me to do the interviews that put flesh on the bones of this book. Here's how it all began.

September 28, 2009. Yom Kippur, the Day of Atonement. I spend hours in synagogue, doing what Jews are supposed to do: I resolve to be a better person in the New Year, which, according to the Hebrew calendar is 5770.

September 29. I start the year by going in for my annual mammogram. No big deal: routine checkup, you know the drill. After flattening your breasts like a couple of paninis, the technician usually takes your films to the radiologist, returns five minutes later, and says, "You're fine. Get dressed." This time the technician says the radiologist, Dr. Julie

Mitnick, needs more X-rays, a sonogram or two or four. The technician goes through her paces then sends me back to the waiting room, where I sit cocooned in my hospital gown and wait. Twenty minutes go by. Half an hour. Finally, Dr. Mitnick herself comes out and beckons me to follow her to a small private consulting room. I already know what she's going to say.

Betty Rollin titled her groundbreaking breast cancer memoir *First, You Cry,* but when I hear "suspicious mass," I don't shed a tear; I go numb. A nurse asks if I want to call my husband. Bert races over from his office in record time and accompanies me from one overly air conditioned clinical room to another, where a CT-scan and MRI confirm the presence of a tumor in the upper quadrant of my right breast.

My calendar chronicles the ensuing events in a terse chronology:

September 30. Biopsy. Tumor definitely malignant.

October 2. MRI. Establishes exact location.

October 19. Meeting with breast surgeon.

October 22. X-rays. Blood work.

October 28. CT Scan.

October 29. Injection of nuclear dyes (to map tumor). Scan. Tattoo marks breast for eventual X-ray beams and positioning of radiation treatments.

October 30. Lumpectomy surgery.

During one of my delusional postsurgical reveries a scrap irony zips by in headline form: "Feminist Activist Stricken with Quintessentially Female Disease." Just as construction workers get mesothelioma from overexposure to asbestos, it seems entirely possible that I contracted breast cancer from overexposure to women's troubles. After all, I'd spent four decades immersed in the thick of the women's movement as a founding editor of *Ms.* magazine, the bible of mainstream American feminism. I was a veteran of a feminist consciousness-raising group that met once a week for four years. I was the cofounder of more than a dozen women's organizations, commissions, and dialogue groups.

I'd been privy to the most searing particularities of male sexism and female pain and heard countless stories about the indignities and abuse visited upon women by their partners, spouses, fathers, brothers, uncles, bosses, teachers, and classmates. As an activist, I'd marched, demonstrated, picketed, petitioned, sat in, and rabble roused on behalf of gender equality and women's rights. As a journalist, I'd covered pro-choice conferences and rape speak-outs, written hundreds of articles about the exploitation and intimidation of women, pregnancy discrimination, domestic violence, sex trafficking, sex stereotypes, women in poverty, gender bias in schools, sexual harassment on the job, and male supremacy on the home front.

No surprise, then, that I become convinced, in my semi-anesthetized state, that my body had absorbed all that female angst and compacted it into the tumor whose excision would eradicate the misery afflicting womankind. This hi-falutin', self-referential fantasy was overtaken, when I came to, by a stabbing pain under my arm and the realization that, though the tumor had been removed from my breast, sexism's sins were still intact.

January 2, 2010. Begin radiation.

Okay, so I got diagnosed the day after the Jewish New Year, and I'm starting my journey back to health the day after the secular New Year. Nice frame, but try as I may, I find no mystical meaning in it. All I know is that when I leave my apartment on that cold winter morning and walk across Central Park to MSK for my first treatment, I'm revved up to get zapped in the breast and stunned to find that the X-ray monster and its operatives aren't ready for me. Don't they know how nervous I am, how desperate I am to get this over with, how fragile, skittish, and scared I feel?

The first day my wait is forty-five minutes. Often I wait more than an hour for my treatment room to open up. The radiation itself takes just a few minutes, but the time I spend beforehand in the waiting room and the time it takes the technicians to set up the machines properly add uncountable hours to the process. Once I realize that great chunks of my life are about to coagulate into shapeless sludge within the walls of MSK, I stop wearing a watch. I train myself to ignore the A.M. and P.M. line on my BlackBerry screen, the clock on the wall, the watches on other people's wrists. The least I can do is spare myself the quantification of time slipping away—another loss.

Like my fellow wait-ers, I sorta-kinda keep track of who arrives in what order so that none of us gets taken out of turn. I gaze out the window at the schoolyard below. I drink too many cups of coffee, check my e-mail, study the changing cast of characters, the receptionists' family photos, the Christmas cards still taped to the walls, the communal tissue box set within easy reach to accommodate our sniffles and tears. Before long the waiting room at MSK is as familiar to me as my apartment.

It angers me that sick people have to wait for everything and everybody—doctors, nurses, callbacks, lab results, prescriptions, medications, technicians, treatment rooms. If illness is the embodiment of powerlessness, which, believe me, is true, then waiting is its temporal incarnation. Waiting is time's carnivore; it eats away your life. It's the enemy of sublimation, the ally of anxiety and fear. It mires the mind in a stew of what-ifs, fatality statistics, the perils of a foreshortened future. I wait for my name to be called; when it is, I proceed to the women's locker room, strip to the waist, don a hospital gown, and schlep myself to another waiting room where I wait for my treatment chamber to become available. Once inside this holy sanctum I wait for the technicians to set up the machinery that must be tilted, tuned, and calibrated to the precise location of my former tumor.

"Why is nothing ready on time?"

"Sorry, Ma'am."

"How come no one's available when they're supposed to be?"

"Can't be helped."

"Any idea when they'll get to me?"

"Nope, you'll just have to wait!"

Which is exactly what I do every day for six weeks because I have no choice, no control whatsoever, and I know it. Were I to complain, I'm afraid the technicians who *are* in control might retaliate by making me wait even longer for the zapper that's supposed to burn my chest but save my life. Once, when I log nearly three hours in a chair in the waiting room, I mouth off a little to a passing technician. With fatigue in his voice he explains that the schedule for my treatment room first got bollixed when they had to wait for a patient who'd recently had a stem cell transplant to stop vomiting long enough to lie down under the machine. The patient after him, a three-year-old with brain cancer, was so panicky and fought the technician so frantically that she finally had to be anesthetized to stop her from squirming. Needless to say I'm ashamed of myself and quickly apologize for my impatience. That's the last time I grumble. How dare I complain when others are going through so much worse?

Not just my type of diagnosis but my radiation experience makes me one of the lucky ones: though serious burns and debilitating fatigue are common hazards of these treatments, mine are painless. My skin tans rather than fries, and I feel no lag in energy. Still, in six weeks I smile only once, when Lenny, the technician with the thin mustache and the plummy British accent, greets me with a courtly bow, gestures toward the long metal slab on which I'm to stretch out under the X-ray monster, and says, "Good day, Madam, your table is waiting."

This particular morning I awake to a howling blizzard. Having committed myself to trekking to the hospital on foot every day for fitness's sake regardless of the weather, I bundle up, pull on my snow boots, and set out across Central Park. The serpentine paths are blanketed in white, and my footprints, the first to despoil the snow, leave deep marks.

I'm reminded of my surgery of two months ago and how the scars from the lumpectomy and node excision have left their marks on this phase of my life just as deeply as the jagged belly-button-to-pubic-bone incision from my emergency C-section marked me decades ago when I delivered full-term twins. The scars on women's bodies tell the stories of our lives. Men show off their battle scars. How odd that we hide ours when we should be flaunting them as proof of our heroism.

Thick flakes swirl in the wind like goose feathers unloosed from a gigantic pillow. I cross Fifth Avenue and head east on Sixty-Seventh Street, mini-icicles dancing on the tips of my eyelashes, snow melting between my neck and the collar of my parka. Soaked and shivering, I finally push through the doors of MSK, telling myself that if I come down with pneumonia, at least I'll be near hundreds of doctors.

Then again, I'll probably have to wait for one of them to see me.

The technicians stay the same, the routine stays the same, the out-of-date magazines stay the same; only the patients in the waiting room keep changing. This morning the room is a beehive of activity, people stomping caked snow off their galoshes, shaking their wet coats like dogs after a swim, spreading their sodden gloves on the radiator grill to dry—and talking to each other! I'm stunned to find our normally leaden waiting room abuzz with convivial camaraderie and light-hearted banter. The snowstorm has broken the ice. Rather than hide behind their newspapers, my colleagues are trading stories about how they got here, where they started out, what weather-related hardships they endured en route. A woman with wind-burned cheeks is grousing about the neighbor who didn't show up that morning as promised.

"She said she was gonna take the subway with me and keep me company in the waiting room. I don't need company, y'know. I just need to count on someone when she says she's gonna do something."

"It's about being reliable," says the thin woman in rimless glasses, casting a soft smile at the teenager beside her, probably a grandson. The man in a Mets hoodie nods, and the young couple lock eyes in a way that suggests that they too have been let down by someone they trusted.

My mind slaloms down a mountain of recent memories, past all the friends who, in the current parlance, "have been there for me" every day in every way. It skids to a stop at the one friend who hasn't—a close pal who, after I told her I had cancer, never called or wrote or asked how I was, though we often found ourselves in the same room together. I wonder how many other people in my situation have experienced such wild extremes of fealty and neglect. I think about the people I had expected to be the most supportive and the people who actually were as well as how hard it was to forecast who would be which.

I ponder what made me allow some friends to get in close while keeping others at a distance. I wonder what other sick people do to protect themselves against annoying friends and what sort of friends make them feel comfortable and safe. I Google "friendship and illness" on my BlackBerry: 7 million results. A scroll through the first couple hundred suggests that most entries seem to focus on mental illness and New Age philosophy. A search of Amazon.com yields 117 titles, mostly kids books (*My Friend Has Diabetes, My Friend Has Epilepsy*), teen novels about the impact of illness on adolescent social life, and for the rest of us a slew of spiritual guides, sorrowful but uplifting fiction, and memoirs by people who helped a friend through a crisis. Several sound interesting, but none directly address the questions that have captured my interest: What's the best way to be a friend to a friend who's sick? What happens when illness becomes the third party in a relationship? Does everyone agonize as I did about whom to tell and how much to divulge? Do life-threatening illnesses deepen people's desire for intimacy or make them retreat into themselves? Are others as persnickety as I am about protecting their privacy? How do they deal with friends who are insensitive or say stupid things? Are other sick people as eager as I am to *not* need help? Do their friends' ministrations sometimes make them feel burdened, and if so, have they figured out how, without sounding mean or ungrateful, to ask an overbearing pal to back off? Once or twice I actually felt like shouting, "Thank you for caring. Now leave me alone." Didn't mean it literally—didn't want to be ignored or abandoned—I just wanted my friends to dial back a bit. Is there a nice way to tell someone what you want without sounding like an ungrateful bitch? Even when there's something I need done, why, when my friends ask what they can do for me, do I always say, "Nothing?" What's *that* about?

A new idea begins unspooling in my head. Rather than bewail my daily incarceration in the waiting room, I could write a book on the subject of friendship and illness that would answer all those questions. I'd already established a toehold on the general topic of friendship twenty-five years ago when I published *Among Friends: Who We Like, Why We Like Them, and What We Do with Them.* Back then, however, the depredations of illness and the strains it puts on friendship had barely dented my consciousness. Neither I nor any of my friends had yet been stricken with cancer, heart disease, stroke, Parkinson's, or Alzheimer's. Now, a quarter of a century and uncountable maladies later, life has ripened me for the subject.

I resolve that, as soon as this morning's treatment is over, assuming I can make it home through the blizzard, I'll type up everything I can remember about my interactions with my friends since the day I sent out the group e-mail that divulged my cancer. I'll revisit their reactions to news of my diagnosis, my reactions to their reactions, their questions, my answers, their deeds, my needs, and so on. And because I can't possibly have experienced every permutation of friendship and illness, I decide to start interviewing people of all ages, racial, ethnic, and geographical backgrounds—people like the elderly African American now warming his hands over the radiator, the woman in the green turban at the coffee machine, the emaciated guy with the Walkman, the girl holding her mother's hand.

At this point I'm gripped by an idea that changes everything: I'll use my waiting time to interview my fellow wait-ers, who, like me, are killing time at MSK in the hope that time won't kill them. No need for me to go out and report this story; all the human diversity a writer could wish for passes through this poignant, maddening waiting room every single day. My subjects would be my fellow patients and their accompanying spouses, partners, parents, children, or friends. Cancer is what brought them here, but all of them surely have had other illnesses as well. They all must have friends who have either helped or hurt them, and friends whom they've helped or hurt. And their companions must have been patients themselves at one time or another and have memories of how *their* friends treated them.

Suddenly, the waiting room is transformed from a locus of confinement to a journalistic cornucopia. Because MSK schedules patients' treatments at different times on different days, I would have daily access to a revolving group of subjects who, by virtue of being in this hospital, are authorities on illness and, by virtue of being human, are authorities on friendship.

This book could not have been written without all of them. From the day of the blizzard until the end of my radiation, I spend my waiting time interviewing anyone who is willing to talk—and of the talkers, everyone has a story. When my treatments end I consider returning to the waiting room for more interviews, but I'm too superstitious to tempt fate by hanging out in a cancer hospital when I don't have to. Instead, I conduct additional interviews at random, seeking out those whose experiences might flesh out the story. I talk to sick people, people whose friends are sick, and friends of people who, though not sick themselves, are in pain because someone they love is sick. I log onto disease websites and patients' blogs, solicit anecdotes by e-mail, trawl the Internet for first-person accounts. I interview people who used to be sick but got better, those with chronic illnesses and permanent disabilities, those whose friends received dire prognoses, and those whose loved ones didn't make it.

Ancillary to their illness stories I hear memorable charges that the medical community favors family members and discriminates against friends. One patient is annoyed because his best friend was shooed out of his hospital room at the end of visiting hours while his brother was permitted to stay. A flyer announcing, "Art Therapy Group for Families Coping with Breast Cancer" incenses a patient who tells me that her whole family lives on the West Coast, so the people who've been helping her cope with her breast cancer are her friends, and if anyone needs some art therapy, it's them. At another New York hospital the postsurgical waiting room is called, "The Family Atrium," though some of the most anxious wait-ers aren't family; they're friends of the patient. Visitors are permitted into the recovery room one at a time in five-minute shifts, and the hospital staff summons them by calling out "Murphy family," "Cohen family," "Rodriguez family," and so on. This pisses off at least one person, who tells me, "Hospitals shouldn't assume every visitor is a relative! Why can't they say, 'Visitor for Murphy.' Or, 'Who's here for Cohen?' Or just call out, 'Rodriguez?' Friends shouldn't be invisible at a time like this. We're here. We're waiting five hours for our friend to get out of surgery. This is *not* a second-class relationship."

I love that quote!

Some of my interviewees are comfortable speaking under their own names; others ask to be given a pseudonym or quoted by their first name only. Despite the stylistic inconsistency, I honor everyone's request so they can feel free to speak honestly about their experiences. Though I try to give equal time to both positive and negative stories, you may notice a tilt toward people who failed Friendship 101. That's because I take seriously Eleanor Roosevelt's advice: "Learn from the mistakes of others. You can't live long enough to make them all yourself."

When all is said and done, this book is a hybrid, a quirky amalgam of reportage, memoir, and Baedeker, with some armchair philosophizing tossed in for good measure. Interposed among its ten self-help chapters is my personal sickness story in the form of seven Interludes. In short, rather than a one-size-fits-all formula, what you'll find in these pages are multiple voices—confessional, cautionary, inspiring—and all sorts of practical advice that I'm confident will help you be a better friend to a friend who's sick.

|||||||||||||||||||||||||||||||||||||||||||||||||||||||||||||||||||||||||||||||||||||||||||||||||||||||||||||||||||||||||||||||||||||||||||||||||||

I CAN'T BELIEVE
YOU SAID THAT!

*Goofs, Gaffes, Platitudes, Faux Pas,
Blunders, Blitherings—and Finding
the Right Words at the Right Time*

"A CLOSED MOUTH GATHERS NO FEET."

It's a charming axiom, but silence isn't always an option when you're dealing with someone who's sick or in despair. Say a friend calls to tell you he just found out he has a fatal blood disorder, or your child's teacher shows up on the first day of school with her bald head clearly visible beneath a scarf, or your coworker returns after vacation looking like hell, or you've Googled your friend's ailment and learned that it has a 5 percent survival rate. To forestall a future blooper, let's speculate in advance on how you might react to such common scenarios.

Though the natural human reaction is to express shock and blurt out some cringe-worthy cliché, craven remark, or blunt question, a better option might be to tamp down your unfiltered feelings and come up with a more appropriate response. Otherwise, there's a good chance you'll say something you'll regret.

Most of us feel dis-eased around disease, and colloquial English proffers a sparse vocabulary for embarrassment, fear, anxiety, grief, or sorrow. You don't want to sound like a Hallmark card, but anxiety thickens your tongue. You want to say something real, but the words that come to mind add insult to your friend's injuries. Some verbal gaffes may be amusing to read about; however, when you're the one who misspeaks, words can humiliate you and hurt your friend.

This chapter focuses for the most part on what *not* to say to all sorts of aggrieved people—victims of accidents, stroke, blood poisoning, HIV/AIDS; a wounded veteran or the parents of a dying child—because once you've banished the worst no-nos from your conversational repertoire, you can't do too much damage. You'll also read about the one exclamatory phrase sick people hate to hear, advice about giving advice, reasons why military metaphors are annoying to many patients, and why "You look great!" isn't always a compliment. You'll also learn how to talk to people who are terminally ill as opposed to people who are sick but sociable, and why truth telling should be the new illness etiquette. Finally, to distill the essence of everyone's advice, this chapter will end with ten commandments to help you feel more comfortable conversing with a sick friend.

SELDOM IS HEARD AN ENCOURAGING WORD

||||||||||||||||||||||||||||||||||||||||||||||||||||||||||||||||||||||||||||||||||||||||||

"How'd it go?" Pete, one of the men I interviewed in the waiting room, was asked by his friend Fred.

"Great!" said Pete. "They got it all."

"Really? How do they know?"

If the tone deaf ever need a poster child, Fred's their guy. When Pete told him how demoralizing his remark had been, Fred's excuse was a paltry, "I was nervous, man. I just said what popped into my head."

We're all nervous around illness, misery, and mortality. But these anecdotes, gleaned from my interviews with people in the waiting room and elsewhere, prove that what pops into your head should not necessarily plop out of your mouth.

- When Marian Fontana was diagnosed with breast cancer eight years after her husband, a New York City firefighter, died in the collapse of the World Trade Center, a friend exclaimed, "Wow!! You must have really bad karma. How come you always attract bad luck?"
- After a friend poo-pooed Kathleen Peratis's hip replacement operation as "minor surgery," Kathleen said, "The definition of minor surgery is surgery done on someone else."
- "God, you look awful!" cried a visitor upon entering the sickroom of John Rosove, who was recovering from blood poisoning and a raging fever. "Not helpful," said John.
- Janet Avery, a marathon runner, weight lifter, motivational speaker, and job training specialist, who had a stroke in her early fifties, was often greeted by friends who said, "I can't believe this happened to you!" "You exercised! You ate right! You were so energetic!" The past tense has become Janet's least favorite. "All it does is remind me of what I used to be."
- "At least you're already married," said a friend to Aisha, who'd just had a mastectomy. (You can't make this stuff up!)
- "Lynn! I just heard! Tell me everything!" That was the chirpy message on Lynn Sherr's answering machine when she came home from the hospital after being operated on for colon cancer. She never returned the call.
- "Wow! A girl in my office just *died* of that!" shrieked a friend when Nel was diagnosed with leukemia. Seeing her horrified reaction, Nel's friend back pedaled. "Wait! It wasn't leukemia! It was *lymphoma!* I mixed up my Ls."

- Patrick confided to his brother that his cancer may have spread to his lymph nodes. "What are lymph nodes?" asked his brother. When Patrick couldn't explain what lymph nodes are, the brother scolded, "Shouldn't you be doing more research?"

- Florence was furious when a friend asked her to recommend a good place for a mammogram. "I don't *get* mammograms anymore!! I haven't had breasts for years! I've had two mastectomies! How could my friend forget something that important? When I objected, she said I should be pleased she misspoke because it means she doesn't see me as a woman with no breasts. I said, 'you're wrong, it means you don't see me for who I am, you don't remember what I've been through.'"

- Frank, about to have his prostate removed, was not reassured when his young business partner said, "Don't worry. My dad had that surgery years ago and his cancer didn't come back until he was nearly eighty!" To Frank, who was seventy at the time, nearly eighty didn't sound all that old.

- "Maybe it's in your head," suggested several of Deborah's friends when her doctors had trouble diagnosing her symptoms. Turned out she had Lyme's disease.

- George, a backseat passenger in a head-on collision that killed the driver of the car, suffered PTSD after the accident. Besides sleeplessness, loss of appetite, and depression, he felt the need to keep talking about the crash. After one of these retellings a clueless friend said, "Isn't it time you reached closure?"

Those are some of the crude and insensitive lines that suffering people have to put up with. The next category focuses on run-of-the mill clichés and fancy phrases that all of us have heard (or spoken) hundreds of times—regardless of how untrue, unprovable, or meaningless they may be.

AVOID HACKNEYED PLATITUDES,
EMPTY ELOQUENCE, AND FEEL-GOOD CLICHÉS

In an interview published in the *New York Times* in September 2012, former President Bill Clinton spoke about the gap between real emotion and packaged eloquence: "'Suppose we've been friends for 40 years,' Mr. Clinton said, putting a hand on a reporter's shoulder. . . . 'If you came to visit me in the hospital and said something pretty and eloquent instead of saying 'God, I'm sorry. This sucks. I wish I could do more about it,' it's an insult."

Formal or fake-fancy lines escape our lips not from a lapse of sensitivity but because we've internalized a culture-wide delusion that they are comforting to people who are sick or suffering. And because they're comforting to *us*. Here are several sentences that my waiting room interviewees found annoying, insulting, or flat-out useless no matter how well intentioned:

"Everything happens for a reason."

"You need to be strong for your kids."

"We're all in the same boat." ("Yeah, but some have bigger leaks," said a veteran who lost both legs from a roadside bomb blast in Iraq and *then* got cancer.)

"Maybe it happened for the best."

"Everyone's dying. No one knows how long they'll live. I could be hit by a car tomorrow." ("That's just blah, blah, blah," said a pancreatic cancer patient who'd heard that speech one time too many. She added, "Enjoy your good fortune and don't pretend you know a suffering you do not. I've lived with a terminal illness and I've lived without one, and living without one is nicer.")

"You're so brave." Or, *" . . . so inspiring."* (Many patients feel pressured by a comment like this. One said it put him in the position of having to live up to his friends' expectations and coerced him to keep

silent when he desperately needed to talk out his fears. Other patients, however, said hearing such a line made them feel strong and good.)

"Just be glad it isn't worse."

"Chin up."

"What doesn't kill you makes you stronger."

"My thoughts are with you." (I write this in e-mails to my sick friends all the time; it's a knee-jerk response. Better to say what I mean, which is, "I feel so bad for you." Or, "I really hope you get better."

"You don't deserve this." (As if anyone does.)

"God works in mysterious ways." (Remember that faith-based clichés land more felicitously on religious ears. If you're going to say a line like that, be sure you know your audience.)

"Have you prayed over this?" (Ditto.)

"God doesn't give us more than we can handle." (Tell that to the parents of a dying child.)

"He's in a better place."

"At least she didn't suffer." (My late friend Karl Lipsky heard this incessantly after his wife, Marianne, was killed by a huge tree limb that suddenly cracked off and landed on her while she was walking down a country lane. "*I* suffered," Karl replied. "I'm *still* suffering.")

"I know ten women who've had breast cancer, and they're all doing fine."

"My sister had a double mastectomy, and she's climbing mountains!"

When the last two remarks came my way, I actually felt encouraged by them, but another cancer patient said she found these kinds of comments "dumb, dismissive, and insulting." The fact that ten women survived her disease and someone's sister was climbing mountains meant nothing to her because "every woman and every cancer is different." Though it's patently absurd to amalgamate your sister's positive experiences into a giant generalization and expect it to be helpful, I somehow found new reason for hope whenever I heard about a breast cancer case with a happy ending. However, had you told me your sister was climbing mountains at a point when I couldn't climb the stairs in my own house, I guess I'd have felt otherwise.

BLOCK THOSE MILITARY METAPHORS

Ever since the 1971 passage of the National Cancer Act, which strengthened federal efforts to cure the disease, the US government supposedly has been waging a "war against cancer," which may explain why the vocabulary of cancer contains so many military metaphors. Words like "fight," "battle," and "survivor" are occasionally applied to other illnesses too (i.e., we're "battling" the epidemic of childhood obesity), but at the level of the individual, you don't often hear that someone is "fighting diabetes."

I never thought much about cancer's appropriation of war-speak until several of my waiting room informants and others complained that violent images militate against their yearning for inner peace. One patient said the word "remission" strikes her ear as a combination of "retreat" and "submission," which together suggest that her cancer is "hiding in some trench, just waiting to pop out."

What's the alternative? I ask her. Does she say she's "cured?"

"Never, since I can't be certain the disease isn't going to return. But instead of using the word 'remission' I'll say, 'I've been treated and I'm doing fine now.'"

Before she died Joan Berkley told friends that she didn't have positive feelings about the word "strong." To her mind it was connected to physical strength, of which she had little at the end. When asked what word best described herself at that point, she thought for a while and finally said, "Free." She meant she felt free to hold onto her twenty-one-year-old grandson and cry deeply with him, free to have the most intimate conversations imaginable with her husband, free to take on each day without knowing what would happen, and free to accept the tears of her friends without feeling she had to comfort them.

Journalist Dana Jennings, who in 2008 was diagnosed with advanced, aggressive prostate cancer and blogs about it at well.blogs .nytimes.com/tag/dana-jennings, also has no use for the "clichés of cancer." He says people call him "brave" because they're afraid of the disease themselves. But he insists, "There is nothing brave about showing up for surgery or radiations. . . . Bravery entails choice and most patients have very little choice but to undergo treatment." Dana doesn't refer to himself as a "victim" because it "implies an assailant, and there is no malice or intent with cancer." Nor does he use the word "survivor" because he "didn't crawl from a burning building or come home whole from a tour of duty in Afghanistan." Finally, he wishes people would stop saying, "Well at least it's a good cancer." There are no good cancers, "just as there are no good wars or earthquakes," he writes. "Better to say nothing, and offer the gift of your presence, than to utter bankrupt bromides."

TRY NOT TO MANGLE YOUR MEANING

The wrong word at the wrong time can be devastating; it can also be pretty funny. When Mary Lindsay, wife of New York's then-Mayor John Lindsay, was seated beside Yogi Berra in a parade grandstand on a sweltering summer day, she commented on how cool Yogi looked despite the soaring temperature. The baseball legend replied, "You don't look so hot yourself, Mary."

Misused idioms, errors in syntax, botched translations, faux pas, double entendres—all lie in wait for careless speakers and writers. A foreign-trained gynecologist said he specialized in "women and other diseases." A note on the bulletin board at my mother-in-law's senior citizen's residence informed the residents that "Sid Green entered the hospital today for testes." This inadequately punctuated item appeared in a Catholic newsletter: "Eileen Flanagan remains in the hospital and needs blood donors for more transfusions. She is also having trouble sleeping and requests tapes of Father Anthony's sermons." Seen on a T-shirt: "I've upped my pledge to the LGBT Health Center—Now up yours." After being told that his grandfather had a terminal illness, a twelve-year-old asked his grandpa, "When were you at the airport?"

If the Internet can be believed, the following bloopers have appeared on church bulletin boards in various parts of the country:

- "Due to the Rector's illness, Wednesday's healing services will be discontinued until further notice."
- "The outreach committee has enlisted 25 visitors to make sick calls on people who are not afflicted with any church."
- "Remember in your prayers the many who are sick of our community."

If you can't imagine anyone misspeaking, misspelling, or misinterpreting in quite those ways and, therefore, you're wondering how in the world you can prepare for or prevent such bloopers, the answer is that you can't. But should you happen to make a spectacular illness-related blunder, what you can do is laugh at yourself, apologize profusely, and hope the patient has a good sense of humor.

THE "HOW ARE YOU?" PROBLEM

Believe it or not, the most basic opening line in human discourse, "How are you?," can upset a sick person.

My friend Susana Leval was able to discern her friends' anxieties in the tone of their "How are yous." When someone called and asked questions about her condition, she could instantly tell whether that person was thinking about her or themselves. While she was undergoing thirty-two weeks of chemo for breast cancer, some of her closest pals and family members exhibited such high levels of anxiety about the possibility of her dying that she had to keep them at a distance. She said of that period in her life that she had to conserve her energy and protect herself from other people's anxieties, so she drew a curtain around herself and only let in those who had "the quality of tranquility."

Once they knew about my condition, I noticed in some of my friends a discomforting change in emphasis. Instead of a simple, light, "How are you?" or "How ya' doin'?" I'd be greeted with a weighty, conspiratorial "How *are* you?"

I, too, hated that tone, its intimations of tragic foreboding, its invitation to confide the worst. The three-word question, asked ominously, instantly telegraphed that rather than see me as *me*, the asker viewed me as a *cancer victim*!

"I'm fine," I'd reply when I didn't feel like amplifying the specifics.

"No, I mean, *really*!" they'd say. "How are you, *really!?*"

"I'm *fine*," I'd repeat, this time more firmly. I wished they could intuit what I meant, which was, "Look, I want to *believe* I'm fine, though I can't say for sure, but it would make me feel better if you treated me as if I *am* fine while also recognizing that I'm physically compromised and more consciously mortal than I used to be."

Conversely, I'll admit that when I ask other people how they are and they say they're fine, I'm tempted to reply, "Really? How do you know? Maybe you're just *undiagnosed*." To earn the right to say we're fine, we would have to pass every test known to modern medicine, and even then our bodies could be harboring some nasty little mutant cell that's just starting to subdivide. And it doesn't matter how terrific we feel either. The day I went for my routine mammogram, I walked three miles to the radiologist's lab, felt great, and had no symptoms.

Being asked, "How are you?" requires us to decide on the spot, questioner by questioner, friend by friend, situation by situation, how candidly to respond. If we sense you're just being polite and don't really give a fig how we are, we're not apt to tell you the truth (which you may not want to hear anyway). Some of us will finesse the question, having decided our condition is too complicated or personal to explain, our discomfort too difficult to put into words, our symptoms too embarrassing to share. Some will shut down altogether if your queries about our condition sound too formulaic or you seem oblivious to the nuances in our voice, eyes, or body language. Then, too, if we tell you we feel lousy and you don't follow up with a phone call or e-mail within a reasonable time, we're going to regret opening up in the first place and we may well shut you out of our inner circle for good.

Don't be surprised if, in replying to your "How are you?" we dwell at length or in detail on our affected organ, system, cells, or body part. In that case, we need our friends to do two things at once: indulge our fixations (be sensitive and tolerant) and also facilitate our return to "normalcy"—that marvelous mindless state in which one has the luxury of taking one's body for granted. And we can't feel normal until our friends stop pelting us with those portentous "How *are* yous?"

The natural question, then, is what *should* I say, if not "How are you?"

Donna, who's had recurrent cancers, says, "Friends should gently ask, 'Are you well?' This I can answer simply and honestly, but the critical word is *gently*."

Sandy Smith, who lost a child to brain cancer and also had cancer herself, suggests, "Just say, 'It's good to see you today.' Or say 'How are you?' then add, 'I know that's not a great question, but I really do want to know.' And if our friends really *do* want to know, they should ask us in a place and situation where we actually have time to answer, and they should know that if we're battling cancer or we're grieving for a loved one, the answer is not going to be a simple one."

In short, "How are you?" should not be a robotic question but instead a genuine expression of interest, and the asker should be prepared for a longer than average answer.

Here are a few more useful tips from people in the waiting room and others who've been there.

- "Instead of 'How are you feeling?' people should ask me, '*What* are you feeling?' That's a much easier question for me to answer."
- "Listen to how I am, don't tell me how I should be."
- "Respond to what I say, don't just move right along or talk about yourself."
- "Don't interrupt my answer unless you want to inject a sympathetic comment or a relevant vulgarity. After I finish telling a buddy of mine how I am, he always says things like, 'Man, what a fuckin' nightmare.' Or, 'Jesus Christ, how can you stand that shit?' I love that."

ADJUST YOUR CONVERSATION TO THEIR CONDITION

When the late Geraldine Ferraro was being treated for multiple myeloma, her bones were so weak that her ribs cracked just from breathing. One day, when I called to see how she was doing, she shared with me how burdensome it had become to respond to her friends' queries: "I appreciate everyone's calls, but I need them to first ask if I feel up to talking, and I need them to tell me it's all right if I don't feel like talking. Real friends understand when you can't deal with them because you're dealing with your pain."

While patients are stymied in one way, their friends are stymied in another. With someone whose capacity to provide feedback is limited by their condition or hampered by their misguided sense of illness etiquette, you may not know what to say or do or when to say and do nothing. It's especially hard to respond appropriately when the patient is in no shape to advise or guide you.

I know how frustrating this can be. Not long ago my sister, Betty, who lives two hundred miles away, underwent chemotherapy for ovarian cancer, after which she developed a horrifically debilitating autoimmune reaction that atrophied her swallowing muscles and required her to be fed through an IV. Next she got a virulent infection. Now she was not only weak, bald, and hungry but listless and miserable and talking about wanting to die.

In a scant ninety days I'd seen Betty, a fiercely independent woman with wide-ranging interests and the metabolism of the Energizer Bunny, utterly drained of her intellectual curiosity, physical vigor, and will to live. She couldn't eat, speak without effort, walk, read, or watch TV. Her world had shrunk to her apartment's four walls. Given the distance between our homes and the demands of my own medical issues, I couldn't visit as often as I would have liked, but when I did, she became visibly exhausted after we'd exchanged just a few sentences. I'd ask if she wanted to nap, or I'd offer to go out for a walk to give her a break from talking, but she always insisted I stay. So I stayed, though at times her side of the conversation was so muddled and fragmentary that I feared my attempts at distraction were too enervating to be useful. When I couldn't visit, I called her every few days to lift her spirits and catch her up on family news. On her bad days she really couldn't hack it on the phone; mostly she slept, sucked ice cubes, and dozed off. On her good days she might enjoy hearing about my kids or talking haltingly about hers. Nothing else really engaged her. Once she dropped the receiver on the floor in the middle of our conversation. Nevertheless, I kept calling because, even at her lowest point, she seemed buoyed by the sound of my voice.

After the infection and autoimmune problem were under control, Betty was able to eat soft foods and conversation flowed more easily, but our subjects remained circumscribed by her limited purview: how she felt, what she ate, who visited. As I accommodated to her new situation, what struck me most—beside the radical change in my sister—was my own powerlessness. I felt useless, confused, incapable of alleviating her misery, and unsure of how to brighten her day when I was with her or what to say to her when we talked on the phone—in short, powerless to make her feel better. Sometimes, we have to accept that doing the best we can isn't quite enough.

FOUR GRADES OF ILLNESS
CALL FOR FOUR TYPES OF RESPONSE

Undoubtedly, this overwhelming sense of frustration and powerlessness underlies most people's difficulties in relating to their sick friends. But once you realize you can't "fix" everything and once you understand that different grades of illness require different behaviors, you're more likely to respond in ways appropriate to each situation. Although the following points will seem obvious to some readers, I need to elaborate on them for those who haven't thought things through as methodically as perhaps you have:

1) *With patients who are terminally ill or in continual pain,* have difficulty communicating, or require assistance with basic life functions such as eating and going to the toilet, remember that the primary purpose of your presence is to make them feel comfortable and valued. Don't talk *at* them. Don't pressure them to talk. Even answering a nurse's or doctor's questions can be taxing to a patient in extremis. Be clear that the reason why you're in the room or on the phone is to *listen* to whatever they have to say and help them in any way you can. That's it: to listen and help, to comfort and affirm.

2) *With people who are very sick but seem willing to talk and answer questions,* start with basic patient-oriented queries. Ask what they're feeling and ask about their prognosis, but don't push where you meet resistance. Patients will tell you as much as they want you to know.

Only after their health issues have been addressed, and only if they're so inclined, should you move on to Other Things, by which I mean subjects unrelated to their illness. It's important to honor the patient by assuming they're still interested in Other Things; if they aren't, they will let you know by shutting down. Don't expect all your interactions to flow smoothly. Don't be insulted if the patient gets fussy, brusque, or cranky. A person who's sick and tired of being sick and tired must be excused for losing patience with questions that cover the same ground again and again. Some patients may "overshare," describe their symptoms too graphically, or provide more details about a procedure than anyone needs to know. Let them talk about whatever they want. It's not going to kill you to hear about their bowel movements. Having been on the receiving end of any number of meandering "organ recitals," I know how mind-numbing TMI (too much information) can be. Bear in mind that what strikes you as oversharing may constitute the entirety of your sick friend's current reality. If you care about the person, you'll want to practice "active listening" (a psychologist friend's term for concentrated attentiveness punctuated by brief sympathetic comments or relevant expletives). Just take in what they put out and offer feedback where appropriate without being prescriptive.

3) *With people who have a congenital, permanent, or genetic condition* (which may not always be readily apparent, like Lupus or Crohn's disease) and with those who live with visible disabilities (like paraplegia, blindness, or ALS), you need to understand and accept that they're never "getting better" in the conventional sense of those words. Spiritual healing is possible, accommodation to their limitations is possible, a full and productive life may be possible, but their core problem is not going to disappear—and neither should their friends. Seldom do patients in this category want their condition to be the primary focus of conversation; in fact, they're usually among the most driven seekers of normalcy. So if they want to talk about Other Things, please comply. Your goal should be to give them all the help and support they need

without making them feel as if their problem is the most salient thing about them.

4) *With people who are ill now but expect to recover,* who *were* ill and are now convalescing, or who, like me, had something scary happen to them but are intent on putting it behind them, your conversation should briefly touch on their condition—just long enough to show that you remember what they have, had, or what they've been through— then seamlessly move on to Other Things. Since completing my radiation I spend very little time thinking about my cancer. I listen to music. I go out. I read, take walks, see friends, and follow the news. I worry about what "normal" people worry about—the leak in the ceiling, the unincorporated business tax, what to make for dinner.

We who are trying to heal sometimes feel held back in that effort by friends who persist in perceiving us and addressing us as if we're still sick. As we process their words or sense their attitude, it becomes a measure of our progress back to health and "normality." A fourteen- year-old cancer victim put it best: "When my friends treat me like they always did, I know I'm getting better. If they were too nice to me, I'd think I was going to die."

"YOU WANT COMPANY?"

A half-dozen friends of mine asked if they could keep me company on my walks to the hospital and sit with me in the waiting room or accompany me to my many doctor's visits. Much as I appreciated their offers, I declined them all because I knew they would ask me a lot of questions, and I didn't want to have to explain what I was going through. I told them that I enjoyed walking across the park by my- self, it gave me time to clear my head, and, as for having company in the waiting room, it was hard enough doing time there myself—if I had to worry about friends frittering away hours at my side, I'd be doubly stressed.

My fellow patients must have had the same desire to be on their own, as relatively few showed up in the waiting room with a companion. But I recently read about a wonderful use of shared waiting time. When his mother, Mary Anne Schwalbe, a former educator and college admissions director, was dying of pancreatic cancer, her son Will, an editor and author, often accompanied her, and what they usually talked about was books. Will writes, "It wasn't until one day during her second month of treatment that we realized that we had created a very peculiar book club, one with only two members. . . . From then on, until my mother died almost two years later, at age 75, we read dozens of books of all different kinds; classic novels and modern ones, mysteries, biographies, short-story collections, self-help books, histories. . . . We didn't meet over meals, like so many book clubs, or a set number of times. But we were forced to keep coming back to that waiting room as Mom's health got worse and worse. And we talked about books."

Will Schwalbe has written his own book about their experience, *The End of Your Life Book Club* (see Resources, page 265). If your sick friend is someone who does want company in the waiting room, you might want to replicate Will's two-person book club.

I've always preferred to go it alone at the hospital, except twice when I didn't. The first time, I asked my daughter Robin to accompany me to the surgeon's office for my pre-op consultation. I wanted her with me because she's a calm, steadying presence and a professional journalist, so she knows how to listen and takes great notes. Without her verbatim documentation of that consultation, I could never have absorbed my surgeon's complex diagrams and medical explanations. It was TMI to absorb in my anxious state. My mind turned to mud the minute the doctor started talking. However, in the ensuing days I frequently referred to Robin's notes to better understand what was going to happen during my surgery and to realistically anticipate its expected results.

That experience leads me to underscore the importance of having a second set of ears at every *major* medical consultation—not routine office visits but rather those during which various options are being presented or decisions must be made. The ideal friend to play such a role is someone who can be more detached, take notes, and ask questions on the patient's behalf, and who can function both as an advocate and a reality check. If you're that someone, your primary job is to listen carefully and write things down. But you also should feel free to ask the doctor questions yourself because if something isn't clear to you, chances are it's probably not clear to your friend, the patient, either, and you'll want to be able to discuss it or explain it later.

The second exception to my "going it alone" rule was my husband, Bert, who took me to the hospital on the day of my surgery, stood vigil in the waiting room, and was the first face I saw when the anesthesia wore off. I was grateful to him and Robin for being there when I needed company, grateful to the friends who asked, and grateful to those who understood that when I declined their offer, it wasn't about them; it was about me.

So here's your takeaway: make sure you mean it when you say you're willing to accompany a friend or sit there no matter how long it takes—and make sure the patient understands that they can accept your offer of company when they want it and decline it when they don't without you being insulted. This isn't international diplomacy, people, it's common sense. Your job is to offer; the patient's job is to accept or reject. (Disclaimer: there will be times when your instincts will tell you to "just show up," but more about that in the chapter on visits. Here we're talking about talk.)

TRUTH TELLING: THE NEW ILLNESS ETIQUETTE

In essence, there are three things you ought to be able to say, simply and forthrightly, to someone who's sick:

1) "Tell me what's helpful and what's not."
2) "Tell me if you want to be alone and when you want company."
3) "Tell me what to bring and when to leave."

Those sentences, I know, are easier for me to write than for the average person to speak, and it's going to take a paradigm shift to make people feel comfortable saying them. Traditional illness etiquette leaves little room for such exchanges. Lacking the permission to speak openly or the talent for mind reading, sick people and their friends continue to spout bromides, fly on instruments, and sometimes miss the runway.

But giving your sick friends permission to tell you the truth about what they want and what they're feeling doesn't mean they have to tell you absolutely *everything*. When friends of mine asked me, "How are you?" I used to answer in detail until I started noticing how often (usually at first mention of a sentinel node or estrogen receptor) their eyes glazed over. If we were talking on the phone, I'd hear the audio equivalent of a glazed eye—the soft click of computer keys or the whoosh of running water, a sure sign that they were multitasking. I took no offense. They didn't mean to be rude, but medical terms are daunting and minds wander. Finally, I realized that I didn't have to report *every* detail. I wasn't under oath. Besides, most people aren't interested in our blood count or oncotype; they ask questions because they're not sure what else to say. Yes, they care about us, and yes, they hope we're on the mend, but what they really want to know is pretty straightforward: Are we feeling better or worse? Are we hurting? What can they do to help? And what they really want from us are clues to how we wish to be treated.

We patients should provide that information not in coded messages but in just so many words. We should tell you whether we want visitors and, if so, when to come and how long to stay. We should admit it if we're exhausted or we don't feel like talking. We should be clear about whether we want you to make us dinner and hang around while we eat or just deliver a covered dish. And because you're probably going to bring us a present anyway, we may as well mention the book we've been eager to read, the edibles we most crave (and are permitted to consume), or the kind of flowers that make us happy.

Candor is absolutely essential when dealing with disabled people and their spouses and partners. To give you the best possible advice on this subject, I cannot improve on the piece written by my friend, Mary Pleshette Willis, whose husband broke his neck forty-two years ago in a surfing accident that happened two months before they were to be married ("National Disability Awareness Month: The Best Compliment Is No Compliment at All," October 17, 2012, http://www.huffingtonpost.com/mary-pleshette-willis/national-disability-awareness-month_b_1971167.html). It should be required reading for anyone who ever interacts with disabled persons or those who love them. Here are excerpts from Mary's blog, which was published in October 2012 to commemorate National Disability Awareness Month:

> It's always a shock to me when people single him (and me) out for his disability rather than for our respective accomplishments. [Mary is a published writer; Jack is an award-winning documentary filmmaker] . . . Just the other day, a woman at a dinner party whom I hardly know said, "I think you are so amazing. I really admire what you do."

. . . I've struggled for a long time to explain why remarks that are often well-meaning are so offensive to me, why singling me out for being married to a man who's disabled diminishes rather than enhances my place in the world. The only thing that makes my husband different is his difficulty walking. . . . When we use the wheelchair, I have to push; when he's on the scooter, I walk alongside him. We don't feel very different from other couples who go to the park, to restaurants or to the movies until someone makes an earnest, but ultimately gratuitous, remark. More upsetting is when they address me but ignore my husband (in his presence) . . . like the airline clerk who asked me where he would be most comfortable. . . . When they address me as if my husband isn't there or when they infantilize him with silly remarks (another favorite when he's on the scooter is, "Watch out not to speed") they make us feel separate, objectified, other.

. . . For those who say, "I could never do what you do," I say you have no idea what you could do until you have to do it. It's scary to think that the same thing could happen to them that happened to us, and I understand that the remarks are their way of distancing themselves from a terrifying scenario.

. . . But when people praise me for the worst thing that ever happened to me, I want to tell them . . . to stop projecting their own anxieties onto me.

So what do you say to someone who's handicapped or to his spouse/partner? More times than not, you say nothing. Or you don't say anything you wouldn't say to someone who isn't handicapped. Rather than an unsolicited expression of sympathy, the woman at the dinner party would not have offended me if she'd asked me a direct question: "How do you travel with a wheelchair?" or "What do you do when the bathroom is down a flight of stairs?" Or even "Is your husband in pain?"

I appreciate it when someone says, "You two seem to handle your life with grace and humor," or "I never hear you complain." There's a big difference between commenting on the way we negotiate our life and making us into martyrs.

... So for those who are tempted to tell me how amazing I am, I hope they'll understand that the best compliment is no compliment at all.

I'm absolutely convinced that in illness, as in every other aspect of our lives, honesty *is* the best policy. It's high time for the tyranny of politesse to give way to the frankness of truth telling. Were candor to become the prevailing modus operandi, patients could be direct and honest without coming off as arrogant or demanding, and their friends would no longer flounder around trying to strike the right chord. Frankness may feel weird at first, but once both sides sign onto it, you and your friends will have one less thing to worry about.

ASK AND ACT

||||||||||||||||||||||||||

I'm never sure why but, to my ear, "How can I help?" or "What can I do?" always sounds more authentically credible than "Can I help?" or "May I do something?"

However they're couched, such questions often ignite controversy among patient advocates, many of whom believe sick people should not be put in the position of having to order their friends around. According to this view, patients don't always know what they need and shouldn't have to sit (or lie) there, racking their brains for assignments to give to others. Friends should simply act, anticipate the patient's desire and provide it, and not ask questions. What's more, asking for something is bad for patients because it reminds them of their vulnerability.

A cancer survivor I talked to in the waiting room also espoused this view: "If you want to help me, you have to *do* something. Don't tell me to call you if I need anything. You have to push sometimes. Otherwise, I won't want to inconvenience you."

The opposite perspective, which mirrors my own, is expressed by Dr. Kimberly Allison, a breast cancer pathologist who, at age thirty-three, discovered *she* had breast cancer: "People want to help, but you have to let [them] know what you need so you don't end up with six casseroles on the same night."

What's lacking in most sickbed conversations is not the question; most people feel comfortable asking, "What can I bring?" or "How can I help?" What's lacking is the patient's willingness to answer honestly. Were truth telling to replace knee-jerk politesse, rather than "No thanks, I don't need a thing," sick people could answer, "Actually, I need an ice pack" or "Could you bring me a *Sports Illustrated?*" or "Gee, I'd love a brownie." When they answer truthfully, patients get their needs met and their friends get the chance to feel genuinely useful.

Ask or Act is a false choice because either/or isn't the only option. No reason why you can't visit bearing a CD as a gift for the patient *and* also ask, "What would you like me to bring the next time I come?" Or why you couldn't rake the leaves on their lawn *and* also ask, "What else can I do?" It's possible to act *and* ask, or ask *and* act, as long as when you ask, you mean it, and when you act, you either follow through with a full heart or get someone else to do it if you can't.

Should you lack the time, money, or ability to provide what your sick friend needs, say so. Honesty is a two-way street. Explain why you can't personally deliver on the patient's request then figure out another way to fulfill it. Let's say you ask, "What can I do?" and your friend says, "It would be great if you could do some weeding and deadhead the petunias—the garden's gone to seed since I've been laid up." And let's say you have a bad back or a black thumb. What should you say? Tell her gardening's not your thing, then hire a couple of teenagers to do the job for ten bucks an hour.

ADVICE ABOUT ADVICE

||||||||||||||||||||||||||||||||||||||||||||||||

Dolores, a woman I met in the waiting room, said she got some good advice about advice from her husband. It seems Dolores was worried about Gena, her obese friend who regularly binged on sweets and fried foods and had just been diagnosed with breast cancer. Convinced that Gena's poor diet would exacerbate her condition, Dolores was planning to speak to her about her eating habits and give her advice about healthy alternatives, until Dolores's husband dissuaded her. "He told me, 'Gena has a doctor to worry about her health. What she needs you to be is her friend.'"

On Michele's first morning home after ten grueling days in the hospital, a friend called and asked how she was.

"Pretty good," she replied. "I'm watching funny movies and practicing denial."

"Oh *no*! You can't do *that*!" cried the friend. "Denial is so wrong. You've got to face up to your mortality! You must!'"

That was the last thing Michele wanted to hear. Suddenly the specter she had temporarily banished from her thoughts came leaping back. She ended the conversation politely but has been avoiding the advice giver ever since.

Advice can be dangerous, unsolicited advice infuriating. For instance, Vincent Lee has a virulent form of pancreatic cancer. Ninety-five percent of those who have his disease die within twenty-four months of their diagnosis. In August 2012, having survived for twenty-seven months, he published some tough advice about advice in the *Berkshire Eagle*: "The primary reason I don't tell new acquaintances [about my illness] is that so many people unthinkingly and offensively try to be amateur oncologists as soon as they find out. . . . My oncologists have been Harvard clinical professors. But somehow people who are not MDs and have never seen my scans or read my charts start telling me what to do, where to go, who to see for treatment.

"When these unthinking jerks start to tell me, 'Oh, well you should do . . . ,' I want to punch them in the face. . . . They think they are cancer experts because of something they read in *People* magazine or because their cousin had a different cancer. Not so. If you don't know what to say, say 'I'm sorry . . .'

"Even some people who have survived cancer can be like this, thinking that if they survived with a positive attitude then anyone can. Not so; some cancers unfortunately are incurable."

A friend I'll call Jeb, clearly motivated by concern for his fellow cancer survivors, myself included, e-mailed us a health bulletin from the Johns Hopkins Medical Center that sent me into a panic. It said that surgery can cause cancerous cells to spread, radiation can make leftover cells mutate, and cancer patients shouldn't eat dairy products because they make the body produce the mucus "cancer feeds on!" At that point I'd already completed my surgery and radiation and my fridge was packed, as always, with cheese, yogurt, and a dozen other dairy products. I felt like a condemned woman, until about twenty minutes later a second message arrived. Subject line: "CORRECTION!!" Thanks to Snopes.com, Jeb had discovered that the "Johns Hopkins" bulletin was a scam designed to get cancer patients to buy herbal products.

Despite that scare, I still tend to heed advice proffered by friends who've had what I had. Marcia Seligson, for instance. A breast cancer survivor and dutiful researcher, Marcia alerted me to new studies, anti-cancer meds, and an accelerated radiation protocol that she suggested I ask my doctor about in case it might be right for me. (It wasn't).

"I hope I'm not intruding," she wrote in an e-mail shortly after I was diagnosed, "but I believe information is power and we need to be each other's advocates. Keep me posted. I'll also have some alternative dietary supplements to recommend when you get to that point. Meanwhile, please buy as much *organic* meat/produce as you can find."

It's easy to take advice from someone as genuinely concerned and well informed as Marcia but not from someone who fires a torpedo at a friend and acts like it's a life raft. This was made clear to me by Judy, a waiting room colleague, who received a wig catalog in the mail with a note from her friend Nora that said, "Check out the hairdo on page 5. You'd look great in it!"

"Sounds like a considerate gesture," I said.

"Maybe for someone who's having chemo," said Judy, "but I've told Nora six times if I've told her once that I'm having radiation and radiation doesn't cause hair loss. I'm done confiding in people who don't listen."

Bottom line advice about advice: don't bully or guilt-trip your sick friends into doing something. Don't insist that they take ginkgo biloba and acidophilus because ginkgo biloba and acidophilus always makes *you* feel great. Don't make them feel bad if they haven't read the book you recommended or visited your massage therapist or changed to your orthopedist. The difference between a coercive command and a gentle suggestion is the difference between "You've *got* to go to this spa! It'll save your life!" and "I just read about a beautiful spa that caters to cancer survivors. Would you like me to check it out for you?"

"YOU LOOK GREAT!"

In her one-woman show, *I Got Sick Then I Got Better,* Jenny Allen, who survived the double whammy of endometrial and ovarian cancer, does a hilarious riff on the phrase that Ben Brantley, the *New York Times* theater critic, rightly identified as the world's most "discouraging encouraging words": "You look great!"

Jenny heard that line all too often when she was having chemo, she said, and then mimicked how different friends of hers had delivered it, in tones ranging from astonished to reassuring to patronizing—but never quite convincing. However her friends accentuated these energetic effusions ("You look *great!*" "*You* look great!" "You *look* great!" and "You!! Look!! Great!!"), all they did was convince Jenny that she must really look awful. Either that or her friends expected her to be dead by now, so anything short of rigor mortis was a relief.

When I was having radiation, my friends, too, kept telling me I looked "great!" Because nuking the chest does nothing for the face, I knew it was a lie, or rather a compassionate fib, but still I always smiled and replied, "So do you!"

Three problems arise when friends focus on a sick person's appearance. First, if the patient looks awful and knows it, your little white lie will cast doubt on whatever truthful things you may say to them in the future. Second, talking about how they look may dissuade them from telling you what they're feeling. Third, if you said they looked great the last time you saw them and you forgot to say it this time, they may assume they look worse this time. I confess that after constantly hearing how great I looked, I expected everyone to greet me that way, and when someone didn't, I got depressed.

Despite those three reasons not to, I suggest that you keep saying "You look great!" simply because everyone else is probably saying it, and if you're the only one who doesn't, your sick friend may come to associate you with negativity and depression.

"OMIGOD!"

||||||||||||||||||||||||

Most MSK patients showed up in the waiting room in jeans or sweats, so I assumed the man in the three-piece suit was the husband or father of a patient. However, when I asked the small group sitting near me what they *least* wanted to hear from their friends, he revealed himself to be one of us.

"I hope I never hear these words again: 'Oh my *God*, Roger, I just heard! I am *so* sorry.' I swear I'm going to choke the next guy who grips me by the shoulders and says, 'Oh my God, Roger . . .'"

"Me too! I hate that!" cried a young woman with a Caribbean accent. "This friend of mine, she comes to my hospital room, this girl I haven't seen in forever, and she goes, 'Omigod!! You're *emaciated.*' I go, 'Two brain tumors, two weeks of Jell-O, you'll lose weight too.' Next day another girl shows up and she sees me and she's screaming, 'Omigod! Your face is so *puffy.*' I go, 'You do Botox. I do steroids.'"

"I hate that word too," says the woman in the green turban, who I hadn't seen since the day of the blizzard. "Oh-em-gee should be banned from e-mail. Omigod should be banned from the English language. When I told a friend of mine I got lung cancer even though I never even smoked, she screeched, '*Omigod!* You poor thing! That is *soooo* bad!!' I swallowed my tears, and I told her, 'Don't call me until I call you.' She's a good person, but I need to be surrounded by positive energy right now. It's part of my healing process."

The young woman high fived the turban lady, then turned to me. "Put this in your book, okay? *Never start a sentence with 'Oh my God!'*"

SUPPORTING A FRIEND WHO HAS HIV/AIDS

For people living with life-threatening illnesses, how they look is the least of their problems. On top of its scary symptoms and an often grim prognosis, many HIV/AIDS patients endure social prejudice and ignorance, rejection from their families, and estrangement from judgmental friends. During the early years of the epidemic, when death was a common outcome and fear of contagion was rife, parents, siblings, sex partners, colleagues, and friends often abandoned people with AIDS, and this probably explains why so many of those who were infected kept their condition hidden for as long as they could.

Rae Lewis-Thornton lived with her secret for seven years before finally deciding to share it with the two friends with whom she'd been insepa- rable since college. "I felt I had a responsibility to prepare the people who love me for this process that's eventually going to happen to me. I didn't want to find myself in a hospital and people just totally flabbergasted."

"I remember the day she told me," said one of the friends in a TV interview. I couldn't believe this was affecting somebody I knew. I knew how she lived her life, and [long pause here] it was not one where you would think that somebody would become HIV-positive."

"It certainly won't affect how much I love Rae," said the second friend, "or how much she has affected my life, and I hope to be her friend forever."

Rae was first diagnosed when she volunteered to give blood. A mo- tivational speaker and writer, she now chronicles her experiences with full-blown AIDS on the blog "Diva Living with AIDS" (www.raelewis thornton.com). In one post she wrote, "When you have AIDS, friendship takes on a whole new dimension. Your friends aren't just your friends, they become your support system and your caregivers."

The slogan of the UN Development Program's global AIDS- awareness campaign is, "We have the same feelings, the same dreams, the same life. HIV/AIDS will not affect our friendship. We Are Friends!" If someone in your life has the virus and you're anxious about con- tagion, talk to them, let them educate you, and you too may declare, "HIV/AIDS will not affect our friendship!"

The questions young people pose on the HIV Prevention Message Board mostly center on whether they can get AIDS by hanging out with a friend who has it, by touching him, using her computer, or shar- ing a drink. Though the Board's medical experts explain that no one gets AIDS from casual contact, this doesn't always persuade a fright- ened teenager. "Yeah, but what if she's bleeding, which has happened, and she touches the blood and then touches something that I touch right after her and then. . . . "

Michael Adams, executive director of services and advocacy for GLBT Elders, says it's still common for friends of HIV/AIDS patients to be nervous about physical contact. "Education about how HIV is transmitted has been around for years, but there's what people know intellectually and then there's irrational fear. I think part of being a friend to a friend who's sick is being willing to overcome your own fears and anxieties in order to care for them and to be the support they need."

Michael told me about caring for his friend José, a vibrant young man who became ravaged by AIDS. "It was a profound experience in terms of deepening our friendship and creating an amazing level of honesty. He became very dependent on me. When he was still living alone, I made sure he went to the doctor and took his medicine, but mostly I made sure he felt loved. I'm not talking about sex but about intimacy. That meant getting in bed with him and watching TV together so he could be physically close to somebody because he still wanted contact and warmth. Caring for someone with full-blown AIDS is a deeply intimate relationship, something like what you would engage in with a very sick parent. You carry the person from one room to another, you clean them up. It can get very down and dirty. You have to get over your fears about body fluids."

Michael assumed his friend's working-class Mexican immigrant family would not accept a gay son, but when José became critically ill, his parents, who ran a storefront hair salon, set up a bed for him in the supply room behind the shop so they could take turns watching over him. "They couldn't afford home-care attendants, no nurse's aides, no nothing, but they were beautiful with him, totally involved and supportive in ways that blew away my own stereotypes about culture and class. Once they took over, my role was just to sit and talk with him and be his friend."

Here comes another obvious point that nonetheless bears repetition: people with HIV/AIDS need friends and family to love and care for them, stay close to them, and not stigmatize, ostracize, or abandon them—and they don't always get what they need. The day Trevor came out to his parents and admitted he had AIDS, they disowned him. They did, however, attend his funeral. At the end of the service his mother stormed up to his long-time partner, screaming, "You gave it to him! How come you're alive and my son is dead?!!" The partner walked away, but he wanted to scream back, "Where were you when he was sick? I stayed. I took care of him until the very end. Where the hell were *you*?!"

Echoes of this dialogue are heard in Michael Cristofer's powerful play, *The Shadow Box*. Mark, the lover of Brian, who has advanced AIDS, describes in excruciating physical detail what Brian has been going through, and then turns on Brian's ex-wife, howling, "Some of us have to live with it and clean up after it. I mean, you can waltz in and out of here like a fucking Christmas tree if you want, but some of us are staying. Some of us are here for the duration."

LET US NOW PRAISE THOSE WHO GOT IT RIGHT

Here are seven lines sick people said they *do* want to hear:

"I'm so sorry this happened to you."

"Tell me how I can help."

"I'm here if you want to talk."

"Just give me my marching orders."

"That sounds awful; I can't even imagine the pain."

"I'm bringing dinner."

"You must be desperate for some quiet time. I'll take your kids on Saturday."

What makes those sentences register so positively? The fact that they express empathy, availability, or both.

In his cancer memoir, *[Sic]*, Joshua Cody writes of a friend: "I will never forget her words on the phone, just two words, 'Oh Josh,' . . . low register, somewhere between *piano* and *pianissimo*, and I detest hearing my name pronounced but these were the two purest words ever addressed to me."

Two of the purest words ever addressed to *me* were spoken by my friend Kathleen, who had the aforementioned unminor hip surgery. When I told her I had cancer, her reaction both summed up her empathy and captured my feelings in a nutshell. She said, "Oh, fuck!"

A longer but equally pitch-perfect response came from another friend, Sandy Edelman, a two-time breast cancer survivor.

I know how overwhelming the initial news can be, and the shock of being thrust into the medical treatment vortex, the appointments, second opinions, tests, waiting around for results, all seeming endless. I also know it can be a little daunting to be cast in the role of decision maker on your treatment choices. I'm happy to explain why I made the decisions I did.

Even though diagnoses, pathologies, and profiles can differ, sometimes it's helpful to talk through your options with a number of people—not so you can do what they did but to help clarify in your own mind the right thing for you.

I also want to share with you a few of the unexpected blessings that arose out of my experience. First, I realized it was OK to let people know how they could help me. Second, I focused on what would make me happy while I was undergoing treatment. Third, I realized that I didn't have to accept every social and professional invitation extended to me. And most importantly, I reconnected with an old friend who reached out to me during the experience and who, a year later, fixed me up on a blind date with the man who would become my husband.

I don't wish the breast cancer experience on anyone, but now that you have it, I wish you unexpected blessings as well.

Though you may feel powerless in most illness contexts, remember that you do have the power to normalize your sick friends by the manner in which you address them. Your tone of voice, what you talk about, and the attitude behind your words can keep your friend from feeling typecast as Cancer Girl or Heart Attack Guy. Your normal behavior is the Get Out of Jail Free ticket that lets people like me leave the prison of the sick and return to the square that says Go.

When navigating through tight verbal straits, you can quickly brush up on your Ps and Qs by reviewing the rules I've distilled from my interviews:

TEN COMMANDMENTS FOR
CONVERSING WITH A SICK FRIEND

|||||||||||||||||||||||||||||||||||||||||||||||||||||||||||||||||

1) *Rejoice at their good news. Don't minimize their bad news.* A guy tells you the doctors got it all, say "Hallelujah!" A man with advanced bladder cancer says he's taking his kids to Disneyland next summer, don't bite your lip and mutter, "We'll see." Tell him it's a *great* idea. (What harm can it do?) A friend tells you with palpable relief that her biopsy was negative, break out the champagne and toast her—don't let it slide by uncelebrated. A friend on crutches insists he's going bowling next week, say, "More power to you!" Endorse his plan; don't point out its implausibility. Your job is to support your friends. Leave the fact checking to people at the *New Yorker.* I don't mean you should slap a happy face decal on a grim diagnosis: "Nowadays breast cancer is like having a cold" is *not helpful.* A better response in almost every encounter with the sick is, "Tell me what I can do to make things easier for you—I really want to help."

2) *Treat your friends as you always did before they got sick—but never forget their changed circumstance.* I know that sounds contradictory,

but I promise you can learn to live mindfully within the paradox if you do the following:

    a. Keep your friends' illness and its attendant constraints in mind, but don't treat them as if their illness is who they are.

    b. Acknowledge their newfound awareness of their mortality, but don't treat them as if they're defective or doomed (unless they are, in which case see Chapter 8).

    c. Speak to them as you always did, which means tease them, make demands on them, kid around with them, get mad if they piss you off, but indulge their occasional hissy fits.

    d. Start conversations about Other Things as soon as possible to help speed their journey from the morass of illness to the miracle of the ordinary. When Julie Silver was being treated for breast cancer, her friends brought her meals for months. "It was fantastic," she said. "But around the dinner hour my kids would say, 'Not again. Please don't talk about cancer.'"

3) *Avoid self-referential comments or anecdotes.* Don't tell a depressed friend, "I know what that's like" or "I understand how you feel" unless you can back up the claim and use your experience as a springboard for greater support. Don't tell someone with congestive heart failure that you have a migraine headache, painful as it may be. Don't complain about your colicky baby to the mother of child with spina bifida. I'm not saying sick or suffering people have lost their capacity to empathize with others, just that solipsism is insensitive and rude. Cancer survivor Sandy Smith, now a grief counselor, says, "Just as it's not helpful to tell your childbirth story to a pregnant woman, it's not helpful to tell your illness story to a sick friend. You shouldn't burden people with information they don't need. You can't compare the death of someone's child to the death of your elderly grand parent. You can't compare any death to something bad that happened to you at work." Someone with a hacking cough doesn't need to hear,

"You think that's bad? I had double pneumonia." The truest thing you can say to a sick or suffering friend is, "I can only try to imagine what you're going through."

4) *Don't assume, verify.* Michele was upset when three different friends reacted to her breast cancer diagnosis with "Well, at least you caught it early so you'll be all right!" In fact, she did *not* catch it early and never said or hinted otherwise. Her friends just assumed it. She's not sure if they said it to cheer her up, to cheer themselves up, or simply to fill the awkward pause after she told them her news, but she was so frightened by her disease that whenever someone uttered the words, "You caught it early," she thought, "No, I *didn't,* so I'm going to die." Please repeat after me: assume nothing.

5) *Get all the facts straight before you open your mouth.* Did your friend have a heart or liver transplant? Chemo or radiation? Mumps or measles? Don't just ask, "How are you?" Ask questions specific to your friend's circumstance. "How's your rotator cuff feeling these days?" "Did it turn out to be an ulcer?" "Are your new meds working?" Some people (especially people of a certain age) have trouble keeping track of their friends' troubles because so many of their cohort have problems. If you need help remembering who has shingles and who has lupus or the date of a friend's cataract operation, enter a note under the person's name in your iPhone, BlackBerry, or address book and update the information when things change: "Dennis: gall stones surgery Oct. 5." "Karen: eye infection Apr. 28." "Charlie: bad knee." Luddites can write the health note on a Post-it and stick it near the phone. Just do whatever it takes to put the facts at your fingertips before a word comes out of your mouth.

6) *Help your sick friend feel useful.* Zero in on one of their skills and lead to it. That's what Susan Plum did when she asked a writer friend

with stage IV breast cancer to help her craft a speech. Susan's request focused the patient on her strengths and reminded her that she's a writer while her other friends made her feel as if all she is is sick. Many people who are ailing but not incapacitated wish they had something meaningful to do with their time and talents. You could ask a cybersmart patient to set up a web page for you; ask a bridge, poker, or chess maven to give you pointers on the game; ask a retired teacher to help you research summer camps for your disabled child or to help guide your teenager through the college application process. In most instances your request won't be seen as an imposition but rather an opportunity for the patient to feel valued and needed.

7) *Don't infantilize your sick friend.* Never talk to a grown-up the way you'd talk to a child. One posthysterectomy patient said a few condescending friends treated her "as if they thought that because I'd lost my uterus I'd also lost my mind." Objectionable sentences include "How are we today, dearie?" "That's a good boy." "I bet you could swallow this teeny-tiny pill if you really, really tried." And the wince-worthy "Are we ready to go wee-wee?" Remember that words can wound a person's dignity more deeply than the point of a sword. It's within your power to protect those who already feel helpless and vulnerable—especially when clad in a hospital gown, the most undignified garment on the planet—from verbal humiliation.

8) *Think twice before giving advice.* Remember that bogus "Johns Hopkins" bulletin my friend Jeb sent around? Don't forward medical alerts, newspaper clippings, wig catalogs, or your Aunt Sadie's cure for gout. As Dolores's husband pointed out, sick people have a doctor to tell them what to do. Your job is simply to be their friend.

9) *Allow patients who are terminally ill to set the conversational agenda.* If they're unaware that they're dying, don't you be the one to

tell them. If they know they're dying and want to talk about it, don't contradict or interrupt them; let them vent or weep or curse the Fates. If they cry, give them a tissue, and feel free to cry with them. If they confide their last wish or their final instructions or they trust you with their life's regrets or tell you their lifelong secret, don't feel you have to say anything; just listen hard. Someday you're going to want to remember every word they say.

10) *Don't pressure them to "keep up the fight" or practice "positive thinking."* It's cruel to imply that negative thoughts—that is, feeling discouraged, not battling hard enough, not having the "right attitude"— caused their illness in the first place or may have compounded their suffering. If your friend keeps getting sicker, the last thing they need is to blame themselves. The masculine ideal of stoicism is of little practical use to a man who is deathly ill. Don't say, "You're gonna beat it!" when you know they probably won't. Positive thinking can't cure Huntington's disease, ALS, or inoperable brain cancer. Telling a terminal patient to "Keep up the fight!" isn't just futile; it's mean. Don't make a dying patient feel guilty for having lost the fight. Don't make death into a personal failure. Positive thinking may help patients endure unpleasant tests or agonizing treatments, but it's not a prescription, palliative, or cure. Furthermore, insisting that terminal patients see the glass as half full may deny them the truth of what they know and the chance to tie up life's loose ends while there's still time. As one hospice patient put it: "All I want from my friends at this stage is the freedom to sulk and say good-bye."

Although each of those ten commandments addresses a different conversational hazard, they can be summarized in this paraphrase of Hillel's famous dictum: "Do not say unto others what you would not have them say unto you. All the rest is commentary."

||||||||||||||||||||||||||||||||||||||||||||||||||||||||||||||||||||||||||||||||||||||||||||||||||||||||||||||||||||||||||||||||||||||||

MY CANCER
AND MY FRIENDS

THIRTY-SIX HOURS AGO, when we were at our dining table with our kids and their families, stuffing ourselves in anticipation of the Yom Kippur fast, my biggest worry was how to survive twenty-five food-free hours without fainting from hunger or blasting a friend with an unsavory whiff of my nutrition-deprived breath. Now, though the Jewish New Year is only one day old and I haven't had time to commit a single sin, I'm worried I might die. But first I have to tell my children I have cancer.

Phone's out of the question; my voice would crack on my opening line. Summoning the family to an in-person meeting would be too melodramatic, and seeing my kids' faces crumple would send me over the edge. To avoid false bravado, vocal quivering, and tears all around, I decide to break the news to my three grown children, Abigail, Robin, and David, in writing and leave it to them to tell their children (of which each has two), who at this point range in age from seven to twelve. Though arguably inappropriate for a health bulletin of this magnitude, e-mail strikes me as the best way to break the news. I'm at the computer struggling mightily to find the right words. Ultimately, I take refuge in the phrases my radiologist had used that morning to talk me down from the tree of panic: "Caught early." "Tiny tumor."

"Noninvasive." "Nonaggressive." I cling to those words for dear life. From now on they will be my mantra.

Once my cancer has been given a name, I decide to tell my friends in the same manner—electronically. I want them to know my world has been upended, but I can't bear the thought of calling each of them separately, hearing their stunned responses one by one, or fielding questions I'm not yet equipped to answer. I'm also loath to hear myself keep saying, "caught early," "tiny tumor," and the rest of my refrain for fear that repetition will drain the words of their redemptive power. In an e-mail I believe I can control the conversation. I write:

> *Bummer! I've just learned I have breast cancer, a "tubular carcinoma" to be precise. My oncologist says it's one of the least invasive, least aggressive tumors, and my comedian-internist says it's the best cancer to have if you're having only one. Despite this mordantly celebratory prognosis, I'll definitely need surgery—not sure yet if lumpectomy or mastectomy—then radiation and maybe chemo.*

I sign off with the request that my friends keep this news confidential. Not that I buy into the fifties mentality, when cancer was hush-hush. Today, a diagnosis like mine is neither shameful nor (necessarily) fatal—but I don't want to feel exposed. My misery would be compounded were I to become grist for gossip or an object of pity.

It's always been hard for me to strike the right balance between intimacy and privacy, and right now these contradictory needs seem irreconcilable. I want my dearest friends to stay close no matter what happens next, but I also want to preserve a zone of solitude in which I can sort through my thoughts and feelings without a lot of surrounding chatter. So the question is whom and how many friends to tell?

DEFINING A CIRCLE OF INTIMACY

Illness and misfortune lay bare the anxiety of proximity: only when we're ready to share a major problem do we discover where our friends fall on the spectrum of closeness, whether they have a place in our emotional inner sanctum and at our bedside, or whether they're to be kept at arm's length and out of the loop. The ultimate power of one friend over another is the power to grant or deny intimacy. When we trust someone with the turmoil of our body, soul (or bank account), we give them the key to our core and, in so doing, define them as the closest of the close, our Uberpals. Other friends may be good and dear to us, but when we're thinking about whom we want to confide in, listen to, and lean on, only the Uberpals make the cut.

Sitting at the computer screen mulling over my contacts list, I start typing names on the To line. I know that some of the people I love and who love me, people who undoubtedly consider themselves close enough to merit my confidence, would be wounded were they to discover I'd withheld my diagnosis from them. But I can't tell everyone, can I?

I end up with twelve names and press Send. A dozen "intimate" friends may sound like an oxymoron; however, their responses alone attest to why each of them deserves that definition. Sympathy, empathy, encouragement, and reassurance; invitations to breakfast, lunch, and dinner; offers to bring us meals, do our marketing, come over and keep me company—all twelve respond fast, all twelve want to do something, anything, to help, all twelve generously declare their devotion and love. Their e-mails, phone calls, and visits fill me with gratitude and wonder. I begin to believe I can beat this.

The following Monday I get an e-mail from someone who was not among my designated dozen, a lovely woman, a good friend, but not one who'd met my need-to-know test. The next day there's a message on my voicemail from a former colleague. The rest of the week brings a get-well card and two more e-mails from friends whose names weren't in the To box, all of them nice, kind people who are sorry to hear about my diagnosis, all of them asking how I am and how they can help.

Clearly, news of my cancer has metastasized. One or more of my Uberpals must have squealed, and I suppose it was naive of me to expect otherwise. Gossip, as Dave Barry once put it, is "the most powerful force in the universe." The compulsion to transmit bad news was either wired into the human genome or evolved as an early warning system to protect members of primitive societies against contagion. Our biblical forbears were always jabbering at the well. Native Americans used smoke signals. Early moderns hogged the party line. Now we need only tap a few keys for gossip to go viral. People have talked about each other behind each other's backs since the beginning of time. I've done it myself.

Years ago, during drop-off at the nursery school my children attended, a group of fellow parents were talking about one of the mothers who had been seriously injured in a taxi accident after dropping her son off at school. None of us knew what to do: fetch her son out of class? Call the hospital? Visit her? Send flowers? We wondered how and if we could reach her husband (this was before cell phones)? Should one of us pick up her son after school and offer to keep him overnight so his father could stay with his mother at the hospital? What would the little boy be told, we wondered, and what should we tell our children, his classmates, so that, going forward, they'd be sensitive to his feelings? How else might we help? What if the mother was permanently disabled and had to quit her job? They weren't rich—would they have money problems? Did they have health insurance? Should we take up a collection to cover their medical bills? Should we call other parents on the class list and tell them what happened so that they too could discuss whether to call, visit, send flowers, bring food, or offer help?

Some would call that gossip. I've always thought of it as "constructive intervention" because we weren't just talking about a friend's mishap; we were figuring out how to cope with its repercussions. I can't know if all the friends who disseminated my cancer diagnosis thought of themselves as gossips or constructive interventionists, but one woman told me that gossiping about my situation helped her deal with her "there but for the grace of God go I" reaction to my news because it gave her an excuse to share her fears and vulnerabilities in the act of worrying aloud about me. When my friends who are take-charge personalities felt overwhelmed by their inability to do anything to help me, gossip became their substitute for action. (If they were talking about me, at least they were doing *something*.) Rather than retreat into frustration and impotence, they were actively discussing my situation, commiserating with mutual friends of ours, and enlisting others as partners in their powerlessness.

Just for the hell of it, I ask each new caller how she heard.

"Oh, let's see now, who told me?" they muse aloud and inevitably come up with something like, "Gee, for the life of me, I can't remember."

Imagine that! Not one person who's become privy to my private information can recall her source! What's more, a few people express surprise, even dismay, that I didn't inform them myself, which puts me in the odd position of apologizing for having cancer and not telling them. "I didn't want to burden you," I reply. From their reactions it appears that's a paltry excuse for my icing them out. I may as well have said, "You're unworthy of my confidence" or "None of your business." Worse yet, by withholding my diagnosis from my second circle of intimacy—another oxymoron by which I mean people who are close friends but not Uberpals—I may have conveyed the impression that my cancer is more serious than it actually is. As with any cover-up, a secret once revealed is magnified by its prior concealment.

In November a friend invites us to dinner. I accept. She e-mails back, "So glad you can come. I just heard from XX about your cancer and I got very worried, but she said that the tumor was contained and all is well, so we can celebrate. . . . Shall we say 7:30?" The name she mentions is neither that of an Uberpal nor a second-circle friend, so I'm never able to follow the gossip trail to its origin. Then on January 1, 2010, this e-mail arrives from a friend I'll call Emma, who identifies her source in the first sentence:

> *I hope I am not intruding on your New Year's Day, but I had dinner with Dorothy [not their real names] the other night and she mentioned that you were starting radiation this week. Having gone through it ten years ago—after nine months of chemo—I can imagine your feelings. If you have any questions or just want to chat, I am happy to do so at any time. I can only relate my experience, of course, but it was pretty easy: 33 days and I went to work every day, went for the radiation and right back to my office.*

I've known Emma and Dorothy for years, and no finer women walk the earth. I adore both of them for their gentle warmth and their good hearts. Moreover, Emma's offer is generous, sensitive, and lovingly expressed (and it turns out to jibe to the letter with my radiation experience). What bothers me about Emma's e-mail is its further evidence of the still-spiraling, ever-widening ripples of gossip. It is January 1, a new year. I have to put a stop to this. I write back,

> *Dear Emma, I deeply appreciate your concern, and not only am I grateful for your kind offer, I'm comforted to know that you've come through your treatments with all your smarts and energy intact. At the moment, I'm not at all worried about the upcoming radiation, as I've talked to several other friends who've been through it and not one of them has described troublesome side effects.*

But I have a different problem now: every day or two someone new calls or writes to tell me that someone else has told them I have breast cancer. In response to each fresh query, I've had to revisit my diagnosis to answer her questions, which has made it impossible for me to put it behind me. That's why I'm asking you to please not pass the information along to anyone else. I'm going to e-mail Dorothy and request that she do the same, as I know she has a huge social network, and I shudder to think of how many more calls and e-mails I might get if she chooses to mention my situation.

Please know that I welcome your love and reassurance and I think you're wonderful to reach out to me, but for the sake of my privacy and peace of mind, I need to nip this in the bud (or rather in its full flower) so that I may, as my oncologist suggests, stop thinking about my lump and start living my life.

Less than a minute after I send the e-mail Emma calls to reassure me that she hasn't told anyone else, nor would she. When I e-mail Dorothy asking her to do the same, her reply is so abjectly remorseful, I regret raising the issue in the first place.

Dear Letty, I am so, so sorry! Clearly, though it was not intentional, I see now that it was wrong of me to disclose the information about your cancer to Emma, and I hope I did not hurt you by having done it. Had I known it was confidential, I would not have said a word. I would have honored your privacy. I also want you to know that this was not a full-fledged conversation about you, it was a passing remark, which never should have come out of my mouth. I should have realized that if you and Emma were close friends, she already would have known about your condition, and I wouldn't be the one telling her. But now, going forward, I want to emphasize that you can tell me anything and I can be trusted. Please, please forgive me for this one indiscretion, and please don't hit the Delete button when you next see my name in your e-mail box. I would be eternally grateful, since you hold a very special place in my head and heart. Thank you for your honesty, and again, I apologize for being so careless and insensitive to your needs.

||||||||||||||||||||||||||

I HATE MYSELF for making Dorothy and Emma feel so guilty. In retrospect, I think I should have kept my feelings to myself and accepted Emma's offer with grace. After all, any friend worth her salt is going to ask about you, worry about you, offer to be helpful, and occasionally talk about you behind your back—mostly with the goal of "constructive intervention." However, twelve weeks have passed since my fateful mammogram, seven weeks since the surgery, and, though I have no idea how I'm going to react to the radiation, I'm already functioning pretty much as I did BBC (Before Breast Cancer). I'm ready to move on, but to do so I need my friends to quit talking about me and relating to me as if I might be doomed. After the go-around with Emma and Dorothy, however, I decide it isn't worth the effort to put out a privacy policy if it's going to arouse all that guilty angst in my beloved friends.

I hadn't included my friend Martha Lear in my original Uberpal bulletin, but after I have the surgery and radiation, I tell her about my situation and deliver my usual litany—"tiny, noninvasive, nonaggressive, no big deal but definitely discombobulating though I'm well on the way to recovery."

"The real big deal is this happy outcome," writes Martha in a return e-mail. "Onward!!"

After reading the word, "recovery," she doesn't need chapter and verse, and with that singular exclamation—Onward!—she gives me permission to default to normal. Since then Martha and I have seen each other at three or four parties, and each time, she's asked, "You okay?" and I've replied, "Yup," and with that, we've moved on to Other Things.

Another just-right reaction comes my way after I mention during dinner with some old pals that I'd be starting radiation the following week. I thought everyone at the table knew my diagnosis, but the gossip had not yet reached one friend, Linda Gottlieb, who e-mails me the next day:

> I was so taken aback last night to learn that you are dealing with breast cancer—taken aback because I had no idea of it and felt that you must think me a dreadful friend not to have called you or acknowledged your illness; and taken aback because in the setting last night I couldn't come over and just give you a hug.
>
> I know that you are going to be just fine, and I even understand your wanting to cope with this by not making a big deal about it—I think I would do the same thing—but nevertheless, dealing with this illness, getting such a diagnosis, and trying to readjust your life around it is a profound experience. Surely one must take a pause in the 'business as usual' lives we all lead to tip one's hat to the terrifyingly random nature of the universe.
>
> We need not talk about this again (I surely respect your privacy), but I just wanted to give you—electronically—what I couldn't stop the party last night to give you: a great big hug.

I can't imagine a more sensitive, eloquent response to a friend's illness than Linda's. The first time we see each other after that e-mail, she asks how I am.

"Doing great!" I say, and that's the end of it. We've met in different settings since then, and she has neither grilled me on my condition nor given me one of those deep stares of compassion (bordering on pity) that people bestow as proof of their concern. Our relationship has also defaulted to normal, for which I'm grateful. However, I've been kicking myself for not including her in my first e-mail blast, for I might have taken early comfort in her wise remarks.

So here's what I've learned from the Whom-to-tell quandary and all the leaks that followed: calculating who's in and who's out of your inner circle is a no-win proposition. Nearly everyone you know and care about and everyone who cares about you will eventually find out anyway (trust me on this one too), so if you're sick, you may as well be more expansive in your definition of "close friends." Tell more, not fewer people from the get-go, and you'll end up with less explaining to do.

TWO

HOW TO GIVE GOOD VISITS

*Behaving Well with the Unwell
Under Almost Any Circumstances—Even If You're Shy and
Awkward, Hate Hospitals, Hardly Know the Person, and
Wish You Could Be Anywhere Else*

VISITING THE SICK IS A COMPLICATED BUSINESS. In this chapter you'll meet people who pop in on their sick friends eagerly, reluctantly, or not at all; people who used to visit and stopped; people who'll gladly visit a friend at home but won't step foot in a hospital; and people who get flustered by what they see when they visit a sickroom. If you like lists, you'll find several: fifteen common excuses for not visiting, ten suggestions for more satisfying home visits, seven ground rules for attitudinal honesty, and twenty tips for good behavior at the sickbed. Other subjects under discussion include religious approaches to visiting the sick, gender differences in visiting habits, how often to go and how long to stay, why not everyone wants to be visited or should be, how to accommodate to the needs of the disabled, and how to help your children give good visits.

Again, let's start with some sinus-clearing truth-telling. If you're like me, your motivations for paying a visit aren't always pure. It goes without saying that you mostly visit to show your concern for your sick friends, to see how they're doing, and to lift their spirits with your presence and presents. But sometimes—admit it—you visit for less noble reasons: because you were taught that it's "the right thing to do," your faith demands it, or the patient has power over some aspect of your life (boss, anyone?) and if you don't pay them a visit, you fear you may suffer for it later.

Notice the verb: to *pay* connotes compensation, obligation, the discharge of duty. When you make a sick call, you're paying in multiple currencies—your time, love, care, words, and gifts. It may be an attempt to compensate for your past neglect of that person, a kind of gratitude tax to the cosmic health department, a symbolic installment on your "There-but-for-the-Grace-of-God-Go-I" debt to the deity who has kept *you* in good health. One man I interviewed admitted that he paid a visit to his sick cousin to clear his conscience before going off to the movies without her. An honest woman I'll call Rosalyn confessed to a fairly venal reason for visiting Carole, her fellow school board member: after years of feeling diminished by Carole's superior airs, Rosalyn derived a guilty pleasure out of seeing her friend laid low in a hospital bed; it felt like a corrective adjustment to the scales of justice.

What undergirds all motivations for making a sick call is the fact that it's the one thing you can do when you feel powerless to do anything else. Which is not to say the dynamics of the encounter are uncomplicated. Through no fault of their own, the unwell have a way of making the well uneasy, causing visitors who are unpracticed in the bedside arts to botch the encounter due to awkwardness, misinterpretation, or ignorance. No one visits a sick room for the fun of it. Some of us just show our discomfort more overtly than others.

- Natalie Robins, a survivor of MALT non-Hodgkin's lymphoma, recalled when a couple of friends dropped by after she first came home from the hospital. "They acted so somber and strange, you'd have thought they were paying me a condolence call."

- Kate, a vibrant middle-aged woman, told me she visited her friend Alison, who, though roughly the same age, was seriously debilitated by emphysema and only able to breathe with the aid of an oxygen tank. So stark was the contrast between the two of them that Kate felt overwhelmed by pity, which made her extra solicitous, which, she realized belatedly, made Alison feel weaker and worse. This obviously was not what Kate had intended her visit to accomplish.

- During his friend Robert's visit to his hospital room, Steve, who was recuperating from a stomach operation, had an attack of postsurgical gas. His discomfort made him act snarky to Robert, who concluded he ought to leave (even though he'd just arrived ten minutes ago and had traveled an hour to get there), which made Steve feel obliged (even though his gut was wheezing and gurgling) to beg his friend to stay. This defeated the entire purpose of Robert's visit—to make Steve feel better.

- Years ago my friend Barbara Barrie had a colostomy that requires her to wear a small plastic pouch on her stomach and a long, clear plastic irrigation sleeve that's attached around her waist with an elastic cord. I later learned that the apparatus is used once a day to irrigate her system, like an enema. The pouch is discarded each time she showers, but the sleeve gets washed and hung on a hook to dry. The first time I visited her at home after her surgery I went to use the bathroom and was taken aback to see the plastic sleeve looped over her shower rod as casually as a pair of handwashed pantyhose. I didn't know what to say or whether to say anything at all. I was curious about it and how she used it, but despite our long friendship, I was too embarrassed to ask. Turns out not asking was the wrong call by far.

Unlike some colorectal cancer survivors for whom the apparatus is a shameful symbol of their dysfunction, Barbara sees the pouch and sleeve as "trophies of my survival . . . a miracle of my life as they never show beneath clothes." If she thinks about it when she has company, she puts it out of sight so as "not to force my visitor's attention upon my ablutions, which is the last thing I want to do. However if it is hanging in the shower (and it often is) it doesn't matter one whit to me. I am not the least bit ashamed."

This "miracle" is what lets Barbara pursue the activities she loves—exercise, tennis, swimming, museum-going, and travel. Recently, in an e-mail, she reminded me of the time both of us were on a bike trip with an organized tour group. Before we set out each day on our route, she recalled, "the group often sweetly waited for me to irrigate in the morning. Even now, when friends call, they often say, 'are you irrigating . . . should I call back?' And whenever I travel, all the equipment never leaves my side, and the people I travel with always help me protect the valise it is in."

In a return e-mail I admitted that when I first saw the sleeve hanging on the shower rod I was uncomfortable and embarrassed. "Interesting," she wrote back. "Because I think the whole thing is life giving and a blessing."

Such minidramas explain why some people don't visit their sick friends as often as they think they should whereas others opt out of the enterprise altogether.

Fifteen Common Excuses for Not Visiting a Sick Friend

- "Once his Parkinson's got really bad, I couldn't stand to see him so shaky and shrunken. It was painful for us both."
- "I can't do anything for her, and sitting there just makes me feel useless."

- "I'm not good around really sick people. Suffering scares me."
- "When I hear him gasping for air, all I can think is, please God don't let him die on my watch. I'm not proud of being so self-centered, but that's why I don't go."
- "I can't bear to see him like that; I want to remember him the way he was."
- "If it was me, I'd want to be left alone."
- "She told me I didn't have to come."
- "She knows I love her. I don't have to prove it."
- "He was asleep all the time, so what's the difference if I'm there or not?"
- "I never really liked her that much to begin with."
- "He doesn't care if I come."
- "My visit isn't going to make her better."
- "I sent a fruit basket."
- "I couldn't get a sitter."
- "We were never really that close."

VISITATION PHOBIAS

||||||||||||||||||||||||||||||||||||||||||||||

If you have a visceral resistance or a psychological block to visiting the sick, it may have nothing to do with the patient and everything to do with your childhood or an incident in your past that left you with negative associations regarding doctors, hospitals, or something in the illness environment.

I'm thinking of Kyle, who kept coming up with reasons why he couldn't visit Aaron in the hospital. One day his car died; the next his roof leaked; Wednesday he had to help his mother move; Thursday he woke up with a cough. Yet when Aaron came home from the hospital Kyle was the first one there. He hadn't been dissing his friend; he just hated hospitals.

"Bad things happen there," said Kyle. By which he meant staph infections, bloody tableaus he'd rather not have imprinted on his retinas, morgue-chilly temperatures, beeping machines, flashing lights, strange smells, and the sound of patients moaning on stretchers in the halls. Very simply, he found hospitals inhospitable and couldn't rise above his repulsion.

Another man, Brett, confided that the day he brought his wife to MSK for cancer surgery he'd had a vivid flashback—a repressed trauma dating from when he was four years old. Suddenly he saw himself lying in a hospital bed in a children's ward, having awakened after his tonsillectomy, unable to swallow. He remembered his mother feeding him ice cream with a flat wooden spoon from a Dixie cup—half vanilla, half chocolate—when his father announced that grown-ups weren't permitted to stay overnight, so Brett would have to be a big brave boy and stay there by himself and *not cry*. Panicking, young Brett had grabbed his mother around the neck and held on so tightly that his father had to smack him to make him let go. It took two nurses to restrain the little boy as his parents were shooed out. Twenty-five years later Brett expended a lot of self-control to douse that flicker of childhood terror before he could be truly present and able to assist his wife in her time of fear and stress.

Betsy, another of my waiting room interview subjects, said she never used to visit anyone in the hospital because the smell of institutional disinfectant reminded her of the night her brother was in intensive care. When the man in the next bed died, an orderly came and cleaned up his space to prepare it for a new arrival, and a few hours later her brother died. For decades Betsy had associated that odor with his death and refused to step foot in a hospital. Of course, now that she was at MSK every day, she had no choice but to get used to the smell.

VISITING RELIGIOUSLY

!!!

However deeply felt or psychologically determined, no excuse for hospital aversion would pass muster with the three major Western religions.

Christianity teaches the faithful to visit the sick *not* to meet their own needs but rather the needs of the afflicted. "Visit the sick and bury the dead"—an obligation listed among Catholicism's "Corporal Works of Mercy"—is said to originate in Jesus's words: "I was naked and you clothed me, I was sick and you visited me" (Matthew 25:36).

The Koran cites visiting the sick as one of five fundamental duties every Muslim owes to "a brother in Islam." Believers are instructed to visit a patient repeatedly, not just once, and in return for performing this *sunnah* (an act that emulates the conduct of the holy Prophet Muhammad), visitors are promised such heavenly rewards as "the blessings of seventy thousand angels" and "a garden in Paradise."

Observant Jews must perform the *mitzvah* of *bikur cholim* (the commandment to visit the sick) whether or not the patient is Jewish. According to the Talmud, each visit removes one-sixtieth of the sufferer's pain. Moreover, "Anyone who does not visit the sick, it is as if he has spilled blood." "Anyone who visits the sick causes him to live, and anyone who does not visit the sick causes him to die." Talk about one's actions having consequences! If paying a visit to a friend has even the slightest potential to save a life, you can bet I'll show up.

HOW LONG SHOULD YOU STAY

!!

If a sickbed visit were a stage play, Act One would establish what you did and worried about up to the moment when you arrived. Act Two would show you in the sick room, behaving well or blundering comically, being helpful or messing up. In Act Three you would either say your good-byes perfectly, blither your way to an awkward departure, "go up" (i.e., draw a complete blank on the lines you'd rehearsed a hundred times), or overstay your welcome and spoil the final scene.

I once paid a visit to two friends who happened to be in the same hospital at the same time—Liz, a woman in her mid-forties who had fractured her leg by stepping into a three-foot-deep post hole, and Esther, eighty-two, who was recovering from a quadruple bypass.

Liz, ensconced in a sunny room, her leg in a cast up to her thigh, recounted how she'd gotten stuck in the hole that had been dug in preparation for installing a wooden fence, how she'd frantically twisted and yanked her leg in an attempt to pull it out (which caused it to break in several places), and how it felt to be wedged in the earth up to her hip. In great detail she told me about the person who finally extracted her leg from the hole, how it was done, what the doctors did to fix it, how her leg felt now, when she was expected to be able to walk again, and so on. She didn't just describe what happened; she animated the story with both hands and one leg, embroidered it, embossed it, decorated it with sequins, and, in so doing, was able to reframe a terrifying experience into an engaging anecdote that, repeated again and again to each of her visitors, helped tame the trauma. (Behavioral psychologists call this process desensitization.) I found her narrative riveting, but had it been dull as dust, I still would have given her my rapt attention because I sensed that's what she needed—enough time to restate her ordeal and enough ears to hear it. I stayed about twenty minutes.

Next I strolled over to the cardiac unit where Esther was recovering from bypass surgery. I asked her about her operation. "Too boring!" she said, and flatly refused to talk about herself. All she wanted was to ask *me* about "the outside world." Books, plays, movies, Obama's press conference, Mayor Bloomberg's anti-smoking law—that's what we schmoozed about, to her obvious delight. About half an hour into my visit I saw her eyelids droop. Her tank had finally run dry. I pecked her cheek quickly, saying I'd just remembered I was late for an appointment. She was snoring before I reached the door.

Both visits are worth recounting in detail because they illustrate why no one can tell you exactly how much time is the right amount to spend at the bedside of your friends. It depends on too many variables—their medical condition, degree of infirmity, and level of fatigue; their temperament and loquaciousness or lack thereof; the history and depth of your relationship (how intimate or how casual); the time of day; the hospital's rules; the atmosphere in the room; and who else is there. I can only say that in my experience twenty minutes is about right for a hospital visit, ten or less if the patient is woozy, weak, or in pain. You can stay longer for a home visit, and if some of your time is spent helping out, you *should* stay longer. I suggest, however, that you not hang around more than ten minutes if the patient's parents have just arrived from out of town or you found your friend and his wife holding hands when you arrived. Chances are that in such situations your friend would prefer to be alone with those closest to him.

I recently visited a friend in New York Hospital four days after her surgery. Though she was perky and peppy enough to be sitting at the edge of her bed and chatting freely, we kept getting interrupted, first by a nutritionist, then a social worker, then the technician who'd come to teach her how to use her new urinary apparatus in preparation for her discharge the following day. With each staff member's arrival I left the room and waited in the hall (did I mention that you should do that too?). In the end, although I was technically at the hospital for about thirty minutes, I was probably with my friend for ten, which was the right duration for that particular patient on that particular day.

Ultimately, if forced to answer, "How long is the right amount of time for a sickbed visit?" I'd have to say, "Long enough to show that you care, but not as long as you think."

HOW OFTEN SHOULD YOU VISIT?

IIIIIIIIIIIIIIIIIIIIIIIIIIIIIIIIIIIIIIIIIIIIIIIIIIIIIIIIIIIIIIIIII

It's not easy to maintain the same frequency over the long haul.

Janet Avery had much to say on the subject of frequency and consistency: "The worst thing about illness is being left alone, especially if you live by yourself like I do. When my stroke first happened, dozens of my friends came by every day. Then they fizzled out. I think they disappeared because I'm not the same person anymore. I'm no longer bedridden, but I'm boring. I'm this dull old lady now, and I wouldn't want to be around me either. I have nothing to talk about. I have no energy. It's understandable that their visits petered out.

"I believe people *are* what they *do.* Our lives are made up of our energy and interests. When I had a full life, I saw my friends sporadically, and that was okay because I was in my world and they were in theirs, and we came together now and then to share each other's world. But when my world shrank and they were still active in theirs . . . ,"—her voice trailed off for a long moment—"I try not to make people feel guilty for not visiting. There's nothing worse than a friendship based on guilt. At the same time I feel like telling them, 'What happened to me is going to happen to you! It just happened to me sooner.' I think they should have gotten together and organized a committee to make sure at least one of them was always looking in on me and checking up on me." [For help organizing a support group, see Resources, page 265.]

Suppose you have a friend you like a lot but see only once or twice a year. Are you socially obligated to pay repeated sick calls to someone who is more than a casual acquaintance but not quite a gal pal or buddy boy? I can only tell you what I did when a woman who answers to that description in my life broke her hip. I went to the hospital with a mesh bag full of Clementines and spent about twenty minutes at her bedside. She told me how the accident happened—a jogger slammed into her and knocked her down. We talked about the prognosis for her recovery. We talked about Other Things. She said she'd probably be discharged from the hospital by the weekend. I left, promising to call. A week later I left a voicemail message on her home phone, something like, "I hope to see you back on the dance floor soon." By my lights our friendship, which is more than casual but less than intimate, dictated no more outreach than that. I'm not in her inner circle; I'm someone who cared enough to express my affection once in person, once by phone. Given our history, that felt appropriate, sufficient, and right. Since then we've seen each other a couple of times a year. Her hip is healed, and our relationship is as warm and comfortable as always.

Had a beloved family member or intimate friend broken her hip, however, I probably would have turned up at her bedside every day, helped her home from the hospital, and spent a considerable amount of time with her throughout her convalescence. But you can't be there for *everyone* all the time. I'd say you're a good enough friend if you're there for those who matter most and if, when you're there, you give good visits.

TEN SUGGESTIONS TO PERK UP YOUR VISITS WITH THE HOUSEBOUND

While your world continues to expand and you're actively pursuing your interests and amassing experiences, the world of the invalid, infirm, or incapacitated is bound to contract, and they are likely to bring less and less to the table. Unless they have enormous inner resources, your relationship with them, which formerly was one of equals, eventually tips out of balance. Though still fond of them, you may find yourself visiting less frequently, and when you do, it may be harder and harder to make conversation.

The secret to more satisfying visits with a long-term housebound friend lies in advance planning and creative activities. Here are ten ways to make your time together more relaxed and rewarding.

1) *Rehearse the visit in your mind.* Don't count on spontaneity or serendipity to start the conversational ball rolling. Decide in advance on three or four subjects that might stimulate discussion. Bring along an item of interest—a newspaper clipping, a CD, a new app.

2) *Watch a movie or TV show together and talk about it with them in detail.* Don't just ask, "How'd you like it?" Ask what they thought of the direction, script, casting, scenery, background music. Challenge them to think of other actors who might have played each role more convincingly. Discuss the pivot points of the plot. Housebound patients may have lost their mobility, but they haven't necessarily lost their ability to form an opinion. Before you leave, ask your friend what movie they would like you to bring on your next visit.

3) *Convene a book group composed of the two of you or add a few others to the mix.* The idea is for everyone to read the same book and meet in the patient's home once a month to discuss it. (These days discussion guides are often included at the back of the book.) Be sensitive to the limits of the patient's concentration. Don't choose *War and Peace* or the two-volume biography of *Emma Goldman* if *Freakonomics* or a breezy novel is about as much as your sick friend can handle.

4) *Bring a jigsaw puzzle.* Offer to do it with them, and if the two of you don't finish it by the end of your visit, encourage your friend to continue without you. Tell her you look forward to seeing the finished product on your next visit. (Before buying, check the puzzle box for the number of pieces it contains: three hundred–piece puzzles allow for more immediate gratification and less chance that the patient will quit in frustration. Thousand-piece puzzles can be daunting.)

5) *Play checkers or chess, and keep score.* If your friend is enthusiastic about either game, buy them a unique-looking set that will always remind them of how much you care about them.

6) *Use poker chips when you play cards.* They feel good and add gravitas.

7) *Play one of the "With Friends" games.* Try "Words with Friends" for starters. Available on Facebook, Android, or http://www.zyngawith friends.com/wp/category/blog/.

8) *Create a Trifecta of game classics.* Scrabble, Monopoly, and Battleship could together comprise a tournament that lasts for months. Trivial Pursuit, Bananagrams, and Uno could be another. Whoever wins the first three games gets to choose the next three.

9) *Ask other friends of the patient to send artifacts*—photos of themselves, mementos of shared events, personal anecdotes, written messages—and collect everything in a scrapbook or dedicated box. Go through the stuff with the patient, and as you do so, encourage them to share whatever thoughts each item evokes.

10) *Combine forces with other friends to create different cadres of visitors.* Stagger your visits. Coordinate who comes when and which group brings what. With each constellation of visitors, the chemistry of each visit will change, providing a variety of stimuli to the patient. (See Resources, page 265.)

JUST SHOW UP

Woody Allen, not my favorite source of usable wisdom, once said, "Eighty percent of success is showing up." That's certainly true of friendship.

Here's how my daughter Abigail put it in a recent e-mail: "So much of friendship is just being in the room. Not necessarily what you say, give as a gift, or write in a note—just showing up when it matters (and not making a grand entrance or expecting trumpets in return). That's the fabric of friendship. All of us remember who paid us a visit soon after our kids were born or who traveled farthest for a wedding or funeral. We remember people who just *came*. They didn't expect to be knighted because they got on a plane or cleared a night to come and sit with us when we were sick, but to me, their simple presence in the room spoke powerfully. It said, 'This is important. I'm here to be with you.'"

Lisa Alther's experience underscores that point. When her ninety-five-year-old father, Shelton Reed, was near death, Lisa rushed from her current home in Vermont to her childhood home in Tennessee to sit with him, even though he was often asleep and sometimes didn't know who she was.

"I felt it important to be present, that there was some part of him that was intact, that he was still in there somewhere, and my being in the room was a comfort. This was confirmed when, amazingly, he opened his eyes at one point and said, '*Please* don't go back to Vermont.'

"There's a difference between the hard work of caring for a child and the hard work of caring for an elder. With a child, when you're done, they're raised; with a sick parent, there's no happy ending, so there's a kind of poignancy about just being with them and caring for them. It's bittersweet."

Lisa's father outlived almost all his contemporaries, but his best friend, Bob Jones, is still around, elderly himself but still able to drive. Bob visited Shelton twice a week and sat with him for two or three hours, whether they talked or not. Bob was a witness to Shelton's life. He knew him in his prime, loved him then, and loved him still.

"I don't know if he was a support to my dad, but he definitely was to my three brothers, my sister, and me," said Lisa. "Other visitors were *our* friends; they would take us out to dinner to distract us from our reality, which was so depressing and physically exhausting. But Bob was my dad's friend; he knew my dad in his prime, so the two of them could revisit their happy memories of when they were at college and played basketball together or when they were in medical school to-gether or did their residencies together in New York. It was wonderful for us kids to be able to look at my father, who was bedridden, ill, and confused, and to imagine him leaping up, playing basketball, and being vital and vibrant."

Dick Bailey was another old friend of Shelton's who visited often. The two of them enjoyed talking about their experiences in World War II, about Paris and the Occupation. "My dad was a surgeon on a fleet of Liberty ships going across the Atlantic that were constantly being circled by German submarines. He worked in field hospitals where they brought trainloads of sick people in from concentrations camps. I guess he didn't want to bring all that unpleasantness home to us kids, and that's why he didn't talk about the war until he was old and sick. But when Dick came over, they reminisced about that time, and I could see that they were proud of who they were and what they did."

THE QUESTION OF GENDER

Back in the eighties, while doing research for my book *Among Friends,* I plowed through hundreds, maybe thousands of studies on behavioral sex differences—which of them are supposedly innate and which are acquired. Rather than reopen that can of worms, I think we can agree that in general men and women "do" intimacy differently. Nowhere is this difference more striking than in each gender's typical response to illness, whether as patient or visitor.

"I love my buddies, don't get me wrong," rasped Nick, a widower, who had cancer of the larynx. "But every day I thank God for the fe-male of the species!" The day he was discharged from MSK, his friend Joe took the day off from work to drive him home, then stuck around to set up his TV so he could watch it from his bed. "I really appreciated that, and I appreciate it when Joe brings a couple of other friends of mine to see me, but I've noticed that guys don't really know how to act or what to say around you when you're sick. Girls just walk in the door and *do* things." These days Nick speaks through a battery-operated vibrating device pressed to his throat. On days when his chemo knocks him out, his late wife's best friend does his grocery shopping. Two women from his workplace take turns bringing over a pot pie or a sandwich and soup. His neighbor down the hall, a young mother, checks on him in the evening after putting her kids to bed.

"Here's my advice for bachelors and widowers," said Nick. "If you don't have women friends, don't get sick!"

Most of Stuart's male friends took off for the hills when he got cancer. "I think they feel insecure and vulnerable around me now," he told me one day in the waiting room. "I'm single and I'm needy, so they don't want to get too involved. They're afraid if they visit me, they'll get sucked in. If I didn't have my family and Wilma, I'd be alone. She was a class behind me in high school, but we hit it off—not romantically, humor-wise—and we've been good friends ever since. Nowadays she acts like my mother. I guess that's what I need right now. She takes me to my doctors' appointments. She comes over to cook a meal, or we'll order in and watch TV. I like having someone around who's helpful but not hovering. Wilma doesn't hover; she just hangs out with me.

Jorge, overhearing my conversation with Nick and Stuart, came to the defense of men, or rather to *his* men friends. "They've been very encouraging and pretty expressive about their feelings, considering how most guys are. They were Marine officers, so they're used to being in charge and they're pretty forceful. When they tell me to take my medications or to eat something, it's an order. They bring pizza and beer and make sure I finish every last drop. I get the feeling they want me to survive."

"His friends are great guys, but they're nothing like *my* friends," interjected Jorge's wife, Sabrina. "When he was in the hospital, my best friend didn't just call me up or take me out for coffee. She made me sleep over at her house. She absolutely refused to let me stay alone when my husband wasn't there."

Harriet, another waiting room interviewee, said all the important women in her life stop by regularly to visit with her—friends, neighbors, members of her church, coworkers from the charity thrift shop where she volunteers. Harriet considers the husbands of a couple of her friends to be *her* friends too, but she said they only visited her when she was in the hospital. They never came back. "Men show up in a crisis," she said. "After that you're on your own."

NOT EVERYONE SHOULD (OR WANTS TO) BE VISITED

My husband, Bert, insisted on no visitors after his hip surgery. First he said it was because he was woozy from the painkillers. Then he said he didn't want to have to entertain anyone; he just wanted to lie in bed, watch the Winter Olympics, and nap. Next he said he didn't want his friends to see him looking so scruffy and shuffling around. Finally he admitted he didn't want visitors because he considered hip replacement surgery "kind of self-indulgent, like a face-lift" and not an illness, and if people came to see him at home on a workday, it would make him *feel* sick.

I reminded him that he'd been limping for months. All summer long, he hadn't been able to walk without pain or play tennis, his favorite sport. Now the doctor practically guaranteed him he'd be ambulatory in six weeks and back on the court in twelve. "Nothing self-indulgent about wanting to be functional," I insisted.

"No visitors," said Bert.

Days went by before I resumed my campaign: "Joyce and Max want to come visit you." (Old friends both, Max is a tennis partner of Bert's, Joyce, a friend of mine and one of my cancer mavens.) "Let's have them over for Sunday brunch. I'll make a frittata."

Bert shook his head.

"Why not? You're feeling better. And you know you can relax with them."

"I told you, I don't want visitors."

"Dammit!" I said. "We've been cooped up all week. *I* want visitors!"

With that, he relented.

Bottom line: not everyone wants to be visited. Bert didn't, I didn't, and dozens of people told me they prefer to be left alone when they're sick. Yet rather than ask our friends, point-blank, if they want company, we keep visiting each other on the assumption that we should and that they want us to. We don't ask if we should come because we don't want our sick friends to think we're trying to weasel out of a visit. Our friends don't ask us *not* to come for fear of making us feel unwanted or as if we don't count enough to be at their bedside. The whole issue is muddied by the dictates of traditional illness etiquette and the same old tape running in our heads: How can we *not* visit them? We're their friend. How can they *not* want us? Don't we belong there?

I'd like to believe that my presence at a friend's bedside always had a positive impact, but a recent sick call made me wonder whose needs were actually being met, mine or the patient's. This time I did everything by the book: I called my friend Phyllis to ask when it would be convenient for Bert and me to drop by to see Ira, her husband, who was recovering from back surgery. On the appointed day and at the appointed hour we arrived bearing chocolate chip cookies from one of Manhattan's best bakeries—the perfect treat, I thought, for someone who'd presumably ODed on hospital fare.

Before heading to the kitchen with our cookies, Phyllis schlepped two extra chairs into their bedroom so we could sit closer to Ira's side of the bed. I thought it odd that his pajamas were creaseless, as he'd spent all day in them, until I realized that he must have been lolling about in his rumpled skivvies before we came and changed into freshly pressed PJs just for us. Phyllis returned with mugs of steaming coffee and the chocolate chip cookies set out on a pretty platter. None for her, thanks; she'd had a late lunch. Ira declined too, saying he'd gained weight from being bed-bound and needed to cut calories. That left me and Bert to make short shrift of the cookies, which were scrumptious with Phyllis's coffee. While Ira was answering our questions—How did the operation go? How long did it last? How do you feel now? Any pain? Medication? Physical therapy—it crossed my mind that, having entertained several visitors prior to us, all of whom undoubtedly asked similar questions, he must be tired of reiterating the same story.

We were careful not to stay too long. I got up, kissed Ira's cheek, and started clearing the mugs as Bert made a move to return the extra chairs to the living room. Phyllis insisted we leave everything as is. She retrieved our coats from the closet, thanked us for coming, and hugged us good-bye.

The dynamics of that visit are instructive. We phoned first, didn't overstay, and had a nice conversation, but in the end I think going there did more for us than for Ira and caused him and Phyllis more trouble than comfort. Both had clearly expended extra effort to accommodate us—he to freshen up, change pajamas, and rev up his motor to retell his tale, and she to interrupt whatever she'd been doing, make coffee, and schlep furniture. All Bert and I had to do was to turn up with cookies (on reconsideration, not the best gift for a sedentary patient) and sit there and chat.

What should we have done differently? Though at the time it was inconceivable for us *not* to come, I should have asked Phyllis not *when* would be convenient but *whether* Ira really wanted visitors. I should have insisted she be truthful and assured her we wouldn't take it personally if he didn't. I should have told her we had felt the same way when we were sick. Or, if that put her on the spot, I could have suggested the four of us get together after his recovery rather than while he was still bedridden, and we should have invited them to dinner at our place, where *we* could have fussed over *them*.

Enough with the woulda, shoulda, couldas. Here again, what's needed is a radical new norm of simple truth telling, one that holds for both sides of the equation. And we have to recognize that not everyone qualifies for a place at the sickbed.

When word reached Bruce that his friend Ted was injured in a motorcycle accident, he called the hospital. Ted's wife answered the phone in his room. Bruce said he was coming right over. Ted's wife said his injuries were grave and the family was asking friends not to visit for now. Bruce felt shut out: he wasn't just a "friend"; he was Ted's *best* friend. He wanted to see Ted, and he was sure Ted wanted to see him, so he drove to the hospital and walked into the room without knocking, only to find Ted unconscious, in traction, and trussed in a full-body cast, with his wife, parents, and two brothers standing vigil at his bed.

"I asked you *not* to come," said the wife, seething. Mumbling his apologies, Bruce excused himself and left. Ted eventually recovered and the two men still see each other, but Bruce senses their friendship was irreparably damaged when he overstepped an intimate boundary and offended his best friend's wife.

Although that anecdote argues against unwanted pop-ins, my daughter Abigail takes the opposite position just as persuasively. The night her husband, Dave, had an emergency angioplasty, she e-mailed their friends not to visit, yet her pal Jamie showed up at the hospital anyway.

"She just appeared, and I felt kind of held up by her. She came for *me*, not for Dave—just to be with me for a little while. She didn't bring a gift, but her presence was a gift because it gave me an excuse to take a break, get a cup of tea, and talk to someone about what I was feeling. She taught me that sometimes you should come even if the person in charge tells you not to."

Abigail's anecdote reminded me of what a woman named Ursula told me she'd said to a friend whose child was in a coma. "Unless you forbid me to come or you lock the door, I am coming over right now to sit with you." Ursula came, and as far as she could tell, her friend, the child's mom, was grateful.

This in turn reminded me of the night before my operation, when Nancy and Miles Rubin, longtime friends of ours, took me and Bert out to dinner. At the end of the meal Nancy said she would see Bert tomorrow at the hospital. Bert insisted he didn't need company; my surgeon had assured him the procedure would be routine and I'd be out of the operating room in about an hour.

"I'll have my briefcase with me," said Bert. "If it lasts longer, I can do some work."

"Great," said Nancy. "I'll bring work too."

"You really don't have to do that, Nancy," I put in firmly. "He'll be fine on his own." And, repeating my usual mantra—tiny, noninvasive, etcetera—I added, "Really, it's no big deal."

The next morning, like the intrepid, unstoppable activist she is, Nancy turned up in the hospital to keep Bert company. Only after I came out of the anesthesia did I learn what happened next: my surgeon had emerged from the operating room in her scrubs to tell Bert she'd found a malignant cell where least expected, in one of the sentinel nodes under my arm (sentinel nodes guard the entrance to the lymph system), so she was keeping me on the table for a second procedure, the removal of eleven additional nodes that she would send to pathology to see if the cancer had spread.

Spread? Wait a minute! What happened to early, tiny, noninvasive? When "no big deal" turned momentarily ominous, Nancy, having known so many women who'd survived breast cancer, helped Bert keep things in perspective. In the end I was grateful to her for having disobeyed us and come anyway.

But Jamie, Ursula, and Nancy didn't visit a *patient* unannounced; they showed up to support, respectively, the wife, mother, and husband of a patient. From the testimony of several interview subjects, I've concluded that dropping in unannounced to keep a caregiver company is quite different from an unbidden visit to a patient. Caregivers may be dealing with fear, worry, and exhaustion, but on top of that they're also dealing with weakness, pain, or embarrassment, and therein lies the difference.

Ground Rules for Truth Telling in Action

If you buy into my honesty-is-the-best-policy approach to visiting, here are some ground rules of the new Truth Telling Etiquette:

1) *Ask the patient to be honest with you and all their friends and express their druthers,* whether it's zero visitors, certain hours of the day when friends are welcome, a limited number of people allowed in the room at once, or a time limit for each visit.

2) *Be honest with yourself about* your *attitude toward the visit.* The everyday demands of work and family are stressful enough, so it stands to reason that, however much you may want to see your sick friend, you also may feel yourself begrudging the time it takes to drag your ass up to their hospital ward, time you would otherwise spend with your kids or meeting a work deadline. If resentment is your first reaction, let your guilt barometer be your guide. Would you feel more guilty disappointing your friend than disappointing your kids or shortchanging your work project? If so, swallow your stress and visit the friend (assuming they want visitors). But if you'd feel more guilty disappointing your kids (say because you've been out every night this week) or facing your boss (who's been unusually critical lately), then explain the situation honestly to the patient, and I'm pretty sure they'll understand.

3) *Think through your role in the visit.* This is yet another instance of the obvious having to be spelled out. Ask yourself: what am I prepared to do and what do I expect my visit to accomplish? Some friends show up with an inflated idea of the impact of their presence on the patient. They imagine their words are going to have the power to heal their friend's brokenness, jolly them out of their funk, persuade them to change medications, or induce them to turn vegan. Other visitors waft in and out of the sickroom without expecting to do anything for the patient—even if something clearly needs doing. To avoid misconceptions and misapprehensions, it's a good idea to review your expectations in advance. Do you feel that, having taken time out of your day, you've done enough, or are you prepared to make yourself useful by pitching in on one or more of the following chores while you're there:

cook a meal

tidy up

clean the kitty litter

fix the DVD player

offer to make a pick up at the drugstore or dry cleaner

water the plants

sweep the floor

walk the dog

do the dishes

dress the patient's wound

help them bathe or dress

take them to the toilet

change their sheets

rub their aching back

pay their bills

pack or unpack for them

babysit their kids

shovel their drivway

make calls to cancel any appointments or explain the patient's absence to friends or colleagues

ask what else you can do to help

You may not know what your friends need until they tell you, or what you have to give unless you make the effort to notice what's needed. Remember to Ask and Act, or Act and Ask. It's not either/or; it's both/and.

4) *Don't visit if you can't abide silence.* There's a chance that all your sick friends want from you is to "be there." Are you prepared simply to sit at their bedside without talking? If so, how often and for how long? Do you think you can absorb someone else's despair without succumbing to it? Can you let your friend ventilate without you feeling compelled to problem solve? Are you someone who has to fill every auditory gap with chatter? People who give good visits are good listeners. They pick up vibes. They know when to comfort and when to keep still.

5) *Be prepared to respond without flinching to whatever scene or circumstances greet you during your visit.* Some illnesses leave a brutal imprint on their victims' appearance, capacities, and state of mind. Are you willing to stay the course even if your friend is hideously unsightly? Even if they're not getting better? Even if the sick room is odoriferous or depressing or there are weird-looking mechanisms or illness-related objects around the house?

6) *Be sensitive to your friend's losses.* Discomfort, pain and misery are hard enough to witness. What can break your heart when you visit a friend is the confrontation with their multiple losses, whether it's loss of hair (chemo); facial and bodily contours (steroids); energy and vigor (from the illness or medications); loss of their time, freedom, and independence (from being bed-bound or disabled); or their forward

motion (a stalled education; interruption of their social, sexual, and developmental progress). Loss of fertility, a side effect of some treatments, can devastate young people who have yet to start a family. Adolescents can lose ground in the race toward puberty (and be bullied and stigmatized because of it). Children can lose their childhoods.

Beyond your control are the aching, sometimes irreversible losses that often go hand in hand with grave illness, but the one loss you have the power to prevent is the loss of your sick friend's friends, starting with yourself. The future of your relationship largely hinges on *your* attitude. If you're someone who turns tail when confronted with profound suffering or physical disfigurement, the transformations of a friend's illness may send you running. But if you're loyal and committed, then consider your first entrance into the sickroom to be your Oscar-worthy opportunity to smile and appear unastonished by whatever you see. You may have to steel yourself against the shock and work hard to control your facial expressions and body language, but with a little preparation, you can do it. Rehearse in your head in advance how you'll react to a friend who's been mutilated by an industrial accident, what you'll say if a burn victim asks, "How do I look?," what you'll do when you first visit a friend who's paralyzed and can't hug you or shake your hand. Once you've assessed their condition and circumstances, it would be a kindness for you to prepare other friends of your friend for what to expect, and encourage them to visit as well and stay connected.

7) *Talk honestly with your children about the demands illness makes on friendship and how important it is to visit people who want company.* If you're currently involved with a sick friend, you should model good behavior not just to help your kids become empathic adults but also to influence

their behavior with friends of theirs who may be sick or struggling. Be ready to ferry your child to visit an ailing classmate. Obviously, I don't mean a child who's in bed with strep or flu but rather one who is gravely ill or incapacitated and may have been shunned by their peers.

I'll never forget the girl who was diagnosed with cancer and had to drop out of school and miss most of the ninth and tenth grades because of it. Two of her friends stuck by her and visited often, but the rest dropped her like the proverbial hot potato and when she finally returned to school, they acted as if they didn't know her. Then there was the fourteen-year-old boy who sent an e-mail to his social group when a classmate of his was diagnosed with stomach cancer. It said something like, "If you haven't been his best friend until now, don't act like one now. And if you *have* been his best friend, this is your chance to behave like one."

Ask your children to put themselves in the sick child's place and imagine how they would feel if their friends abandoned them the way some classmates have abandoned the sick child. Tell them that friendship can alleviate suffering and how important it is to resist peer pressure. Challenge them to take the high ground and treat the sick child with kindness and respect.

Ask *and* Act applies here too, but where kids are involved, it's the adult who does the asking and the child who follows through. Call the sick child's parents and ask if she or he is able to receive visitors. Make sure there's no threat of contagion in either direction. Ask the parent if their child's appearance or capacities have been severely compromised, and prepare your child in advance for what to expect. Encourage the parent to suggest activities appropriate to their child's level of energy and ability. Coach your children in advance about the sick child's limitations, whether he's too fragile for roughhousing or her speech is going to sound slow and arduous. To minimize awkwardness during the visit, rehearse some possible interactions before your children leave home. Make sure they visit the sick child more than once, and remind them to remind other friends of theirs to do the same.

ACCOMMODATING TO A DISABILITY

Our late friend Marianne Lipsky suffered from Multiple Chemical Sensitivity, a pernicious syndrome that required everything and everyone in her environment to be fragrance-free. Substances that most of us take for granted—cosmetics, cleaning products, pesticides, construction materials, phones, computers, TVs, and even fluorescent lighting—can be as harmful to people with MCS as poison gas might be to you and me. Because the slightest whiff of moisturizer, aftershave lotion, deodorant, or dry-cleaned garments made Marianne sick, her friends knew they had to be as scrubbed as a newborn baby before stepping foot in her house. Everyone accommodated.

When photojournalist Thilde Jensen suddenly developed MCS and experienced her Brooklyn neighborhood as a "toxic war zone," she moved to Tucson and lived in a tent under the sky. Maintaining friendships was nearly impossible because she couldn't drive a car, use a cell phone, operate a computer, or watch TV. She had to wear a respirator at the supermarket, post office, or anywhere that required interaction with the public. Eventually Thilde built a house in the woods in an ecovillage in upstate New York, where the houses are far apart and community members live fragrance-free for the sake of their chemically sensitive residents.

If no accommodation is made for individuals with disabilities, their friendships will inevitably suffer. Arnold, a Vietnam War veteran who uses a wheelchair, told me he couldn't visit a dying Army buddy because the man's house was not wheelchair accessible. My friend Martin, who was paralyzed from the waist down many years ago after falling to the ground while pruning a tree, told me that before he could attend a meeting at my home, he needed me to check if the doors of my building were wide enough for his wheelchair. The building was erected in 1903, long before passage of the Americans with Disabilities Act, so I wasn't hopeful, but after measuring all the doorways from the ground up, I discovered there was room to spare on all the doors except the door to our bathroom. Martin said he could handle that. Unfortunately, however, there was something I missed. Though I'd been going in and out of our building for years, I had never viewed it from the perspective of someone in a wheelchair, and therefore I had overlooked one obstacle—the high concrete step at the street-level entrance. On the day of the meeting Martin had to sit in his wheelchair on the sidewalk for fifteen minutes while our doorman rummaged around in the basement looking for a plywood plank that would allow the wheelchair to be rolled over the tall step.

A few months later our friend Jack Willis, who uses a motorized scooter, came for dinner with his wife, Mary, whose essay I quoted earlier (see p. 34). I knew we had the plank and asked the doorman to get it ready for Jack's arrival. The couple arrived on time so I assumed all had gone well downstairs and I thought nothing further about their experience until I received this e-mail from Mary:

> Jack and I wanted you to know that the night we had dinner at your house, the only way to get Jack's scooter up the step and into your lobby was with a rather pathetic piece of beaver board that the doorman used as a ramp. We needed two people to get Jack over the hump. We have a metal ramp in our building that costs less than $100 and can easily be stored in your lobby. We're not planning to move in, but we think a ramp will come in handy again at some point. Here's the URL for the online store where we bought ours: www.portable-wheelchair-ramps.com/Wheelchair_Ramps/signature _suitcase_ramps.aspx. Again thank you for a lovely evening.

Our building can thank Mary Willis, the patron saint of candor, for the fact that we now own a metal ramp and *every* visitor, regardless of disability, can enter and leave with ease and dignity. (Though they may not be able to fit through our bathroom door.)

Twenty Rules for Good Behavior While Visiting the Sick, Suffering, Injured, or Disabled
(A summary of tips that you may consider redundant but other people may not have thought of)

1) Call ahead to ask about the patient's condition. Make sure they want visitors. Ask what time would be most convenient for you to come.

2) Check with a family member or nurse before entering the patient's room. Knock first; don't barge in. You don't want to begin your visit by catching your friend in an embarrassing position or indecorously exposed.

3) Don't visit if you have a cold, cough, rash, or anything the patient might catch from you. Likewise, don't visit if there's a chance you can catch what the patient has.

4) Respect the hospital's rules. Most of us would rather visit our friends at home, but if they're in the intensive care unit, where you can't enter without a mask and gown and visitors are only allowed between ten and eleven, don't try to talk your way in at noon in jeans and a poncho. As Florence Nightingale famously wrote, "Hospitals are only an intermediate stage of civilization." It's too much to expect them to be flexible.

5) Don't expect your sick friends to look their best. They may not be well groomed. Their complexion may be wan, eyes rheumy, bedclothes grungy. They may have needles in their arms, tubes up their noses, congealed food on their plates. They may smell funny or have weird equipment around the house. Don't cringe; deal with it.

6) If they're asleep when you arrive, don't wake them. Go out for a walk. Have a cup of coffee. Check your e-mail. Read in the waiting room. Come back later.

7) Try not to stare. For instance, at the automated pen tracking the patient's brain waves in the skittery lines of an arthritic scribe, or the fluid that's drip-drip-dripping in a hypnotic, water-on-a-rock sort of way inside a plastic bag, or the tube snaking its way under the patient's sheets. Don't ask what it is. It's a catheter, okay?

8) Respect the patient's privacy, property, and belongings. Don't even think about propping your feet on their bed, drinking from their water pitcher, or using their bathroom without asking. Even if the thermostat in the sickroom says fifty degrees, you have no right to insist they bundle up and then rummage in their bureau drawers for a sweater. And though it may seem like a great idea to do their wash and surprise them with a clean load of laundry, don't invade their hamper unless they say it's okay. When it comes to a friend's personal space, remember to Ask *before* you Act.

9) Don't stand or sit too close or too far from the patient. Too close and you'll make them uncomfortable; too far and they

may have trouble hearing you, they may feel you're afraid of them, or they may have to strain their voice to be heard.

10) Don't talk too much, too loud, or too soft.

11) Don't whisper to the nurse or attendant as if there's something to hide.

12) Don't chew gum.

13) Be odor-sensitive. (About yourself, not the patient, who may not be able to help how he or she smells.) Visitors shouldn't wear cloying perfumes or aftershave lotions or reek from cigarette or cigar smoke. Have a mint if you've recently eaten onions, garlic, or blue cheese. Even coffee breath can make a sick person nauseated.

14) Ask about their condition, but don't subject them to the third degree.

15) Don't go into your health history or cite someone else's prior experience with the disease. No one cares if your cousin had it worse. The visit is not about you or your cousin; it's about your friend.

16) Keep the spotlight on the patient until they're ready to talk about Other Things. Some sick people never tire of telling you how they feel and what they've been through; others are eager for any distraction—sports, politics, books, music, movies, gossip, or nostalgia. Take your cue from the patient.

17) Unless they're notably chatty and keep insisting you stay, your visit to a patient's hospital room shouldn't last more than twenty minutes, five or less if they're in pain or yawning a lot. Home visits should be similarly brief unless you're doing chores for the patient around the house.

18) Let patients talk about death if they want to, but don't you be the one to bring it up. If they introduce it, don't try to change the subject. Give terminal patients time and space to say what's on their minds even if you think it's morbid. Don't sugarcoat their circumstances or paper over the truth. Don't censor their words or their weeping. Raw emotions can be hard to hear, but you're there to comfort, not to feel comfortable. I have Rabbi David Wolpe to thank for the last two suggestions:

19) Do not greet the sick person morosely. If he is feeling well, he must now accommodate your level of sadness. One who is sick does not spend all day thinking, "I am sick." She may be thinking about lunch. Greet normally, and allow the patient to guide the emotional tone. If you visit someone going through chemotherapy, remember: losing hair is visible and drastic but not catastrophic. Don't make it more important than it is; it is not a symptom nor a symbol—just a side effect.

20) Strength and weakness both are good, and each has its place. When we are ill, our moods shift with pain, medicine, diagnoses, and whim. Do not flaunt your own strength or health. Don't stand above the bed. Sit at eye level. Sick and well are not superior and inferior, just sick and well.

||||||||||||||||||||||||||||||||||||||||||||||||||||||||||||||||||||||||||||||||||||||||||||||||||||||||||||||||||||||||||||||||||||||||

CANCER GIRL

THE FIRST QUESTION MY FEMALE FRIENDS ASK IS, "How'd you find it?"

"Routine mammogram," I say, though the term always makes me think I should stick my breast in an envelope and send it to someone.

"Oh shit! I'm overdue for mine!" is the typical response. Had I discovered my lump in the shower, I'm sure my friends would be scolding themselves for not doing regular self-examinations. Had my gynecologist found it, they'd be wondering if they should switch doctors. Though frankly self-referential, these reactions strike me as justified because my friends know, as I knew and every woman knows, that one in eight of us will get breast cancer in her lifetime, nearly a quarter of a million new cases will be diagnosed every year, forty thousand of us will die of it in the next twelve months, and despite great leaps in research, detection, treatment, and technology, that grim fatality rate hasn't dipped in a decade. So when a friend asks me how I found mine, I know what she's really asking is how can she find hers.

Control is a big issue when you're sick. It's the first thing you lose—other losses come later. Maybe because I lost control of my bodily integrity, I feel it is important to retain control of my emotions, and I manage this partly by answering my friends' questions without getting sucked back into the quicksand of fear. Having powered through my tests and doctors' visits with my fighting spirit intact, I'm feeling strong and hopeful about the surgery and its aftermath until this e-mail arrives from a friend I'll call Madeline:

"O Letty, I was so sad to hear this news! It's almost unbelievable because you've always been so vibrantly healthful and youthful! How ARE you?"

A friend of three decades who lives about a thousand miles away, Madeline is a cancer survivor and a notably kind and empathic woman; I know she would never hurt me intentionally, yet hers is the response that sends me reeling. That single letter "O" takes my breath away: "O Letty . . . " It's the archaic vocative O, now dead to modern speech but vivid in prayers, hymns, and poems. The O of biblical vows and scriptural supplications: "If I forget thee, O Jerusalem, let my right hand forget its cunning." The O of Shakespearean tragedy: "O Romeo, Romeo, wherefore art thou Romeo?" The O-shaped mouth in Edvard Munch's painting, *The Scream*. I'd never met a good O.

My husband and I are supposed to go out for dinner tonight. I undress quickly and duck into the shower, expecting the water to drown out my sobs, but Bert appears on the other side of the glass and, with a glance at my face, leads me out of the stall dripping wet and wraps me in his arms. For the first time since my diagnosis, I lose it. Shuddering against his chest, drenching his shirt and tie, I gasp out fears I didn't know I'd been repressing—that I would never again be "vibrantly healthful and youthful"; that my cancer would make me weak and prematurely old; that I will need chemo and get unbearably nauseous; that I will lose heart, courage, a breast, maybe two, not to mention my hair; that the cancer—unseen and unfelt to this day—has already migrated to other parts of my body; that my life will never be the same. That I could die.

||||||||||||||||||||||||

EVENTUALLY, I CALM DOWN, Bert changes his shirt and tie, and we go out to dinner none the worse for him having been waterlogged. But the feelings Madeline's e-mail evokes underscore yet again how vital it was for me to control the cancer conversation and to nip in the bud, or even at the root, some of the most debilitating exchanges.

Not only do people's questions about my health begin to grate on me and sap my spirit, but my answers—repetitive, sometimes convoluted, sometimes vague—begin to bore me to tears. I know my friends are genuinely concerned about me, yet I can't believe they are relishing these pro forma catch-up conversations any more than I am. Still they keep asking how I am, because that's what friends do, and I keep telling them the same story, one after the other, because I'm trying to be polite. To interrupt the cycle, I consider sending out another group e-mail to my twelve Uberpals and all those who'd subsequently hopped on the gossip bandwagon. I'm tempted to reassure them that I'm fine and they don't have to check in so often. But I'm afraid they'll read my reassurance as a reprimand, and the last thing I want is to make my friends feel that no good deed goes unpunished. So I'm stuck. I don't know how to extricate myself from the conversational hamster wheel without losing my friends' caring love, how to take the pressure off all these kind-hearted folks without making them (and me) feel self-conscious the next time we talk, how to say what I want without sounding imperial or ungrateful. Come to think of it, what do I want?

A few things for sure: I want each person's "How are you?" to be a sincere query, not a knee-jerk substitute for Hello. When I take the question seriously and attempt to answer it honestly, I want people to hear me out and respond with "active listening." I want one friend of mine to stop talking as if I *have* cancer when I need to believe I *had* cancer and now it's gone. I want another pal to quit asking, "How's the chemo going?" when I've already told her that I'm only having radiation—"only" being the crucial word for me, if not for her.

While wishing some of my more solicitous callers would let up a little, I wait in vain to hear a peep of concern from an old friend who has said absolutely nothing and asks no questions whatsoever but rather seems to have shifted into denial gear and acts as if nothing has happened to me. As opposed to the "pain vultures"—friends who love you best when you're weak—this friend relates best to people who are strong. Unable to deal with the salient new facts in my life—my cancer diagnosis, surgery, and radiation treatments—she has closed her emotional shutter, and though we see one another frequently, she hasn't mentioned my cancer since the day she first received my Uberpals group e-mail.

After some heavy lifting in my interior workout room, I either reframe, correct, or forgive each of these friends their perceived transgressions: the woman who'd been referring to my cancer in the present tense stops doing so once I explicitly state that my tumor is gone and I'm cancer-free for now (which, when you really think about it, is the most that anyone can claim at any given moment). The woman who keeps mixing up radiation and chemotherapy wins my sympathy when I find myself, a few weeks later, unable to keep track of seven of my friends (literally) who are coping with various crises at the same time: a melanoma, an ovarian cyst, cracked ribs from steroid treatments, spinal stenosis, a bum knee, a broken foot, and, in the case of the seventh (a female Job), a vast array of issues—her undiagnosed stomachaches, her mother's recent death, her husband getting fired, her brother battling two kinds of cancer, and her daughter admitting to serious alcoholism and announcing that she'd just checked herself into rehab and needed my friend to come immediately (250 miles) to take care of the grandchildren.

I care deeply about all seven people and feel it important to keep track of their conditions and catastrophes, but if I hadn't written them down, I would never remember who had what or where each friend's saga left off. That experience helps me understand how my friend who never had cancer but has problems of her own might confuse radiation with chemotherapy. I give her a pass.

As for the Uberpal who never asks how I'm doing, I realize what should have been obvious all along: that's how she deals with her own health—she ignores it, always has. This is someone who had her first Pap smear when she was sixty, works outdoors all summer but disdains sunblock, and refused to have a complete medical checkup until I noticed she had a persistent cough and badgered her to see my internist. If she lives in denial of her own health issues, why would I expect her to pay attention to mine?

Nowadays paradoxes and contradictions shadow everything I know or feel: on the one hand, the devotion of my friends affirms my sense of worth; on the other, their heightened concern reinforces my vulnerability. Although many friends call on a regular basis or apologize for not calling often enough, I wish they wouldn't do either because, grateful as I am for their solicitude, I also feel stigmatized for needing it. I don't want people to pay too much attention to my illness, but I'm hurt when it's ignored altogether. I want my friends to keep track of my health and cheer my progress, but I also miss the relaxed banter we enjoyed BBC, the rollicking, wide-ranging conversations about Other Things, the relaxed chit-chat that's the making of a friendship. On the one hand, I want to be indulged, cared for, and supported if and when things go wrong, but on the other hand, I don't want my illness to become my identity. I don't want to be Cancer Girl.

THREE

THE PERFECT PRESENT

*What to Bring to the Sickroom When Flowers
Seem Corny and Candy Is a Very Bad Idea
(How Get Well Gifts Can Go Terribly Wrong)*

"I'M DONE WITH HAVING STUFF," said a friend when she was diagnosed with cancer. "No point owning things if I'm going to die."

I had the opposite reaction. Day One after my diagnosis, I bought a pair of shoes I didn't need. Day Two, a raincoat. Day Three, a sweater and some tights. Over the weekend I plundered a flea market for antique earrings.

Linda Grant wrote that shopping is "a balm for the troubled soul," which I suppose is another way of saying, retail therapy makes me feel better. Sandy Edelman, my friend who had a double mastectomy, assured me that my shopaholic urges would pass, but in the meantime I should do whatever it takes to make myself feel better—buy clothes, see two movies a day, eat dessert before lunch. When my credit card bill maxed out, the urges came to a full stop, but for a while there nothing distracted me from my tumor obsession nor helped me escape my mortality as reliably as did shopping.

Remember the joke about the elderly man who wouldn't buy green bananas because he might die before he could eat them? Well, I bought clothes to reassure myself that I would live long enough to get good use out of them. I thought that I would have to survive if only to amortize my investment.

Once I stopped shopping, my friends' get-well gifts provided similar assurance. No one would have brought me a house plant if I weren't going to survive to take care of it, would they? Watching my own upbeat response to material things has inspired me to fill this chapter with ideas for the perfect present, ranging from a Hawaiian fantasy trip to a joint of Acapulco Gold, from a preloaded Kindle to a tiny snail. I also discuss warnings about the perils of misguided choices, including why it might not be a good idea to give a woman silk pajamas.

RESTORATIVE GIFTS

A well-chosen present can embody the promise of recovery. I know that from watching the expression on Bert's face when Max, his friend and tennis partner, arrived for Sunday brunch with a tissue-wrapped object whose cylindrical shape gave it away. The can of tennis balls probably set Max back $3.98, but he couldn't have picked a more perfect present for my husband who, at that point, doubted he would ever again step foot on a court. Max's present told him that he would.

After my friend Janet Avery, a stroke victim, regained sufficient strength to graduate from a wheelchair to a walker to a walking stick, her physical therapist gave her an aluminum cane—serviceable but ill suited to a woman of Janet's style and panache. So on my next visit I brought her a beautiful hand-carved ebony cane. "I'll use it for special occasions!" she enthused, her eyes sparkling for the first time in months. That someone whose body and spirit were so broken could begin to imagine herself attending a special occasion signified the return of hope.

Because her cat had been a great comfort to her, I asked Janet if a pet qualifies as a good get-well gift. She advised against your buying an animal for someone else because the chemistry between people and their pets has to be right. But if the patient is mobile, you might accompany them to a shelter to pick out their own cat, dog, or fish and then buy them some pet accessory—doggie bed, kitty litter box, fish bowl—to get them started. The point is for patients stuck at home to have something to care for and love, another living being who can distract them from themselves.

The object of Elisabeth Tova Bailey's love, believe it or not, was a snail. In her memoir, *The Sound of a Wild Snail Eating,* she describes being felled by a mysterious, seemingly incurable disease that for many years kept her literally flat on her back. One day she received a plant from a friend who had placed a tiny snail in the flowerpot. At first Elisabeth disdained the gift, but that evening, from her prone position, she became fascinated by the creature's industrious efforts to curl up under a petal or inch down the side of the pot. Before long she was obsessed with the snail's nocturnal adventures and meticulous eating habits, and she felt a strange camaraderie with the snail because they "both lived in altered landscapes not of our choosing" and shared "a sense of loss and displacement."

It's not too much to say that a humble little snail rescued Elisabeth from the prison of her inert body. Slowly her condition improved, and when she was able to move and function, she started doing snail research. She tells of the time she fed the creature what she thought would be a treat—a mix of cornstarch and cornmeal—then watched it sicken and how she became distraught at the possibility of losing her companion. When her snail recovered, Elisabeth released it into nature along with its offspring, but she kept one of the babies.

For my money, the grand prize for Most Restorative Gift goes, hands down, to marijuana—alias, pot grass, gange, weed, cannabis. At this writing medical marijuana is legal in only sixteen states, not including New York. Yet in May 2012, on the Op-Ed page of the *New York Times,* a justice of the State Supreme Court in Brooklyn, Gustin

L. Reichbach, a sitting judge who was still hearing cases, was brave enough to out himself as a user. "Inhaled marijuana is the only medicine that gives me some relief from nausea, stimulates my appetite, and makes it easier to fall asleep," wrote Reichbach, who had stage III pancreatic cancer. How did he get the "illicit" drug? With a little help from his friends. "Rather than watch the agony of my suffering, friends have chosen, at some personal risk, to provide the substance." Under New York State law, giving someone as little as one joint can get you three months in jail and a $500 fine. The penalty for up to twenty-five grams is a year in prison and a $1,000 fine; twenty-five grams to two ounces and you're looking at a year and a half behind bars and a $5,000 fine. Yet Reichbach's friends, bless their hearts, risked these consequences in order to give him some relief from his misery. "I find a few puffs of marijuana before dinner gives me ammunition in the battle to eat," wrote the judge. "A few more puffs at bedtime permits desperately needed sleep." If you're willing to risk jail time and a fine, you can't do better than to give a cancer patient in the throes of chemo hell a gift that settles his stomach, awakens his taste buds, and lets him get a good night's rest.

EDIBLE GIFTS

Given my comments about marijuana in the previous section, you'd think the ultimate edible gift would be Alice B. Toklas's hashish-laced brownies. Those without baking skills or access to cannabis sativa, the illegal substance called for in Alice's 1954 recipe for "haschich fudge" (www.subrosa.arbre.us/SubRosaBrownies.html) should consider bringing sick folks some other culinary item that satisfies their cravings while taking into account their dietary restrictions or allergies. For cheese lovers, choose a good gouda, parmesan, or cheddar, not something soft or smelly. Fruit jams, herbal teas, and fragrant ground coffees are safe choices. But you could also bring real food.

In Elizabeth Berg's elegiac, touching, funny novel *Talk Before Sleep*, the main character, Ruth, who is dying of cancer, "opens the refrigerator, scans the contents, closes the door without taking anything. 'I don't recognize my own refrigerator anymore,' she sighs. 'All this sick-person stuff. Where are some lamb chops or something? Where's the fancy lettuce?'" You might take a cue from Ruth and bring your sick friends a great cut of meat, if they're able to eat it, or some fancy lettuce. A present of real food could not just perk up their refrigerator but satisfy ordinary appetites and make them feel more "normal." I'd go easy on the sweets, except for ice cream, which many patients find soothing. The sight of a pint of Häagen-Dazs Vanilla Bean can bring a smile to almost anyone's face, adult or child. On the skids of Parkinson's disease, my friend Bob Broner loved to be fed from a container of his favorite, Ben & Jerry's chocolate. My sister, Betty, even when she couldn't swallow anything else, always managed to get down a few spoonfuls of coffee ice cream. Though I'm a brownie fanatic myself (drug-free but studded with walnuts), I've noticed that for most people ice cream is the ultimate comfort food, and when friends share a pint, they seem to bond over the pleasure of their mutual indulgence. That's why, assuming it hasn't been removed or fallen off, the jacket of this book shows two dishes of ice cream.

Three years after I was diagnosed someone recommended I read Berg's novel. I wish I'd found it sooner. If you have a friend who's dying, don't give her or him the book. Read it yourself. The dialogue between Ruth and her friends will inspire you to listen to your sick friend more responsively, help you initiate difficult conversations, and remind you of the age-old connection between love, pleasure, and ice cream. In one scene Ann is at Ruth's bedside, narrating,

She takes in a breath, looks hard at me. "Do you think I could be getting better?"

"I don't know."

"Oh, Ann, what if I were?"

"Well, that would be wonderful." I hold her tight against me, and say, "I'm so glad I'm here. I want you to know I am exactly where I want to be. I'm so happy to be with you. I don't want to be anywhere else. I don't want to be anywhere but here."

"Ann?"

"Yes?"

Anything. I will do anything for her. I hold her a little tighter.

"Will you make sure I get a lot of ice cream?"

L.D. [another close friend] kicks the door open, sees us embracing. "Break it up. Look what I got." She is holding a tray with three bowls. There are towers of whipped cream over what I know are at least five scoops of ice cream.

Later in the book Ann goes to the hospital to visit Ruth and finds her waiting outside the main door.

"I get to go out," she said. "Yahoo. Let's go get ice cream."

We went to a Friendly's and ordered gigantic sundaes.

Magically, about an hour after reading these passages, I received an e-mail from my publisher asking me to approve the design for the jacket, with a picture of it attached. The two dishes of ice cream immediately struck me as a metaphor for the rewards of friendship during illness. Never underestimate the power of Rocky Road or Cherry Garcia.

PRESENTS THAT ARE PERFECT
BECAUSE OF THEIR PERSONAL MEANING

Obviously, the price of a gift bears no relation to its worth; what makes it meaningful is its unique relevance to the recipient or the effort the giver put into it.

Alison, a French American lawyer who was about to start chemo, received a Kindle from a close friend. A lavish present in itself, this particular Kindle was gilded with love and personality in that the giver had preloaded it with the reading material Alison favored: a year's subscription to the *New York Times* and *Le Monde* as well as a half dozen books about history, Buddhism, and meditation. Alison said it was "le cadeau parfait."

Soon after Natalie Robins was diagnosed with MALT non-Hodgkin's lymphoma, several friends of hers chipped in on an Armani gift certificate that brought tears to her eyes. Though she loves clothes, Natalie is not the type to cry over a designer label. What touched her was the fact that her friends had remembered a story from her childhood about how her mother used the promise of an Armani jacket to bribe her to lose weight and get good grades. Natalie performed well but never got the jacket—until her friends made good on her mom's promise.

"Dammit!" said Natalie's husband, Christopher Lehmann-Haupt, with faux annoyance. "Now she'll have nothing to live for!"

The staff of a Vermont hospice created a perfect present by helping one of their patient's dreams come true. When this particular woman let on that she'd always wanted to take a Hawaiian vacation but could never afford it, the staff reproduced the Big Island for her in the dead of a frost-bound New England winter. Because they believe in affirming each patient's agency wherever possible, the hospice made the woman a partner in the planning process for her Hawaiian "trip" by encouraging her to pick out the palm-patterned fabric for her muumuu as well as choose the orchid lei that was flown in from Honolulu and draped around her neck. The dress code for the party guests was Hawaiian shirts, Bermuda shorts, and flip-flops. Tiki torches blazed in the snow banks outside while everyone drank tropical punch and feasted on skewers of chicken and pineapple chunks to the sound of crashing waves playing on a tape machine. The fragrance of coconut oil sweetened the air. As if that weren't atmospheric enough, the staff burrowed under the snow and shoveled up some sand from the hospice's driveway, baked it in the oven until it turned granular, then piled it on heating pads to keep it warm so that the patient, looking as imperial as a movie director on location, could lounge in a canvas chair overlooking the festivities and beckon her friends to come forward and snuggle their bare feet in her warm sand.

To segue from this elaborate staging of a fantasy trip to the simplicity of flannel sleepwear may sound like a huge tumble, but to Lynn Sherr, after her colon cancer surgery, and to Lisa Deerfield, after her depressing, premenopausal hysterectomy, a "soft snuggly nightgown" was the epitome of comfort. Both women continue to think kindly of the friends who gave them those cozy nighties.

Marian Fontana, who lost her husband on 9/11 and then was diagnosed with cancer, treasured most a gift that the mother of a boy who had leukemia presented to her. It's a silver pendant engraved with Winston Churchill's quote, "Never, never, never give up."

David Wolpe, who's survived multiple cancers, said his favorite presents were an iPod preloaded with classical music he could to listen to during chemo and a prepaid charge account at a local restaurant that delivers.

Michele Landsberg, hospitalized with aspiration pneumonia and reeling from the news that she had breast cancer, was thrilled by the long, gossipy, witty letters she received from a beloved friend:

I can still see their thin tissue-like paper. They were a savory treat for moments when I was conscious. They were read aloud to me by my son, who brought them to the hospital from home. I remember the almost delirious happiness I felt when my entire attention was caught up by one of these marvelous letters. I'd be on a stretcher, waiting for yet another scary medical test, my fever running unchecked, the antibiotic drip plugged into my arm, but feeling flooded with happiness as my son, with a triumphant grin, would bring it out with a flourish: "Another letter!"

In an old copy of *Real Simple* magazine left behind in the MSK reading room I read an article about women with cancer and the gifts they loved best. One of them, Laura Livingston Rubin, gave herself a present before she started her chemotherapy: she hosted a party at which her friends presented her with gift certificates signed with messages like, "Keep kicking ass!" or "You're still hot!" Whenever she felt blue after one of her chemo treatments, Laura said she lifted her spirits by treating herself to "something frivolous—a pedicure, a new dress, organic tomatoes."

Angela Agbasi, a mother of four, said the only thing she wanted was help with her kids. So her family and friends divvied up her child care and household responsibilities among them.

Laura Stratte invited thirty people to witness the shaving of her head. Beth Weinblatt, who dreaded losing her hair, asked her best pal to give her a preemptory haircut—first a mullet, then a Mohawk, then a shaved head—before she started her chemo. "We were laughing at first," said Laura. "But by the time she finally cut it all off, we were both in a flood of tears. . . . It felt good to be proactive and even better to be with a friend who understood."

Lizanne Kelley's cancer returned six years after her breast surgery, this time lodging in her spine, which prompted her closest friends to give her the only gift she could possibly want: their sworn pledge to always love and support her teenage daughter.

In the chemo room Carole Copeland made friends with a woman who turned her on to a new passion: Chinese dragon-boat racing, specifically the Pink Dragons, a Los Angeles boating team made up of breast cancer survivors. Though never much of an athlete, Carole tried the sport and loved it. "I met such amazing, positive women—mostly in their forties, fifties, and sixties, and one in her mid-eighties. Paddling in synch with them helped me regain confidence in my body."

As these accounts suggest, the best present doesn't always come wrapped. Sometimes it takes the form of a passion, a haircut, a challenge, or a promise.

TO PRAY OR NOT TO PRAY

IIIIIIIIIIIIIIIIIIIIIIIIIIIIIIIIIIIIIIIIIIIIIIIIIIII

One of the patient escorts in the waiting room asked a group of us: "What do you do if you're not a believer and your sick friend starts praying in your presence and invites you to join in or asks you to pray for them on your own?" My answer was that religious people may have no difficulty complying, but if you're an atheist or your religion differs from the patient's in ways that would make joint prayer awkward, you need to tell your friends that you respect their faith too much to fake it. Assure them that you're as invested in their recovery as anyone else, and if there's something you can do for them that does not involve the supernatural, they have only to ask. Offer to call up one of their coreligionists and enlist him or her to do the praying. Or send a contribution in your friend's name to their church, mosque, or synagogue. Again, it's important for both you and the patient to be true to yourselves, especially when it comes to their spiritual needs at a time of great tension and distress.

When Christopher Hitchens, the militant nonbeliever and author of *God Is Not Great,* announced in print that he was undergoing chemo for esophageal cancer, several readers, friends, and strangers "either assured me that they wouldn't offend me by offering prayers or they tenderly insisted that they would pray for me anyway."

The British writer, Johann Hari, instantly Twittered, "I forbid everyone from praying for him. He would HATE that." But across the globe believers thought they knew better. Bloggers designated September 20, 2010 as "Everybody Pray for Christopher Hitchens Day." Devotional websites hosted debates on the logic, ethics, and effectiveness of praying for an atheist. Thousands wished him well online.

That's when it struck me that a "wish" is actually a secular prayer. Even a tepid little colloquialism like, "Wishing you a speedy recovery" implies that someone or something has the power to grant one's plea.

If not a deity, then what, or whom? Is it the man behind the curtain? Santa Claus? The first star we see tonight? The wish-fulfillment counter at Costco? The line between a wish and a prayer is up for grabs.

Anyway, Hitchens was having none of it. He wrote in *Vanity Fair* of a new problem that had occurred to him: "What if I pulled through and the pious faction contentedly claimed that their prayers had been answered? That would somehow be irritating."

Bets were placed. Would he embrace his faith in time to enter eternity or "take the hellish consequences"? Religious commentators termed his cancer divine revenge for his blasphemy. One blogger gleefully predicted that Hitchens would "wither away to nothing and then die a horrible agonizing death, and . . . [be] sent to HELLFIRE forever to be tortured and set afire." For some of the pious, Christopher's health clearly was secondary to his salvation.

"I don't mean to be churlish about any kind intentions," he wrote, "but when September 20 comes, please do not trouble deaf heaven with your bootless cries. Unless, of course, it makes *you* feel better."

When he died on December 15, 2011, I wondered if he was thinking, "See! It didn't work!"

THE GIFT OF HUMOR

That old chestnut "Laughter is the best medicine" ain't all hype. Studies done by Robin Dunbar, an evolutionary psychologist at Oxford University, show that laughing triggers the production of endorphins, the brain chemicals that make us feel good and increase our resistance to pain. Indeed, my feel-good meter spiked when a friend sent me a cartoon of a man looking quizzically at a woman whose breasts are jutting out of her chest in the flattened shape of two horizontal Ping-Pong paddles. "Yes, I did have my mammogram today," says the woman. "Why do you ask?"

Many friends forwarded to me a photo that was making the rounds on the Internet when I was first diagnosed. It showed an adorable infant wearing a floppy pink bonnet. On her tiny T-shirt were the words, "FIND A CURE BEFORE I GROW BOOBS."

My endorphins fairly sizzled when an e-mail headed, "Ya Gotta Laugh" delivered these zingy one-liners:

Never take a sleeping pill and a laxative on the same night.
The best way to forget all your troubles is to wear tight shoes.
One of life's great mysteries is how I could gain five pounds from
a two-pound box of candy.
Women over fifty don't have babies, because they would put them
down and forget where they left them.

I also got a big kick out of "The Revised Baby Boomer Hit Parade," which a friend sent to us after my husband's hip operation.

The Bee Gees, "How Can You Mend a Broken Hip"
The Who, "Talkin' 'Bout My Medication"
Paul Simon, "Fifty Ways to Lose Your Liver"
Carly Simon, "You're So Varicose Vein"
Johnny Nash, "I Can't See Clearly Now"
Bobby Darin, "Splish, Splash, I Was Havin' a Flash"
Procol Harum, "A Whiter Shade of Hair"
The Temptations, "Papa's Got a Kidney Stone"
Helen Reddy, "I Am Woman, Hear Me Snore"

Actually, that wasn't the first time I'd seen the list of parody titles. Years ago I ran into Joel Siegel, then the film critic for *Good Morning America,* at my corner drugstore. He was standing in line for the cash register holding a box of Depends. We were friends, so I knew he'd been battling colon cancer. Because Depends is an adult diaper, I deliberately averted my eyes from the box and pinned my gaze to his face. But Joel wasn't into shame. He shot me a wide grin, held up the box as if it were the Heisman trophy, and hollered, "Can you believe it's come to *this*?!" And that afternoon he e-mailed me the Boomer Hit Parade, except his list opened with Ringo Starr, "I Get by with a Little Help from Depends."

Joel Siegel died in 2007 at the age of sixty-three. Whenever I think of him, I see him laughing.

Commiserating with a friend about the high cost of drugs after my oncologist prescribed an anticancer pill that I would have to take for five years, I said I wished I could trust the quality of the Canadian drugs sold on the Internet. My friend said the bad press about Canadian drugs was just a brainwashing gambit by US drug companies to keep us buying US brands, and she sent me this wonderful rant: "American car companies can move their factories to Mexico. American toy companies can outsource to the Chinese. American banks can incorporate in Bermuda to avoid taxes. Americans can buy TVs and phones made in Japan and shirts made in Bangladesh. But God forbid we buy our prescription drugs from Canada. *That's* un-American!"

"I know you're a feminist," wrote a male colleague of my husband's, "but here are six reasons why it's better to be a man":

1) Our orgasms are always real.
2) Our underwear costs $8.95 for a three-pack.
3) Same job, more pay.
4) The world is our urinal.
5) We don't get breast cancer.
6) We can visit a friend without having to bring a gift.

I chuckled but took issue with the last two claims: men *do* get breast cancer, though a hundred times less often than women, and although they often arrive at a friend's sickbed empty handed, that doesn't make it right. Or as Marlo Thomas's Lebanese grandmother always said, "An empty hand is a dirty hand."

In her memoir *Growing Up Laughing,* Marlo mostly focuses on her father, Danny Thomas, and his legendary comedian buddies—George Burns, Bob Hope, Milton Berle, Bob Newhart, and Sid Caesar—who were always trying to crack each other up. But, says Marlo, her mom also liked to get a laugh.

Here's the joke her mom once told to the surgeon who was about to operate on her: "A woman goes to the doctor and says, 'Doctor, I have this problem. I'm passing gas all day long. Just these silent little farts. In fact, as I'm standing here talking to you, I've had three or four silent little farts. What do you think?'

"The doctor says, 'I think you need to have your hearing examined.'"

The joke that made me LOL when I was at my lowest point is the one about Billy Joe, an Alabama good ol' boy, who took to his bed with a nasty cold. Guaranteeing it would make him feel better, his friend, Hershel, a Brooklyn Jew, brought him a container of chicken soup with matzoh balls.

Billy Joe tentatively spooned up some broth with a wedge of the matzoh ball, chewed it, swallowed it, smiled approvingly, and then finished the soup to the last drop.

"Great balls," he said. "What do you Jews do with the rest of the matzoh?"

To give the gift of laughter, you needn't spend money; just spend a few minutes surfing the web, aggregate a great bunch of jokes, gags, and YouTube videos (see Resources, page 265), and you'll create the perfect present for a pal who has a sense of humor but not enough reasons to laugh.

If your sick friends are ambulatory and you have some extra cash, treat them to an evening at a local comedy club or take them to a charity event where a celebrity comic is the headliner. In Sacramento, California, for instance, Jamie Foxx starred in the "Comedy for Cancer" event sponsored by the Bobby Jackson Foundation, a nonprofit started by the former Sacramento Kings star when his mother died of breast cancer. (Proceeds from the event benefited kids whose parent has cancer now or has died of the disease.) In Brooklyn, New York, Garland Harwood, a twenty-something sarcoma survivor, launched "Comedy for Cancer" to raise money for the American Cancer Society. He wanted to pay them back for covering his round-trip transportation to Manhattan for seven months of daily treatments, which otherwise would have cost him $4,000.

If your friends have no stamina for an outing, stay home with them and pump up their endorphins by watching old clips of Lily Tomlin, Eddie Murphy, Tina Fey, Lenny Bruce, Whoopi Goldberg, Chris Rock, or episodes of *The Simpsons*, *Curb Your Enthusiasm*, *South Park*, or *I Love Lucy*. Try Comedy Central. Try Marx Brothers movies or the 2011 feature film *50/50*, a comedy about cancer that also happens to be a paean to male friendship—a grossed-out, arrested-adolescence, "bromance" kind of intimacy, but friendship nonetheless.

Gifts of humor won't always hit the mark. Some of your friends may literally be too sick to laugh; others may have dislocated their funny bone trying to pay their medical bills and make ends meet. But at least you'll enjoy yourself in the process of harvesting jokes and comedy shows, so it's worth a try.

READABLE DIVERSIONS

Books are my favorite gifts to give or get. One night while I was nervously awaiting my biopsy results, my downstairs neighbor Annie Navasky rang the bell and handed me three paperbacks: *Olive Kitteridge* by Elizabeth Strout, *The White Tiger* by Aravind Adiga, and *Snow Angels* by Stewart O'Nan. Annie said a good novel was the only thing that took her mind off herself when she had breast cancer. Fiction worked better than nonfiction for me too.

Some people are charmed by books like *Cancer Schmancer*, or *I'd Rather Do Chemo Than Clean Out the Garage*, or *Not Now . . . I'm Having a No Hair Day*, or *I Put the Can in Cancer*. Other people won't be amused. A woman who has MS said she wished people would stop sending her books about angels. A twentysomething cancer patient told *Newsweek* that she received "stacks of self-help volumes from well-meaning people. Books claiming that cancer was hatred materialized in the body of people who don't love enough. Books promising you can cure cancer by drinking wheat-grass juice. It made me want to throw up, even before my chemotherapy regimen started and I became a vomiting expert. I didn't need more things to make me feel guilty and excluded. I already felt like an outsider."

I think self-help books *can* be helpful, but patients ought to be able to choose this material for themselves.

GIFTS GONE WRONG

The point is that not all presents hit the bull's eye; some miss by a mile and some even make matters worse. Arlene, a Jewish patient, told me an Irish-Catholic friend sent her a bouquet of flowers with a Holy Card attached. Gary, a recovering alcoholic, got a bottle of wine from a friend after his arthroscopic surgery. I doubt you'd make the mistake of bringing candy to a diabetic or books with small type to a friend with macular degeneration, but you need to be similarly alert to gifts that might be inappropriate or considered too personal.

Two male colleagues of Jeannie, a biology professor, chipped in to buy her a pair of blue silk pajamas. Congratulating themselves for selecting a life-affirming get-well gift for a prematurely postmenopausal woman, they underscored the point by writing on their card, "We think you look great with or without your uterus!" (Remember, they were all biologists.) Jeannie loved the PJs but had to return them because her husband thought it unseemly for a married woman to accept lingerie from other men. I'm told his exact words were, "What do they have in mind, a ménage à trois?"

Lisa Alther, a writer who grew up in Tennessee, says that in a crisis the first response of a Brit is to make a cup of tea, whereas in the South, "We bring a covered dish. Typically, we'll leave the dish but won't stay to visit. We'll just hand it to the person who answers the door and say, 'Please tell Alice we're thinking of her.'"

Most sick people I've talked to say they relish receiving an edible gift, be it a tuna casserole, apple pie, or a fruit basket. Still, the food category can also be tricky.

A few years ago I made a whopper of a gift gaffe when I got the bright idea of sending a week's worth of prepared dinners to my friend Ruth Perelson, who was coming home from the hospital after breast cancer surgery. With one Amex charge, I told myself, I could do a double *mitzvah* (good deed): I could feed Ruth and her husband and boost the bottom line of the enterprise of another friend, Gretchen Cryer, who'd started a mail-order business that delivered home-cooked meals to people too sick, frail, tired, or busy to cook for themselves.

The day the basket arrived, Ruth called me and raved about it. "Prettiest thing I've ever seen! Gorgeous presentation! And what beautiful cloth napkins!" That she hadn't mentioned the food seemed odd, but I assumed it was because my gift had arrived in mid-afternoon, and she and her husband had yet to sample their first dinner.

A few months later I met the two of them in our neighborhood. Did the food taste as good as it looked? I asked. Ruth hesitated and glanced guiltily at her husband.

"Uh-oh!" I moaned, fearing for the future of Gretchen's fledgling company. "Was it *that* bad?"

"Actually, we couldn't eat any of it. Not because it was bad," she put in quickly. "Just 'cause it wasn't kosher."

Not kosher? Wait a minute! I'd been extra careful to choose menus that had no pork or shellfish. I'm Jewish, for Christ's sake! I know the dietary laws.

"But we're *strictly* kosher," said Ruth. "We can only eat food prepared in a kitchen certified by a *mashgiach.*"

Gretchen's a good cook, but she's a WASP from Indiana. I doubted she'd brought in an Orthodox *kashrut* inspector to give his stamp of approval to her kitchen.

"Don't worry," said Ruth, patting my arm. "Nothing went to waste. We brought the food to our local soup kitchen. And we still have the napkins!"

CASH ON THE BARREL HEAD

"I hope you're not offended, but I don't know what else to do to help you right now. All I know is, I can afford to do this." With that preamble, a close friend of Deb Kogan's gave her a check for $10,000. Deb hadn't asked for a cent; the friend just knew that Deb's life was in crisis on all fronts, that her father had been diagnosed with pancreatic cancer and given six months to live, her husband had lost his job, and they couldn't afford medicine for the youngest of their three children. As you might imagine, the friend's incredibly generous check made all the difference at a desperate time, and Deb has never forgotten it.

John Tierney of the *New York Times* reported a recent study that found that almost everyone would rather receive cash than any other sort of gift, which means "zealous shoppers have been kidding themselves." Spending extra time and money searching for the perfect present may make you feel better, but it doesn't do much for your friend. (Also, according to the study, the price of a gift matters more to the giver than to its recipient.)

So if it's true that most people prefer to receive money, why am I devoting a chapter of this book to choosing the perfect present? Why don't I just recommend that you put your cash on the barrel head and give your ailing friends whatever amount you would have spent on a bunch of helium balloons? In an ideal world your friends would smilingly accept the money, use it to buy what they need, or put it toward their medical bills or living expenses. But in the real world of the sick and suffering I've rarely heard of a cash transaction as uncomplicated as the $10,000 check given to Deb. To people who are ailing, worried about a loved one, or financially stressed, the offer of money can compound their feelings of weakness, whereas refusing to accept money can feel like a declaration of strength and affirmation of personal autonomy.

Two people I interviewed had negative reactions. Carl was trying to adjust to life with a heart condition when he opened this note from a friend: "I suck at picking presents, so buy something for yourself that makes you happy." Enclosed was a check for $30. Though he was in tight straits and $30 could have helped fill his gas tank, Carl never cashed the check because he felt it would have exposed in him a neediness too humiliating to acknowledge even to a pal.

Amy, who was recovering from eye surgery, received a get-well card with a $50 bill in it. "Don't make me hide this bill in your sock drawer—just take it!" wrote her friend. "I really want to help. Please let me." Amy kept the money, but she didn't feel good about it; she felt like a beggar.

Only you can judge whether the friend in question would feel offended or grateful to receive a cash infusion from you.

AND THAT'S WHY GOD CREATED GIFT CERTIFICATES

You don't need me to point out that gift certificates are convenient and you can buy one almost anywhere—retail shops, restaurants, online stores, supermarkets, pharmacies, and filling stations. But you may need me to underline the fact that for the patient, a gift certificate can be a face-saving, shame-free means of accepting cash (which that study found we all prefer anyway). I've never known anyone who was embarrassed to redeem a gift certificate. It's routine for people to give each other these attractive-looking negotiable instruments as birthday, anniversary, Hanukkah, or Christmas presents. And because no one thinks twice about their impact on the recipient's dignity, no one need ever know that the restaurant vouchers you give to your sick friend are actually going to supplement his or her dwindling food budget.

What sort of gift certificate should you buy? My rule is, "When in doubt, pamper." Most sick people would welcome a creature-comforting indulgence that they would never give themselves. This is especially so for someone facing surgery, starting chemo, recovering from a serious illness, or repairing after an emotional ordeal. For her, consider a certificate for a manicure/pedicure; for him, an old-fashioned shave at a barber shop. If you can afford to splurge, consider a gift voucher for a massage, facial, hair stylist, wardrobe consultant, private trainer, or day spa. Such luxuries can set you back some big bucks, but, as the good book says, if you've got it, give it!

Ten Tips for Good Giving

Again not much new here for the sensitive, caring,
well-bred reader, but worth repeating for the rest of us.

1) Don't stand there waiting for the patient to unwrap your present; let them do it in their own good time—unless it's food, in which case, tell them what you've brought and ask where they want you to put it: counter, cabinet, or fridge. With ice cream, of course, you'll want to offer a serving to the patient the minute you arrive. (Don't be afraid to join them.) And if they're not in the mood for it right now, you should put it in their freezer immediately.

2) Don't expect them to taste your homemade chowder this minute.

3) Check their allergies in advance so you won't bring peanut brittle to a friend who goes into anaphylactic shock upon contact with a PBJ, or chocolate bonbons to someone who gets hives from a Hershey kiss.

4) Don't bring food in a dish or container that you want returned. If you have no choice but to deliver your lasagna in your lasagna pan and you want it back, tell the patient you'll pick it up the next time you come. Sick people have enough on their minds; the obligation to return your crockery would just add another burden to their To Do list.

5) Don't pressure them to eat, use, wear, comment on, or rave about what you've given them. This means don't bring a pie and the next day ask how they liked it, or a book and three days later ask if they've read it. Don't ask what happened to the kabbalah bracelet you gave them last week, and don't expect them to know what it's for. (To you it's a talisman to ward off the Evil Eye, to them it may be a curious-looking strand of red thread.)

6) Steer clear of self-help books. Let men buy *Dr. Peter Scardino's Prostate Book* for themselves. Don't press *Bipolar and Pregnant* into the hands of any woman, even if she answers to both descriptions.

7) Don't give a tome the size of a car battery to a friend who's too frail to hold a porcelain teacup. Consider an audio book and earphones.

8)   Don't regift the book your uncle gave you for Christmas, even if its jacket is pristine and its spine uncracked, until you've read its jacket copy and a couple of online reviews and made absolutely sure there's nothing within its covers that your friend might find weird, offensive, or hurtful.

9)   When giving a book, match the format to the friend. To some (mostly younger) readers, a printed book is to an iPad as a Model T is to a Lexus. Others love to hold the physical volume in their hands. Give traditionalists the real thing and get the tech-savvy a gift certificate so they can download an electronic book of their choice.

10) When visiting someone in the hospital, choose a gift that's small and light enough for them to take home without hiring a U-Haul.

Here's the bottom line on gift giving, and it couldn't be simpler: bring your friends something that might elicit the sensation so many of my interview subjects say they find most elusive during illness: *pleasure*. Whether it's culinary, literary, bodily, spiritual, or sensual, whether it provides diversion, relief, comfort, luxury, or laughter, uncomplicated pleasure is what sick people miss most.

WHY I HATED HOSPITALS AND HOW I CAME TO LOVE THIS ONE

FAIR WARNING: THIS IS A MASH NOTE TO A CANCER HOSPITAL. I'm about to sing the praises of "my hospital" and "my doctors," not because I want to make you feel bad if you don't live near—or your health insurance won't pay for—a hospital with facilities as splendid as those at Memorial Sloan-Kettering or specialists who can take the time to pay as close attention to your case as my doctors did to mine. I'm writing this paean because I want you to know what quality, comprehensive care looks like, at least from the perspective of someone who has spent a lot of time being tested, treated, observed, advised, and operated on. I believe it's possible to deliver superlative, personalized care to a large patient population, because MSK does it every single day. With collective commitment and adequate funding, this caliber of care could be guaranteed to everyone. I'm not happy that I was lucky enough to enjoy this care when other breast cancer patients ten blocks, ten miles, or ten states away are denied it either because they can't afford it, their insurance company refuses to cover it, or their local hospital is overcrowded, underfunded, and understaffed. I think the discrepancy is a disgrace. Even in a stressed economy, quality medical care could become the norm if all of us—people, nonprofits, politicians, foundations, and private enterprise—summoned the political will to reorder our national priorities. It's time to pound on the gates of power and badger the special interests until top-flight medical care is made available, affordable, and accessible to everyone from birth, not as a privilege of the wealthy or lucky but as a basic human entitlement, a civil right befitting a civilized society.

Now, I'll get off my soapbox and back to my story.

For years I had a hospital phobia, and I didn't need Sigmund Freud to figure out why. It started in February 1955 after I visited my mother at Memorial Hospital (a prior incarnation of Memorial Sloan-Kettering), where she had been operated on for what was then called "women's cancer." I thought Memorial would make her well; instead, they sent her home and she got sicker and sicker, and two and a half months later she was gone. In part, I blamed the hospital. My mother was fifty-three when she died; I was fifteen. From then on, other than the cheerful maternity wards where I delivered my three children, you couldn't get me within ten feet of a hospital door. I associated such institutions with grief, loss, and the abject failure of modern medicine.

Avoiding hospitals isn't hard when you're young and healthy and surrounded by young and healthy friends, so my phobia presented no problem until I was in my early thirties, when the son of close friends was hospitalized for radical surgery to remove a tumor lodged between his heart and lung. Shame fills me to this day because I didn't visit that boy. I wanted to, I meant to, I should have, but I couldn't. I've always hoped that my absence was unnoticed or, if noticed, forgiven, but I'm not proud that the one time my hospital aversion was tested, it trumped friendship and my better instincts. I didn't go to see the child until he came home from the hospital and I could visit him on his home turf.

Some years later I was urgently prompted to conquer my phobia when my husband, who'd given himself a hernia by lifting a sailboat, required surgery. Somehow I managed to rise above my mishegas (craziness) and enter Lenox Hill Hospital several times a day to visit him.

Since that breakthrough I've visited too many people in too many medical institutions and been a patient myself often enough for all kinds of hospitals to feel all too familiar.

For the past three years I've been an outpatient at MSK, slogging from examining room to operating room to radiation chamber, from one doctor to another, from mammography to X-ray, from bone density unit to blood lab, so much so that at this point I think of it as "my hospital." I know the smell of the corridors. I recognize the security personnel and receptionists at the hospital's various locations (my favorite being the African American gentleman at the welcome desk in the East 53rd Street building who always greets me with a huge smile and a hearty "G'morning, love!"). I know which waiting rooms are the most comfortable and best decorated; which display the nicest art; which have computer stations, brewing machines that make decaf, espresso, flavored coffees, and hot chocolate, minifridges stocked with enough cold apple and orange juice for a regiment, and baskets with copious supplies of cookies and crackers.

Occasionally MSK personnel turn up in my dreams, and if you ask me, they've earned the right to be there. I can't vouch for other institutions' policies, but my hospital prides itself on its humanized "relationship-based care" and delivers on that promise. MSK takes a holistic approach to every case. It maintains a computerized record of my complete medical history, pre- and postcancer diagnosis, as well as all my test results, medications, and past and future appointments— information that is always readily accessible to me by phone and on the computer screen of each of my seven doctors across all of the hospital's departments. It offers a great variety of extra resources for cancer survivors: quality-of-life workshops, support groups, a Living with Loss Lecture Series (for instance, about how to get through the holidays after a loved one dies), therapy sessions, an Audio Biography Project, various publications, online programs, and in-person meetings that address every kind of cancer and every age group. I have never availed myself of these, as my interactions with my doctors has been so personalized that I feel that my needs have been more than adequately addressed, but I'm glad to know they're there if I need them.

Larry Norton, my breast medical oncologist, remains my primary cancer authority, adviser, and advocate—that is, my main man. Larry, who uses his first name with all his patients, oversees everything relating to my case and assigns me to other specialists as indicated by my symptoms. Once I become the patient of each additional specialist, I see that doctor for all consultations related to that condition. I'm never fobbed off on a strange staff member to suit the hospital's convenience, so I never feel like a name, and "date of birth please"; I feel like an individual, a person, a human being in relationships with other human beings who happen to be cancer experts. Nor have I ever felt, as one often does when dealing with large institutions, that the right hand doesn't know what the left hand is doing. On the contrary, I've been awed by how seamlessly the members of my team coordinate matters between and among themselves.

Though I keep referring to them as "my doctors," I'm also aware that they belong to all their patients. My case is probably most distinguishable for being the one that's proved to be more of a scavenger hunt than a medical mystery, each clue leading to another organ that has another problem that requires another specialist, who, thus far at least, ends up declaring me negative for cancer. This plethora of specialists and my personal relationship with them may be the biggest surprise of my MSK experience. At first I felt trapped in a paradox: I was as scared as any woman in the world who'd ever had breast cancer, yet because my tumor was relatively manageable compared to other patients' tumors, I felt I might not merit my doctors' attention. After I experienced their remarkably personalized care giving, I actually felt the opposite—unworthy of my doctors' attention and guilty for taking up their time.

We cancer patients behave like the stars of our own movie until we realize that we're bit players in a continuing extravaganza and our doctors are the stars, directors, and producers. I nominate mine for medicine's equivalent of an Oscar in every category.

Despite being in constant demand as a world-renowned expert on breast cancer, Larry, my team leader, generally answers my e-mailed queries within the day. He called me on two different weekends to hear how I was doing after I had bad reactions to two estrogen-inhibitor medications. He tweaked the meds until they were right for me and kept tabs on me all the way. (For the pharmacologically curious, Femara caused my fingers to swell and nearly paralyzed my hands; Tamoxifen gave me heart palpitations. Now I'm on Raloxifene, alias Evista.)

After completing his diagnosis and deciding I was a candidate for a lumpectomy, Larry referred me to Kimberly Van Zee, a breast surgeon, who not only explained what she was going to do and why but drew several diagrams until she was sure I understood every detail of the surgery. Dr. Van Zee excised the tumor and enough nodes to get me to clean margins. During my follow-up visits, she always asked about my daughter Abigail because while I was on the operating table waiting for the anesthesia to kick in, one of the nurses had mentioned reading one of Abby's articles just that morning, a coincidence we discussed until I passed out and one that Dr. Van Zee has never forgotten.

Postsurgery, I was referred to an MSK radiation oncologist, Simon Powell, a ruddy-faced, outdoorsy Brit who, besides master-minding my treatment protocol, insisted that I douse my chest with talcum powder every day to minimize the irritation from the X-rays. I credit Dr. Powell with the happy fact that although so many in my radiation cohort complained about searing pain, my skin never burned.

Mona Sabra, my endocrinologist, continues to monitor my thyroid, which only incidentally, during the ultrasounds preparatory to my breast radiation, revealed itself to be possessed of two or three suspicious nodes, thus far benign but targeted for "watchful waiting." During our first consultation, when I asked the origin of her name, Dr. Sabra kindly let me interview her briefly about the politics of the Middle East.

Deborah Goldfrank, the oncological gynecologist who dutifully monitors my reproductive (or, rather, nonreproductive) organs, joined my cadre of doctors when I had some peculiar stomach pains in 2011. My workup included a pelvic ultrasound and diagnostic MRI that demonstrated an abnormal thickening of the endometrial lining of my uterus. Two biopsies and a sonohysterogram failed to produce enough endometrial tissue to test, so Dr. Goldfrank (whom I call Debbie since she turned out to be the daughter-in-law of my old friends, Phyllis and Ira) referred me to a gynecological surgeon for a D&C, an operation to diagnose and remove whatever was causing the uterine thickening. After our first consultation Debbie gave me her cell phone number "in case you have questions," and like an old-fashioned family physician, she calls me at home to explain my test results or just to see how I'm doing. Because she's in her forties, about the age of my kids, I feel confident that she will be practicing long enough to take care of me for the rest of my life.

Ginger Gardner (a dead ringer for the actress Julia Roberts) is the gynecological surgeon who performed the D&C, which mercifully turned up just a few pesky endometrial polyps and no malignancy. During my first post-op visit with her I felt as if I were talking to a friend. Our conversation ranged from the details of our pregnancies and deliveries to the impact on families and friendship circles when a woman gets sick. I asked her why she chose to go into surgery. "Because it offers instant gratification," she said, "and I love working with my hands and I get great pleasure from eliminating disease from a woman's body and putting the intestines back where they belong, and creating beauty and order where there was ugliness and disorder." Captivated, I told Dr. Gardner I was writing this book and asked if she had any pertinent advice. She said, "Be sure to mention that female patients, besides worrying about themselves, also tend to worry about how their family and friends are coping with their illness. Doctors ought to be aware of that fact and pay more attention to the friends and family of their patients and give them the support they need."

From my surgeon's mouth to your doctor's ears.

Monika Shah, an immunologist, entered the picture last spring when I needed shots to get a visa for a trip to Liberia. Naturally, my first call was to Larry Norton to make sure I could go to Africa at all and, if so, whether it was safe for me to have the immunizations that contain traces of the disease they protect against. Larry referred me to Dr. Shah, my seventh MSK specialist, a delightful young woman who ordered shots to prevent polio, hepatitis A, typhoid, tetanus, malaria, and digestive problems. She disallowed the yellow fever shot on the grounds that my immune system had been compromised by my treatments and the shot could actually infect me with yellow fever, but then reversed herself after consulting with Larry who said my system could take it. To me this proved once again the benefit of having one doctor with a global perspective on my case. At the same time, Dr. Shah didn't just prescribe my inoculations and medications and move on to her next patient; she asked me questions about the trip (a study tour focused on women and peacemaking), who our group would be meeting (the president of Liberia, Ellen Johnson Sirleaf, and grassroots activist Leymah Gbowee, both Nobel Peace Prize winners, as well as other women peacemakers). She told me what I should and shouldn't eat or drink, what number of sunscreen to use, what percentage of Deet my insect repellent should contain, what clothing to pack, and what items should be in my First Aid kit. At the end of our lengthy discussion she demonstrated the exercises I should do on the plane to keep my blood circulating.

Besides "my doctors" and the many anonymous staff members who do their part to grease the gears of healing, I'm deeply impressed with—in fact, I adore—Karen Drucker, Larry Norton's warm-hearted, all-competent nurse practitioner. Karen, who's always in the examining room with Larry, contributes her findings and opinions, promptly returns my calls and e-mails, seems to know as much as most doctors, and remembers everything that has gone wrong or right with my body since I first stepped foot in MSK.

Of course, I wouldn't be able to get through to Larry or Karen if not for Ariel Hosey, the physician office assistant (i.e., gatekeeper) who answers their phones with a lilting voice and who never sounds too busy or harassed to listen to my latest problem or to run interference for me with other departments of the hospital. Anyone who's ever become ensnared in bureaucratic hell or the automated maze of a huge institution will understand why I'm so grateful to Ariel.

The last member of my MSK team is Emily Glogowski, the genetics counselor who tried indefatigably, though ultimately without success, to piece together my elusive family medical history in order to create a coherent hereditary map despite several dots that don't connect.

(Regarding the cause of my mother's death, the term my family used, "women's cancer," was politely decorous for that era but utterly useless when it came to genetic mapping. Memorial Hospital's sketchy records from 1955 made it impossible to establish whether her cancer was uterine or ovarian in origin. If uterine, my prognosis would be good, but if her cancer was ovarian, that plus my sister's ovarian cancer plus my breast cancer would justify the prophylactic removal of my uterus and both ovaries. Though I can't know what type of cancer killed her, I tested negative for BRCA1 and 2, the breast cancer genes common to Ashkenazi Jews, and Dr. Norton believes, one, that my cancer is under control and, two, that I shouldn't rush to rid myself of my uterus and ovaries because he's seen it diminish a woman's joie de vivre. Because of this, I've elected to keep the surgical option on the back burner for the time being. When in doubt, my policy is to do what Larry Norton says.)

As you may have gathered by now, "my doctors" have become my heroes not just for their healing prowess but also their extraordinarily intense involvement in my case and their expansive definition of what it means to "take care" of a patient. A similar turnabout affected my attitude toward "my technicians." Disgruntled at first by the persistently long waits for a treatment room, I used to fault the technicians for not timing everyone's sessions more efficiently until I learned what caused the delay behind the scenes: the man who'd recently had a stem cell transplant and couldn't stop vomiting and then the three-year-old who kept squirming and trying to jump off the table.

Every day when I was at MSK I would hear about or interview patients whose illness had prevented them from carrying on with their lives, walking, talking, working, eating, seeing, socializing, making love, conceiving or impregnating, pooping or peeing; patients for whom pain is a constant companion; patients who'd lost their natural immunities, body parts, and hope for survival. In the face of so much suffering, my tiny tumor and overwrought mortality tremors seemed undeserving of my doctors' interest. Yet the minute one of them examined me or questioned me about how I was feeling, I knew I had their undivided attention. I felt I was truly being cared for, cared about, and remembered as a person, not just a name on a chart, from one visit to the next. That is the human reality of my ultramedicalized time at MSK.

And I haven't even mentioned the two side trips I took off campus. In June 2010 it was a grim overnight stay in the emergency room at New York Hospital after I suffered an alarming attack of shortness of breath, an incident never experienced before or since that set into motion much observation and many rounds of tests before a cardiologist declared it "an isolated event." Dr. Norton attributed it to a bad reaction to my anticancer medication and promptly changed me to another drug. My second detour, in August 2011, led me to consult two gastro-enterologists to find the cause of the gnawing pains that for six weeks had attacked my midsection after I ate. I was convinced that either my teeny, tiny tumor had metastasized or I had a new primary cancer site. Ovarian cancer! Had to be. My mother's "women's cancer" must have been ovarian after all. Stomach pain after meals had been my sister's presenting symptom, and she turned out to have advanced ovarian cancer. Ipso facto, I must have it too! I was terrified. The second gastro guy calmed me down and scheduled me for a two-fer (an endoscopy and colonoscopy on one dose of anesthesia). When I woke up, he smilingly identified my "ovarian cancer" as gastritis and prescribed a strong antacid. In less than a week the pains were gone.

Bottom line: after three years' worth of assorted diagnostic tests, ultrasound images, medical consultations, and surgical interventions I was left with only one confirmed verifiable illness—the breast cancer that brought me into the land of the sick in the first place. I'm not complaining. I feel fortunate to have had such a nondebilitating cancer and to be able to claim the title "survivor." At the same time I'm aware that all this hospital-based activity has produced in me an unfamiliar feeling—the sense that my body now belongs to my doctors as much as to me.

Before the mammogram revealed the tumor, my body seldom called attention to itself. But since 2009 my interior landscape has been surfacing "issues" at an alarming rate, giving me ample reason to feel manifestly vulnerable and imminently mortal. I used to be a two-doctor woman, someone who saw her internist and gynecologist once a year, if that, and only when they sent me a postcard reminding me to come in for my annual checkup. Now, however, my body is the purview of seven specialists, and each time I go to MSK to be checked, screened, tested, injected, sonogrammed, mammogrammed, pricked, or probed, I can't help thinking, "Okay, which organ is it this time?"

Another surprising result of this roller coaster ride is that I find myself wanting to get better for my doctors' sake as well as mine—to get well just to please *them*. When they say things like, "Uterus looks good" or when a report shows "No masses or lesions," I feel as if my health is the prooftext of my doctors' talent, as if I'm rewarding them with the one outcome that specifically translates their outstanding devotion and supreme skills into something that might be called success. I want an A on my doctors' behalf.

Thinking in terms of grades feels appropriate to the MSK context. After my last round of visits in the fall of 2012—for a pelvic ultrasound (to ensure that all is well after the uterine surgery), a mammogram, a checkup by my oncological gynecologist, a thyroid sonogram and checkup, my semiannual visit to Larry, and extensive blood work to screen for ovarian cancer among many other things—it occurred to me that this institution is the graduate school I never attended. As much as I'm an alumnus of Jamaica High School and Brandeis University, I think of myself as an alumnus of MSK. I know its campus well. I've spent six semesters in its exam rooms, sampled a large number of its course offerings, availed myself of its state-of-the-art facilities, benefited from the research done in its labs and the expertise of its best brains, and, as befits any well-rounded educational experience, learned from my peers (my cohort of fellow wait-ers in the waiting room). Pushing the parallel, my two surgeries and six weeks of radiation were tantamount to a thesis and final exams, and when three of my cancer doctors—the two surgeons and the radiation oncologist—recently told me I didn't have to see them anymore, I felt as if I'd been promoted from the Master's program and judged qualified to work toward my doctorate in cancer survival.

Yet because I remain attached to the institution at the hip—or, rather, at the breast, thyroid, and ovaries—the only diploma I can hang on my wall at this point is a provisional certificate that says, "So far so good." Dr. Sabra is still in charge of my neck area (may you never have to endure a biopsy of the thyroid; it's the pits). Dr. Goldfrank is still keeping an eye on the calcifications on my ovaries. Dr. Norton remains my advocate of first and last resort. I'm still scheduled for semiannual mammos, pelvic ultrasounds, bone scans, and blood work, all of which bring me back to campus several times a year without benefit of a reunion committee or a class picnic.

Make no mistake: I'm okay with this. By some mystical alchemy—a combination of the frequency of my visits, the hospital's unique hospitality, and my supersatisfied relationship with my doctors—the dread has been has drained out of these encounters. Instead of agonizing for days in advance of a visit or test, I surrender to fate and my doctors, grateful that the institution seems as invested as I am in keeping me well. What's more, I rest assured that if something else develops—or, rather, *when*, as at my age "developments" are all but inevitable—MSK has my full transcript, and each new specialist who joins my team will not have to start from scratch.

The irony of all this is inescapable: after decades of assiduously avoiding hospitals, I now find myself in an affectionate, committed, undoubtedly lifelong relationship with Memorial Sloan-Kettering, the very institution that more than fifty years ago scared me off hospitals in the first place. All I can say is, thank God they take my insurance.

|||||||||||||||||||||||||||||||||||||||||||||||||||||||||||||||||||||||||||||||||||||||||||||||||||||||||||||||||||||||||||||||||||||||||||||||

TWO DEGREES OF SEPARATION, ONE DEGREE OF NEED

What to Do When Your Friend Is Miserable
Because Their *Friend Is Miserable*

WE'VE ALL KNOWN HEALTHY, robust people who are so stressed out and worried about someone they love that they may as well be sick themselves.

Say you have a friend named Jane whose mother has Parkinson's disease. Though there are two degrees of separation between you and Jane's mother, her illness is bound to have an impact on your relationship with Jane who, in the act of devoting herself to her mom, may alter her social priorities and become distracted, anxious, overwrought, withdrawn, even obsessed, and, therefore, less available to you. Rather than interpret Jane's behavior as a personal rejection, I suggest you take it as evidence of her distress, a signal that, despite the two degrees of separation between you and her mom, it's Jane, your friend, who needs first-degree support.

I lost my mother to cancer when I was fifteen, but I still remember how my friends treated me when she was sick and dying. They fell into three camps: those who acted as if nothing had happened; those who were kind, comforting, and sympathetic; and the girls who stared, pointed, whispered, avoided looking me in the eye, and generally behaved as if my sad circumstances were catching.

With those recollections in mind, I asked people who have experienced the suffering and/or death of a loved one to describe how their friends related to them, which of their friends' behaviors exacerbated the ordeal, and which provided a cushion of support. In this chapter you'll meet Deb, who had to cope with several simultaneous adversities and ultimately lost her father; Lauren and Cathy, both of whose husbands have serious cancers; Peggy and other parents whose children are struggling with drug addiction; Harriet, whose family had to cope with three different illnesses at once; and Ruth, who is overwhelmed by catastrophes in her relatives' and friends' lives. I think you'll find wise guidance in each of their stories.

WHEN YOUR FRIEND'S PARENT IS DYING

A few years ago the aforementioned Deb Kogan was slammed with that quadruple whammy—dying father, unemployed husband, sick kid, no money. Oh, and one more thing: her first novel was only weeks from publication, and her publisher insisted she go out on the road to promote it.

Most of Deb's friends who were aware of what was happening in her life responded beautifully. The night after she learned about her dad, her best childhood friend came over with a gift-wrapped package of Kleenex, insisted on taking her out for a good meal, brought the package to the restaurant, put it on the table, then listened to her cry and just kept handing her a tissue when she needed one.

Another friend said the right words at the worst moment—during Deb's book party. "My dad was there and I was trying to give my little speech, but I started to cry and this friend of mine, who'd already lost her mother, pulled me aside and said, 'Try not to mourn in front of him. He's here *now*. Cherish the moment, right here, right now. Don't fast-forward to his death. He knows he's going to die. You know he's going to die. But right now you're both alive, and this party is a celebration of your hard work, and you're lucky he's here to see this day, so try, if you can, to enjoy yourself. That's what he wants to see—your smile, not your tears.' She said all this firmly but gently, and it was life altering in the most profound way. She was like the Buddhist master who finally got me to understand the whole notion of Be Here Now."

There were a few clunkers among her friends too: the woman Deb had to drop for a while because, "Every time we talked, the conversation was about *her*. She kept wondering what *she* would do if what was happening to me happened to *her,* or if what was happening to my father happened to her mother." And the woman who was narcissistic in a different way: "When I told her I had to promote my book despite my father's failing health and I was having a hard time being zippy and happy on TV, this friend, who'd published a novel of her own, barked at me, 'Oh, stop! At least you *get* on TV!' I told her, 'I'm going to hang up right now.' She said, 'You're overreacting.' I kept saying I was going to hang up, and finally I did. When she called back, I said, 'You can't do this to me. I have a book coming out and my dad's dying and I need your support.' It's upsetting when a friend doesn't let you air your sorrow."

Despite her gal pals' missteps, Deb chose not to put an end to these long-term friendships because, she said, "the past doesn't get erased so easily. Still I found it interesting how some people's personal neuroses come out in a crisis."

Deb was grateful when her friends asked about her father, Dick Co-paken, but their questions made her cry, so she started a blog that let her update everyone at the same time or just say, "Don't call us, we'll call you." The blog allowed the family "to batten down the hatches and do our decision making without the constant chatter of friends calling in and to reveal stuff without giving away our souls."

Because her dad had always been an indefatigable optimist, Deb named the blog HappyDickIsSick.com. Members of the immediate family were given a password that let them post whatever they wanted, whereas others had to enter through the family portal before they could access the blog. Not everyone's comment passed muster, for reasons that underscore not just the fragile feelings of the sick but the delicate responsibility borne by a patient's gatekeepers. When a cousin of hers wrote something that poked fun at her father's cheerful nature, Deb responded, "I know you were trying to be funny, but he's quite sensitive right now, and though there are no rules to the blog, as the end of his life draws near I think we should be careful not to cross the line between roasting the man and being mean. Right now is the time for lots of love and support if you can give it or silence if you feel you can't."

The cousin apologized. He also asked Deb to vet his posts in the future, and she agreed, adding, "I'm not even sure I know the right thing to say. We're all stumbling around in the dark here, and the only guideline I can think of is this: Would you, as a dying person, want to read it?"

Four months after he was diagnosed Dick Copaken passed away. Several of Deb's friends "really stepped up to the plate," many of them traveling hundreds of miles to attend his funeral. "You look up," she recalled, "and you see those faces out there and you know they said to themselves, 'Oh, do I have to go to that funeral today?' It's small comfort to see them in the crowd at that moment, but the feelings you have about those people grow exponentially because you know they got on a train at 7 A.M. to be there, and they didn't even know my dad. They did it for me."

WHEN YOUR FRIEND NEEDS A "SECOND MOTHER"

Lauren, who I met in the waiting room, told me she drove her husband, Ralph, into the city—a 110-mile round-trip—for his daily chemo treatments because he was too weak to make the trip himself. The woman who made this possible was her BFF, Joy, a retired teacher who lives a half mile away.

"Mothers are unselfish people who always come through for you. That's what Joy does for me, and that's why I call her my second mother," said Lauren.

Whenever Ralph's treatments were delayed and Lauren couldn't get home by the end of the school day, Joy picked up their seven-year-old, ferried him to his extracurricular activities, and fixed his dinner. One winter day they were stranded in Manhattan by a snowstorm and had to stay overnight at a hotel near the hospital. That evening Joy, who was supposed to host a bridge game at her house, bagged it so she could babysit for the boy (no small undertaking, as he'd been acting out and wetting his bed since his daddy got sick).

"I'm submitting Joy's name to the Vatican for beatification," said Lauren. "She's my Mother Teresa."

Another woman in the waiting room, Cathy, also had a saintly friend, Brenda, who became a second mother to her. "My husband has bladder cancer," said Cathy. "We have two kids. Without a whole lot of fanfare, Brenda does whatever it takes to help me with my children. She understands the strain we live with every day so, to give me and Fred time off, she'll just fold our kids into her family and take them along wherever she goes. Twice now she's had them for the whole weekend so Fred and I can spend some private time together . . ."

Cathy didn't have to add, "before he dies." The words were wet in her eyes.

WHEN A FRIEND'S CHILD IS IN TROUBLE

At this writing Peggy's daughter Hayley has been "clean" for two years, but I remember when her blog, "Helplessly Hoping" (peglud.wordpress

.com) was full of searing entries about her efforts to help Hayley break a heroin habit. I also remember Peggy's disappointment in the friends who couldn't seem to handle her pain.

> My daughter's addiction is so shocking and terrifying that many of my friends don't feel comfortable even talking about it with me, or, if they mention it, they share a moment or two of condolence but that's all. I don't think they know they're being hurtful; I think it has to do with lack of knowledge. They have no experience talking about this subject with anyone. Also, there's such a stigma associated with hard-drug addictions. It's easier to talk to your friends about cancer. People assume that a person with cancer didn't knowingly do anything to "invite" it. With heroin addiction, there's the supposition that the addict is at fault, weak in character, brought it on herself, and, consequently, deserves to suffer.

Peggy very kindly assisted my research by asking readers of her blog who are parents of addicted children to describe how friends of theirs handled their suffering.

- "When a very close friend of mine never even mentions our son anymore, as if it's not still happening, as if he's not currently in his third rehab . . . that hurts."
- "I have close, old friends who act like I don't even *have* a child. They pretend he does not exist. I ask about their kids all the time, but they never ask about my son."
- "A couple of friends made it clear to us that they were so fed up with our son that they would pray for my husband and me but not for him. I wish they could just say they're sorry we're going through this without saying anything negative about our child."

- "I get very defensive when someone says, 'Can't he just stop?' Or 'How does he get the drugs?' Or 'You need to just write him off.'"
- "My least helpful friend is not a parent and knows very little about addiction but keeps trying to tell me how to handle the situation. . . . My most helpful friends are the ones who sincerely ask, 'How's she doing?' without judgment or condescension."
- "It's irritating when someone starts telling me how our son has to stop hanging out with certain people. Or he has to make the decision to want something different from his life, blah, blah, blah. I *really* don't need to hear what we already know *so* well. It was like the time the cops came to our house when our son threatened his father with a hammer, and one cop said, 'Have you ever tried taking away his privileges?' *Geez, why didn't we think of that???*"
- Peggy had her own contribution to the subject: "I sometimes feel that my friends are thinking, 'What the hell must have gone on in that family for that beautiful girl to have become a heroin addict?' I can't really blame anyone for thinking that, but I'm self-conscious about my parenting skills being so miserably measured and judged."

The question Peggy hated most was, how does Hayley get her drugs? "It's insensitive, naive, and hurtful, but people ask it all the time. I mean—duh? It's obvious that my daughter is somehow 'earning her keep' in one way or another, and it's a knife in my heart. Has she resorted to the oldest and most common means women have used to support themselves since the beginning of time—prostitution? That answer doesn't occur to the questioner until after the 'thud,' followed by my long pause."

Sadly, the most judgmental person in Peggy's life was her then ninety-two-year-old mother: "Her remarks to me are almost abusive. She says things like, 'I know why your daughter is a heroin addict—you made her take ballet lessons.' Or, 'Maybe it would be better if we found Hayley floating in the river.'"

On the other side of the ledger from these unfeeling comments are the many kindnesses Peggy recounted. One friend gave her a hand-made box in which Peggy places the names of friends "who are especially on my mind to pray for. . . . I like to think that they're safe in this box, dealing with their struggles and challenges with the support of each other."

Her dear friend Donna sent her poems by Wendell Berry, Walt Whitman, Mary Oliver, and Ellen Bass, lyrics to a Cat Stevens song, and quotations from the Dalai Lama. And when Hayley was evicted from her apartment and Peggy wanted to retrieve some of her belongings before the landlord could haul off everything to the dump, Donna helped her sort through "the devastation of my daughter's life."

The local doctor, who Peggy knew from crossing paths with him almost daily on her rural road as they walked their dogs, became an important friend after she knocked on his door one night and asked if he could properly dispose of her daughter's used drug needles. He did so, and their subsequent conversations about Hayley resulted in a warmth and understanding that Peggy said she didn't share with other casual friends.

Also supportive was the couple who insisted on accompanying her when she decided to drive past the crack house, hoping to catch a glimpse of her daughter or someone who could tell her what was happening to Hayley. Then there was Peggy's friend, Linda, who helped her scope out possible escape routes for her daughter back when Peggy still entertained the fantasy that Hayley was living there against her will and needed help to leave. One of Peggy's more desperate plans was to sneak in the backdoor of the crack house and lead Hayley out through the orchards to freedom and recovery. Linda was going to wait in the getaway car on the farm road behind the drug house while Peggy got Hayley. "Of course, that scenario was never realized, but Linda was a willing, nonjudgmental friend who indulged my compulsions. I could go on, but you get the picture. Friends and neighbors can sometimes be there for you even more actively than family members."

DEALING WITH "SOMEONE ELSE'S HORROR"

In a brief span of time Harriet Brown's family suffered a tsunami of health crises that she recounted in a *New York Times* essay. One of her daughters contracted Kawasaki disease (a rare childhood condition involving the inflammation of the blood vessels), necessitating months of convalescence. Another daughter was hospitalized with anorexia, the starvation disease, and nearly died. And Harriet's mother-in-law fought lung cancer and lost. Many of Harriet's friends stuck by her through all of this, did errands for the family, brought food, kept her company, and cried with her. But a few friends basically vanished.

"During the year we spent in eating-disorder hell, they called once or twice but otherwise behaved as though we had been transported to Mongolia with no telephones or email." She wondered if her family's multiple miseries had made her "lousy company" or if, as some experts claimed, "someone else's horror" arouses disturbing feelings of helplessness and vulnerability in other people and triggers a kind of survivor guilt from which they recoil. "People are grateful that the trauma didn't happen to them, but they feel deeply ashamed of their reactions," she wrote. "Such emotional discomfort often leads them to avoid the family in crisis."

Ruth, the woman to whom I embarrassingly sent a week's worth of nonkosher meals, had barely recovered from her own cancer operation when she was buried under an incredible avalanche of other people's horrors. First her husband learned he had cancer. Then her best friend's husband died suddenly after a medical mishap during a simple laparoscopic procedure. Next her cousin's husband drowned in three feet of water, presumably of a heart attack, a dear friend of hers died of pancreatic cancer, and that friend's wife got lymphoma. Then, believe it or not, another friend was diagnosed with a brain tumor, and *that* friend's husband found out he had prostate cancer. And did I mention that, in the midst of this harrowing onslaught, Ruth's beloved aunt died?

After the first three or four calamities Ruth told me she felt like "Madame of the Large Shoulders." I asked if she would sit for an interview about how she was holding up and what advice she would give to people in a similar situation. She readily agreed but kept having to postpone our meeting as still more crises landed in her lap. I told her to just forget about our interview, that it was more important for her to take care of all those suffering people than to tell the rest of us how to do it.

When friends of yours are coping with *their* friends' traumas, cut them some slack. Let them off the hook for whatever they promised you or owe you, be it a phone call, date, or work product. Take a burden off their overloaded shoulders if you can.

Ten Ways to Help Someone
Whose Friend or Loved One Is Sick

1) *Give them your frequent flyer miles.* If they live some distance away from their sick loved one, and what's keeping them from visiting is a lack of funds for an airline ticket, your miles can make the trip possible.

2) *Babysit for their kids* so they can have more alone time with their loved one.

3) *Take over their personal communications.* Lynn Sherr said she got a hundred calls a day from her husband's friends

and colleagues when he was dying of cancer. "I wished I had someone to intercede and answer those voicemails because they were exhausting." You can be that someone for your friend. Lacking a personal secretary (or traditional do-it-all wife), people who are busy taking care of a sick loved one may need help with routine tasks such as returning phone messages, sorting through the mail so letters and bills don't get mixed in with junk ads, catalogs, and magazines, and separating things into categories so the pile doesn't rise to the sky like one of the teetering towers in a Dr. Seuss picture book.

4) *Create a web page for your friend.* You needn't be a cyber geek to do it. Online sites like CaringBridge.org let you build, at no cost, a personal blog that, once a password and privacy options are established, allows relatives, friends, colleagues, and acquaintances, to stay connected, post messages, ask questions, and contribute photographs. Thanks to such a blog, you, who are two degrees away from the sick person, can keep up with what's happening to your friend's loved one without badgering your friend for updates. And by staying in the loop you'll have a heads-up on when to expect your friend's mood to worsen or improve.

5) *Burn a CD for your friend.* Include music they'll want to listen to through their headphones while their sick loved one naps. (Check the lyrics; omit the sad songs.)

6) *Stock their larder.* Sending food to the patient is a fine act of friendship, but it occurs to few people to send food to the patient's caregiver. Yet friends of yours who are knee-deep in the illness of others have probably skipped a bunch

of meals because they don't have time to shop or cook. You could do their shopping for them. Don't bother them to make a shopping list. Just pick up a few refrigerator basics (milk, eggs, cheese, mayo, juice) and stock their cupboard with staples like cereal, tuna, peanut butter, jam, and crackers.

7) *Feed them.* People who are taking care of others shouldn't have to cook for themselves every night nor should they have to eat alone. Invite them over for dinner, cook for them, or take them out and let them fill their empty stomachs and empty their heavy hearts if they're so inclined. Be prepared to spend the whole evening listening to them talk about the person who is two degrees of separation from you but close and dear to them. Again, remember the definition of friendship that trumps them all: a friend is someone who listens.

8) *Suggest they keep a journal or take an oral history of their loved one.* Writing or taping one's feelings and memories can release lots of tension. Should your friend ask you to read their journal entries or offer to play the tapes for you, recognize this as a sign of trust and an affirmation of your intimate standing in their life.

9) *Call regularly.* Ask how your friend is doing as well as how their loved one is faring. Tell them you're available for whatever they need, whenever they need you. Tell them you mean it.

10) *Offer, but don't impose, your company.* If the answer is no, don't take it personally. If it's yes, don't ask a lot of questions—just go.

KEEPING A FRIEND
COMPANY IN THE CAVE

A SISTER CANCER-SURVIVOR TOLD ME that whoever has experienced a serious illness or tragedy and reaches out to help a friend in comparable circumstances is like the person who is able to go into your cave and sit there with you in the darkness while everyone else is standing outside trying to coax you to come out.

That line spoke to me when I first got my diagnosis. So did a slogan I recalled from the early days of the women's movement: "Laugh and the world laughs with you. Cry and you cry with your girlfriends."

I made a quick count of the breast cancer survivors among my far-flung girlfriends and came up with eight, count 'em eight, women who had been through this particular mill, all of them currently flourishing. Fortunately, two of these women, Joyce Purnick and Lynn Povich, are close friends, and I knew I could learn a lot from them because both are seasoned journalists and had researched their breast cancers as thoroughly as if they were reporting a Pulitzer Prize–worthy story on the disease. They had information and experience that could illuminate the dark corners of my cave, but if I were already resenting and resisting questions that sent me back to the early days of my illness, how could I justify asking Joyce and Lynn, who were years beyond their diagnoses, to revisit that period in their lives? I could, and I did. And being splendid human beings and loyal buddies, both made themselves available to me in every way. Separately they had been my friends and walking partners for some time. Now they became my cancer mavens and personal advisers as well.

Many chilly mornings during the fall and winter of 2009–2010 I trudged around Central Park with one or the other of these women, taking advantage of their candor to learn everything I could about what was happening to me and what to expect next. They tolerated my questions, no matter how personal, and never grew impatient when I was obtuse. They helped me decode my test results and understand my surgical options, described possible post-op complications, various anticancer treatment options and medications, and, after the lumpectomy, they let me vent about the pain of healing and the possibility that a malignant cell may have escaped my surgeon's scalpel. Because I knew I could trust them, I felt free to confide my darkest fears, and because they were as near as our next walk, I never felt alone in my cave.

Lynn counseled me on every topic from mortality tremors to sex after surgery. She warned me early on not to talk to people about my cancer until I knew exactly what type I had and how bad it was or else I'd be bombarded with advice that had nothing to do with my particular tumor. We talked a lot about blood, my bête noire. She told me to prepare myself for a whole raft of blood tests but also assured me that, despite my severe antipathy toward my veins, she knew I could handle it. The combination of her confidence in me and being forewarned helped stiffen my resolve to endure the tests without wimping out.

We were walking the track around the Central Park reservoir one day, with a V-formation of mallard ducks flapping and quacking overhead, when I asked Lynn how she'd broken the news to her children, whether she wished she'd said or done anything differently, and how honest she'd been about her prognosis. The truth is I'd been feeling guilty about having told my children my news by e-mail (and in a minimizing fashion), so I was reassured to hear that Lynn too had finessed her announcement, motivated, as I was, by a desire to downplay the seriousness of her diagnosis. No parent wants her kids to worry, Lynn said, so at first she'd told them "the bare minimum"—hadn't even used the word cancer—saving the details until later and, in the case of her teenage son, much later because he didn't press her for more information. What she'd told them was, "The doctors found this thing in my breast that has to be taken out, so I'm going to undergo surgery, but I'm going to be okay." Her daughter wanted to come home from college, but Lynn insisted that wasn't necessary, that it was "just a procedure." The fact that she had totally understated her condition and her children didn't resent her for it reassured me that my decision not to dramatize my news wasn't so terrible.

In perhaps our most memorable conversation Lynn said, without a trace of sanctimony, that her brush with cancer had heightened her sense of life's fragility and had resulted in some major life-changing decisions. She'd been thinking about quitting her job in cable TV anyway, but the cancer pushed her to do it sooner when she realized that she still wanted to try new things and that the importance of the things she wanted to do outweighed the things she had to do. With a husband to support her, she had the luxury to never again take a job she didn't relish or work for someone she didn't like. She started tutoring in a public school and working on a book. She said cancer sharpened her focus and strengthened her resolve to enjoy life, to love those who mean so much to her, and to act humbly before forces she cannot control. I'd been having many of those same feelings and dismissing them as prosaic, but Lynn's bracingly forthright way of expressing them helped me accept that adversity, rather than pulling me down, could intensify the sweetness of life and put into bas-relief the ordinary pleasures that we sometimes take for granted.

After the lumpectomy and lymph nodes removal, I was sent home from the hospital with a drain that emptied into a plastic receptacle strapped to my ribs. I looked as if I'd acquired a third breast shaped like a Coke can. Because not even my roomiest T-shirt would mask it, I refused to leave the house.

"Don't be silly!" said Lynn on the phone. "Just throw on one of Bert's shirts and a beautiful scarf over a pair of leggings and you'll look totally cool." I did as she instructed. In my "totally cool" ensemble of black tights and black boots, topped by one of my husband's size L dress shirts and a long satin scarf, I sallied forth to meet the world. Four days later the drain was removed and I was back in my own clothes, but without Lynn's counsel I would have spent those four days in hiding.

Joyce, my other cancer maven, was similarly encouraging and edifying. A day after I received my diagnosis she advised me to try to suspend reacting to the news until I had all the facts, pathology reports, and treatment recommendations, because the story would keep changing with every subsequent test result and interpretation. When I was ready to interview oncologists, she warned me to steer clear of a well-known breast cancer doctor whom she'd consulted and found brutally brusque. She underlined how important it was that I feel completely comfortable with my oncologist because I was about to embark on a very long and intense relationship with that person. Thank heavens she recommended Dr. Norton, whose ongoing concern for all aspects of my health, not just my cancer, makes me feel less alone in my cave.

Through it all—diagnosis, surgery, recovery, six weeks of radiation, and bad reactions to two anticancer medications—Joyce functioned as my no-nonsense reality check and resident wise woman on all matters relating to nutrition, medication, exercise, vitamins, rest, and relaxation. We talked about her friends' different responses when she told them she had cancer, and she helped me understand a mutual friend who, rather than deal with this kind of bad news, shrank from it and retreated. Once I knew I was to have a lumpectomy, Joyce kicked into full factual mode. She told me exactly what to expect from the operation and its aftermath. She encouraged me to do lots of research, be my own advocate, and be unashamedly aggressive about questioning my doctors. The day I panicked about what my breast would look like when the surgeon was done carving out the tumor, Joyce listened patiently to my anxieties about scarring, then did something I will never forget. When we found ourselves on a deserted path in the park, she glanced around furtively, pulled up her shirt and showed me her scar. Nothing could have reassured me more than the sight of that simple unterrifying mark on my friend's chest.

Basically, I have no right to complain about anything. Compared to what other women have been through—removal of both breasts, profound disfigurement, complicated reconstructive surgeries, weeks and months of daily ninety-minute sessions in a chemo cubicle where huge vials of horrible red stuff were pumped into their veins, constant agonizing pain, anguish, rejection, depression, fatigue, and the specter of death—I know I got off easy. Still, I bitched and moaned and felt sorry for myself and needed friends like Lynn and Joyce to buck me up.

A third friend—I'll call her Martine because she doesn't wish to be identified—opted to have a mastectomy when her doctor told her the odds of recurrence in her case would increase each year; she didn't want to live with that threat hanging over her head. At the point when I wasn't sure what surgery was going to be prescribed for me, I listened hard to her story. Martine opted for reconstructive surgery after her breast was removed because she didn't want to wake up with a big scar running down her flat chest. She'd talked it over with her husband, who said he wanted a breast to hold, even if it was "fake," and he didn't want to see her so scarred, literally, by the cancer experience. She said if I needed to have a mastectomy and I wanted reconstruction, the doctors would start the process during the same surgery. They would remove the breast and place a balloon under my skin. Over the next few months they would fill it with liquid through a port in my chest, and slowly but surely the balloon would stretch the muscle and skin so that eventually there would be enough space for the permanent implant. She told me I could choose between two methods of reconstruction: one that uses skin from my back or stomach to cover the implant—an operation that takes six or seven hours—or a much shorter one that would use the breast muscle to hold the implant in place.

Then I'd have another operation in which they would insert the permanent implant, which could either be made of silicone or saline. Martine said she chose silicone (even though it caused autoimmune problems in some women) because it was much softer than the saline kind, which is rock hard. Choosing silicone required her to register in a federal experimental trial so that her implant could be tracked for leaks. She considered this a benefit because it would force her doctor to stay on top of the situation.

I asked her about sex, of course. She told me she has some sensation around the edge of the new breast but not in the middle and not around the nipple. Losing feeling in one breast definitely cut down on her pleasure, but what affected her sex life even more was the loss of estrogen, a result of having to suddenly stop taking hormones. In the absence of estrogen, the vagina dries up, and though she uses a local estrogen cream, Martine said the dry vagina plus the unfeeling breast definitely suppressed her libido. She must have noticed me sinking deeper into depression with each new piece of information because she suddenly smiled, put an arm around me, and admitted her secret: "Marijuana has been a great help—really my salvation," she said. "It took me years to figure that out, but once I started smoking grass during sex, my libido returned to normal. If you have to have a mastectomy, yours can too. Take my word for it."

Looking back on the early days of my illness, it's clear to me that my body was the responsibility of my physicians, but my spirit was in the care of the three friends who kept me company in the cave while everyone else was coaxing me to come out. Corny as that may sound, it was their plucky attitudes and practical advice that got me through the dark times. The very fact of their present existence—their vibrancy, good health, and utter normality—embodied the promise of my recovery. I was buoyed up simply by spending time with them, walking with them, sharing their laughter, witnessing how they lived their lives, and reminding myself that not very long ago each of them was where I am now. This suggested that I too might someday look back on this unnerving time with equanimity and the willingness to help another woman through it.

If there's a sick someone in your life who could benefit from your experience as I did from that of Lynn, Joyce, and Martine, I hope you too will turn your friendship into a loving mentorship and keep your pal company in the cave.

FIVE

SICKNESS
AND SHAME

*Problems People Hide, What Happens When Ego
Meets Adversity, and Why Some Friends Are Hard to Help*

BY "HARD TO HELP," I'm not thinking of Justin, Jesse, or Ken.

Justin Canha has a severe form of autism. Until he was ten, he barely spoke, and he had to be taught the most elementary social behaviors, such as what kinds of touch are inappropriate, what questions are rude, and how to control his nonstop "self-talking."

Jesse Saperstein, author of *Atypical: Life with Asperger's in 20 1/3 Chapters*, writes that when he was a child, "making eye contact was as uncomfortable as staring into the blazing sun."

Ken Rosen, once a genial, elegant young man, suffered a head injury when he was thrown from a horse. During our one and only visit after his accident he smiled vacantly and kept repeating, "It's so good to see you," like a record stuck in one groove. I had no idea how to relate to him.

Through no fault of their own, genetic conditions or grievous injuries keep people like Justin, Jesse, and Ken shut off from intimate friendships. But the ones I'm talking about in this chapter—the infertile woman; the man with MS, prostate cancer, colon cancer, bladder cancer, or any cancer at all; the people who suffer from depression or other mental problems—have voluntarily shut *themselves* off because they're ashamed to admit to their friends that they're sick. They don't want to discuss it. They associate illness with weakness, disgrace, failure, and, if they're male, emasculation. Some men are so embarrassed about being sick that they hide their problem as zealously as a state secret, and if someone happens to find out about it, they swear that person to secrecy. Maladies involving one's private parts or reproductive capacity further complicate matters between friends. What do you say to a woman who tries to hide her breast reconstruction? How do you chat up a friend who's had a hysterectomy, prostatectomy, or colostomy? What do you say to someone who considers her illness a personal failing? How do you comfort an AIDS patient who's humiliated by the disease that's killing him? And how do you deal with a friend who's embarrassed about *not* dying—the woman who botched a suicide attempt or the man given days to live whose pals rushed to his side from all over the globe but who's still alive a year later?

This chapter will attempt to answer those questions and then wrap up with three simple tips to avoid provoking shame-based discomfort in your friends.

But first I need to talk about Nora Ephron, the writer so beloved for her warmly romantic movies (*When Harry Met Sally, You've Got Mail*) and her funny, self-mocking essays and books. For someone who was so self-revealing in *Heartburn*, the roman à clef about her marriage and the infidelity of her husband, Carl Bernstein, and so forthright about revealing her physical and other frailties in *I Feel Bad About My Neck*, it was nothing short of astonishing when she died in June 2012, having told almost no one that she was sick. Of her choice to keep her illness a secret until the very end, Frank Rich, a friend, wrote in *New York* magazine that it "was not just out of character but a Herculean task that required an unfathomable scale of compartmentalization and enforcement in the fishbowls of New York and L.A. she swam in. What exactly . . . had Nora intended? What was she telling us by making her final chapter a secret?"

A gregarious social animal, Nora had a zillion friends, 99.9 percent of whom were unaware that she'd had a terminal illness for more than six years. People who saw her as recently as a few weeks before her death hadn't a clue that she was in the final stages of acute myeloid leukemia. Though I was a longtime acquaintance of hers, not someone who could have reasonably expected to know what was going on, I was nonetheless so shocked by the news that I actually let out a scream in the middle of a restaurant when my daughter Abby called my cell to tell me that Nora had died. So I can understand why her closest friends—for example, Meryl Streep, who said at the funeral, "We've all been ambushed by her death"—were not just shocked but, by their own admission, "pissed off" when she died. They felt shut out, almost betrayed, cheated of their last good-byes. As Frank Rich put it, "Her death was a gut-punch that initially landed like a sucker punch. And it came with a vexing mystery. In private, in her public persona, and in her literary voice, Nora exemplified self-awareness and truth-telling, and yet she hadn't let us in on the long battle for her life that finally consumed her."

Though she'd told almost no one that she was sick, she had planned her own funeral down to the list of speakers. Nora's way of death suggests that for her—and undoubtedly for others—there can be another motivation for sickness secrecy: concealment not in the service of shame but to protect one's privacy and preserve the pleasures of daily life. I think Nora was simply trying to tell her friends that she needed normalcy more than sympathy, ordinary conversation more than dramatic farewells. She was determined not to become Cancer Girl. She didn't want anyone to treat her differently, look at her differently, feel sorry for her, or take care of her. Unique in death as in life, Nora wanted to stay Nora until the very end.

Now let's proceed to the more typical motivations for secrecy—humiliation or shame—and how you might build a bridge of friendship across a river of discomfort and denial.

THE SHAME OF INFERTILITY

|||||||||||||||||||||||||||||||||||||||||||||||||||||||||||||||

Years ago a woman I considered one of my closest friends kept me in the dark about the most significant thing happening in her life at the time. Only when she announced to the world (not just me, and not me *first*) that she and her husband had adopted a baby did I learn that she'd been trying to conceive for years and had been undergoing fertility treatments to no avail. The mere fact that she *wanted* a child was news to me. She'd always said she wasn't interested in motherhood, loved her work, wanted to be free to travel with her husband, and so on. I never questioned her choice; I supported it. Though I had three kids, I've never believed biology is destiny, and I'm not one of those pronatalists who think every woman should be a mother. I think the rearing of another human being is a profound enterprise, and only those who are fully committed to it should sign on.

So when my friend took a deep breath in a group situation and announced the adoption, you could have knocked me over with her exhale. As happy as I was for her, I can't deny feeling wounded, bewildered, and retrospectively betrayed by the one-sidedness of our supposed intimacy. All this time I'd been totally forthcoming while she . . .

I never asked why she hadn't confided in me, and she never offered an explanation. But I can venture a guess. Today one hears women openly chatting on the Broadway bus about slow sperm motility, egg donors, in vitro fertilization, and the like, but thirty years ago infertility was discussed in whispers, if at all. So maybe she was ashamed to let me know that either she was infertile or her husband impotent.

Maybe she thought I'd think less of her or view her husband differently. Maybe she just felt bad about herself.

"NONE OF THEIR BUSINESS"

IIIIIIIIIIIIIIIIIIIIIIIIIIIIIIIIIIIIIIIIIIIIIIIIIIIIIII

One morning while I was still doing time in the waiting room, an elderly Hasidic man—black hat, long white beard, ear curls—sat down kitty-corner to me and opened a book printed in Hebrew, a language I speak poorly but read well enough to recognize the word *Shoah*—Holocaust—in its title. The opportunity to interview a member of an insular religious community wasn't going to fall in my lap every day, so I begged his pardon and asked if he would answer some questions for the book I was writing about friendship and illness.

No response. He was a reader; shouldn't he want to help a writer? Was he purposely ignoring me, or did he not understand English? I tried again, this time inserting a few words of *mamaloshen* (the mother tongue) so he'd know I was a member of his tribe.

"I'm sure you've got *tsuris* [troubles] like I've got *tsuris* or you wouldn't be here," I said softly. "I wish you a *refuah shlaymah* [complete recovery] but right now I need help. All I want is a word or two about how your friends have related to you since you got sick."

He stroked his beard but his eyes never left the page.

"Could you at least talk to me about the *halacha* [Jewish law]? I know it says we're commanded to visit the sick, but does it say for how long or how frequently?"

At this, he looked up. It was obvious that I wasn't from his world; no proper Hasidic wife would wear hip-hugger jeans and leave her hair uncovered. "Go ask your *rebbe*," he said. "I don't know the *halacha*. I'm just a tailor."

Chuckling, I replied, "Even a poor tailor is entitled to a little *halacha*." You might recognize that I was channeling Motel the Tailor in *Fiddler on the Roof,* but the old man didn't crack a smile; he had no idea what I was talking about. And why would he? The only time I'd seen a Hasid at a Broadway show was when an actor played one onstage.

"Okay, never mind the law," I said. "Let's just talk about your friends."

"My friends?" Arching an eyebrow, he flicked the air as if brushing away a fly.

"You haven't told them you have cancer? Is that what you're saying?"

"It's none of their business."

"You mean nobody knows you're sick?"

"*Hashem* [God] knows. My wife knows. *Genugg.* [That's enough.]"

"But your friends could be helpful. They could comfort you, do things for you . . ."

"Spread *lashon hora* [evil gossip] about me," he added.

"You think it's a *shonda* [disgrace] to be sick? Is that why you've kept it a secret?"

The Hasid shook his head. "I don't need anyone's *rachmahnis* [pity]."

With that, he clammed up. (Is there an equivalent kosher image?) I told him he reminded me of my mother. "She came from a little Hungarian *shtetl* [village]. She was ashamed of having cancer in the early fifties when it really was a *shonda*. I bet you know why she hid it—because she thought no nice Jewish boy would want to marry me if his parents knew there was cancer in our family. I was a kid when she died, but I still remember friends of hers at the funeral muttering to each other that they never even knew she was sick."

"She should rest in peace," said the old man, his eyes watery and full of kindness.

I asked him about his family. They came from Krakow, he said, but no one made it through the war. He pointed to the word on the cover of his book—*Shoah*.

Both of us fell silent. Just then a technician came to escort him to his treatment room. He stood up with some difficulty, gave me a silent nod, and shuffled toward the men's locker room. Immediately a pleasant-looking fortyish guy in a button-down shirt and corduroy pants took the old man's seat and handed me a sheet of paper.

"I have to leave now, but if you're still here when the Hasid comes out, would you give him this?" The sheet read, *Tefila Lerofeh*. (A prayer for the sick.) "Tell him to give me a call if he ever wants to talk. I wrote my phone number on the top. I'm a rabbi. He probably won't consider me a *real* rabbi, but I know how to be a friend and I know how to be discreet. Tell him my grandparents were from Krakow."

THE SECRETS MEN KEEP

You don't have to be Jewish to feel ashamed of being ill, but judging by my research and interviews, you're more likely to be male.

I found it striking that none of the women I interviewed said they had kept their illness hidden. Then just the other day when I was musing about this fact to my friend Carolyn, she suddenly confessed that she'd had cancer years ago and had never told anyone but her husband. "I had better things to do than to stay on the phone with my four grown-up kids or my friends talking about myself. I didn't want to have to say over and over again, 'Thanks for calling, I'm fine.' I especially didn't want to upset one of my daughters who gets very emotional. I was raised that you close the door of your house and leave your troubles inside."

Carolyn and my infertile friend notwithstanding, based on more than eighty interviews, I found it's men who tend to keep their condition secret. Clearly equating illness with emasculation, many of them said that any hint of impairment or vulnerability would tarnish their image; diminish their status; erode the respect, admiration, and affection of others; or threaten their jobs. So invested were they in maintaining a public face of strength and vigor that they were willing to soldier on without support or succor rather than admit, even to a close friend or relative, what they were going through. Moreover, several of the married men also confided to me that they also had forbidden their wives to tell *their* friends.

One of the most militant secret keepers was Daniel, who told me with discernible pride how he'd succeeded in concealing his bladder cancer from his friends and coworkers and how important it was to keep things that way. "Everyone would look at me funny if they knew. It would be awkward on both sides. They wouldn't know how to treat me. I'd feel them watching me, looking for symptoms, waiting for me to die. I'd be alive but my career would be dead.

"It's bad enough my wife knows. When I went in for surgery, I begged her not to visit me in the hospital. We live in a small city, and friends of ours could have seen her. If she ran into one of them, I'm sure she would have spilled the beans because she's a lousy liar. She came anyway. Luckily, she never got caught."

I wondered how Daniel explained his absence to his boss and coworkers when he left for his treatments at different times on different days.

"I don't have to make excuses. I sell real estate. I'm always in and out of the office showing properties. No one notices when I come and go."

"You're completely bald, you don't even have any eyebrows," I said. "Hasn't anyone noticed *that*?"

"Yeah, they have, but I told them I shaved everything off because it looks cool. My heroes are Michael Jordan and Shaquille O'Neal. I'm just continuing their tradition." Dan cupped his palms on his shiny pate and preened.

What about his family? Did his parents know—his children, his siblings?

"No one knows, not even my kids. I made my wife swear on the Holy Bible that she won't tell them. They're young. They've got enough on their plates. They don't need to be worrying about their dad."

Richard M. Cohen, a television news producer, hid from his friends and coworkers that he had multiple sclerosis, a nerve-destroying condition that gradually steals one's sight, strength, balance, and speech. In the eighties, when he met Meredith Vieira, formerly a cohost of the *Today* show, he told her his secret on their second date, joking that if his illness was going to scare her off, he wasn't about to waste money on dessert. Meredith, empathetic and fatalistic, said she saw no point in worrying about an unknown future.

As their relationship blossomed, her colleagues asked her how she could go out with someone who was such a snob. Didn't she see how rude he was, how he ignored people? Meredith knew he wasn't ignoring them; he just couldn't *see* them, but she didn't blow his cover. The illness remained his secret until he "came out" a few years later. On top of the MS, he eventually had to battle colon cancer too. In 2004 he published a memoir with the double-entendre title *Blindsided*. Now he writes books and columns on chronic illness.

Meredith told AARP magazine that she and her husband didn't discuss his illness with their three children until the kids "saw their father plummet backward down the stairs and land on his head. They were terrified." Later that night, when the seven-year-old asked her a lot of questions, Meredith answered them.

Another morning in the waiting room, another story of shame and sorrow, this one divulged only after I guaranteed the teller an alias for her and her husband: "Jeff has anal malignant melanoma," said Cynthia. "His prognosis is not good, but I think he's more upset by how embarrassing it is. The doctors wanted him to have the radical surgery, but he told them he would rather risk dying than end up wearing a bag or diaper. So he only elected to get the treatments." Cynthia pulled a tissue from her purse.

We have three kids under ten. They know their daddy had surgery, nothing else. He says that's enough for now. We're Presbyterian. We believe whatever happens is God's will. That's how we've made peace with this awful disease. At least Jeff has.

If not for my girlfriends, I don't think I could make it through each day. The support they've given me is beyond anything I could have imagined. Early on I told them Jeff has cancer but not what kind, and I asked them to keep it confidential. I'm sure they told their husbands, because two or three of them have shown up to shovel snow and blow our driveway.

The other night we had an unannounced visit from a couple we like a lot, but they arrived while Jeff and I were researching his illness and making plans for his estate, and it was a profound moment for us and we weren't in the mood for company. Still, how could we turn them away when all they were trying to do is show that they care? Everything's so complicated now.

Various people in Cynthia's life have tried to uncomplicate things for her.

"They're unbelievable! Even when I say not to, they show up on my doorstep with soups and stews," she said as her eyes suddenly grew dark. "I appreciate the help, but I also feel there's a fine line between needing support and not wanting to be treated like I'm totally helpless. I'm still active. I'm still capable."

That was an understatement if ever I heard one. Cynthia said she runs the local theater club, which involves choosing Broadways shows, buying a block of tickets, and arranging bus trips to New York City for about fifty people. When a huge storm put the kibosh on one of her theater outings, the tickets and buses had to be rebooked. Cynthia didn't delegate the job because she knew she could handle it by phone, but one of her friends, assuming she'd be too stressed out, took it on herself to fix the problem and made a mess of things. Cynthia also runs sports clinics for a local softball league. Since Jeff got sick she hasn't been able to promote the league or set up the usual tournaments, so a group of her friends took on the job for her. "This wasn't a one-shot challenge like changing the date of a theater party. It was a full season's commitment, and my friends did it well," she said. Finally, as the class parent who usually organizes special holiday events, Cynthia had to deputize other mothers to create this year's Valentine's Day celebration. To thank them, she bought each a red-covered journal in which she wrote, "Fill its pages with everyday pleasures because you never know when those simple pleasures are going to end."

It's an established fact that most of America's volunteers are women *and* most caregivers of sick people are women (more than forty million at last count). So when a woman is sidelined by illness, the impact on schools, community groups, and neighborhoods is the same whether she's the patient or the caregiver of the patient. Either way, society loses, and either way, those who step in to fill the gap are most often *other* women.

What about Jeff's friends? I ask.

"My husband is very private, so most of his friends don't even know he's sick. He thinks if they knew, they'd treat him differently and he would hate that. He doesn't want a lot of drama in his life; he wants calm consistency. He doesn't like people doing things for us or coming over to visit, and he's not comfortable going out. When a disease affects your bowels, you don't want to be far from home. It's not just that he's embarrassed about the location of his disease; he's embarrassed about having cancer at all. He thinks it's a sign of weakness. Needless to say, we don't see eye to eye on this."

For several months after his June 20, 2011, diagnosis of ALS—also known as Lou Gehrig's disease—Michael Jaillet, forty-one, a senior executive, kept it a secret from his coworkers, his children, everyone in his life except his wife and three brothers. In an AP feature story entitled, "To Tell or Not to Tell?" he said of that initial period of secrecy, "It became, in a lot of ways, a bigger burden than the disease. It's guilt, tiptoeing around, talking in code. It's clearing out your email or your Internet browser every night because your kids are going to get on and you don't want them to see what you've been researching." Once he admitted his condition, he didn't just tell his kids and friends; he became an activist and fundraiser for ALS. "I feel like I've got a torch that I have to carry," he said.

Prostate cancer is among the most common unmentionables. Three men who've had their prostates removed held three different views about disclosure. One, a lawyer in his sixties, freely shares with his friends, partners, and clients the most picayune details of his prosta-tectomy, including the fact that it left him impotent and incontinent. The second, a clergyman in his fifties, announced to his congregation that he was being treated for prostate cancer but left out the surgery's side effects, which he only divulged to his very closest friends. The third man, an eighty-year-old, experienced no side effects whatsoever but told no one other than his wife that he even had cancer. (I found out by accident when the wife let it slip by mistake, then got wildly flustered and immediately warned me in the strongest possible terms not to tell a soul. "He would kill me if he knew you know," she said. "He'd be humiliated.")

SHAME ABOUT MENTAL MATTERS

Years ago, I paid a visit to a colleague who'd taken sick leave for un-specified reasons, and while there I noticed a vial of pills on the side table, its label bearing the name of a medication famously prescribed for clinical depression. Had she overlooked the pills, I wondered, or left them out on purpose so I would deduce her problem without her having to spell it out? Should I mention them at the risk of embarrassing her or pretend I didn't see them and miss the opportunity to connect with her at a deeper, more human level?

Depression carried even more of a stigma back then than it does today. People didn't talk about their mental problems with their friends. Memoirs of emotional breakdown were yet to blossom as a literary genre. William Styron had yet to publish his best seller, *Darkness Visible,* and Art Buchwald and Mike Wallace hadn't gone public with their afflictions. Victims of depression, fearing they would be thought unlovable, unemployable, or nuts, frequently swept such issues under the rug. For all those reasons I chose to ignore the pills on my colleague's end table and say nothing, thus collaborating in her shame.

It was the wrong choice; I know that now. Had I said something, I might have opened the door to a candid discussion of her problems and established that I was comfortable talking with her about her feelings or, rather, listening to her talk about them. I could have told her I sympathized with what she was going through. I could have been a true friend. Instead, my cowardice trumped my empathy, and her secrecy cemented her isolation. When she returned to work, it was clear that the barrier between us would never be pierced.

As promised, we'll end with three basic guidelines to help you avoid shame-based discomfort.

1) *When a friend's issue is genital, sexual, or reproductive, don't be coy or euphemistic.* Open the conversation with a simple, "I'm glad to see you." Ask, "Was it a good day or a bad day?" Or, "What [not how] are you feeling right now?" Pay attention to the patients' nonverbal cues—face, posture, body language. If they seem shy or discomfited, don't probe and don't get too graphic; don't ask about their sex life or digestive facility. Stick to neutral subjects—the weather, last night's amazing tiebreaker, the price of gas. However, with friends who are

more forthcoming, you can encourage them to talk as much as they want about what they're experiencing. The easiest questions to ask include, "Are you in pain?" "Did the doctor say when you can go home?" "Is this going to affect your daily life?" If you forget those lines, you'll never go wrong with, "What can I do to make things easier for you? I really want to help."

2) *Suppress your shock reaction and squelch whatever squeamishness might be aroused by the sight of your sick friends.* Imagine how they feel. Knowing how they look may contribute to their shame. They're already afraid you'll be grossed out by their affliction or its surface appearance. Your job is to reframe what you see as a badge of their survival, not a reason to recoil in disgust.

3) *Expect someone who has survived a suicide attempt to feel ashamed; be sensitive to their embarrassment but don't beat around the bush.* He knows that you know why his wrists are bandaged. She knows that you know she overdosed. Take the bull by the horns and ask if they feel like talking about it. If they don't, say you understand but you just want them to know you care about them. If they *are* ready to talk about it, try not to let your face or voice reveal the shock or horror you may feel as their story unfolds. Don't tsk-tsk. Don't roll your eyes. Don't say, "Oh, God, how could you have done that!?" Listen to them in a compassionate, nonjudgmental way. Nod to indicate you understand even if you don't, and keep listening until they're all talked out. Then ask them future-oriented questions: "What's your schedule like next week?" "Can we make a lunch date?

If they have no family nearby and are going home to an empty house and you're available, you might stay over for a few nights until they're stabilized. Set up a buddy system to keep tabs on them for a while. Make sure they see their therapist, take their medication, and renew their prescriptions. Tell them there's no need to put on a happy act when they're with you. Promise that, should life ever again look grim and futile, they can call you at any hour of the day or night and you'll stay on the phone or meet them wherever they are to help them through whatever it is.

But only make that promise if you're sure you can keep it.

|||||||||||||||||||||||||||||||||||||||||||||||||||||||||||||||||||||||||||||||||||||||||||||||||||||||||||||||||||||||||||||||||||||||

LOSING FAITH
IN MY BODY

FOR SOMEONE WITH ZERO SYMPTOMS, the illogic of my diagnosis was part of its initial shock. The day after Yom Kippur, sitting across from my radiologist in that miniature consulting room, the words "suspicious mass" hanging in the air, stunned disbelief scrimmaging with demons of fear, my first thought was, *Breast cancer! Are you kidding? How could I be sick when I feel so great? How could I have cancer if I'm so healthy?* Cognitive dissonance. The two realities just didn't compute.

My husband used to be tense and anxious about getting to the airport on time, but once he was in his seat on the plane, he usually fell asleep within seconds of clasping his seat belt. He often joked that his problem wasn't fear of flying; it was fear of not flying. Similarly, I'm tense and anxious about pre-op procedures (because of all the blood tests), but once strapped to the gurney en route to the operating room, I'm an advertisement for the Zen of surgery. That was certainly the case this time around because everyone had told me the lumpectomy was going to be a snap. I visualized Dr. Van Zee cutting out my teeny, tiny tumor the way a dermatologist might excise a wart. I thought I would wake up with a Band-Aid on my breast. Instead, there was a drain sticking out of my underarm area because Dr. Van

Zee had discovered—against all odds, given my type of cancer—that my "noninvasive, nonaggressive" tubular carcinoma had already spread to a node. She had not only removed the culprit; she'd also removed eleven more nodes (all those bordering the infected one) in order give me "clean margins"—that is, cancer-free territory around the bad node. With clean margins, my health picture would brighten, but should any of the eleven nodes, which she'd sent to pathology, be found to contain cancer cells, I'd be in big trouble. The pathologist's report wouldn't come through until November 10, eleven days from then, which gave me plenty of time to whip myself into a fearful frenzy.

Why was this happening to me? Was I being punished for the euphoria of my blissful summer? Was cancer God's way of cutting me down to size? Was the Evil Eye taking revenge on my postbirthday contentment? Had I been too lavish in expressing my happiness? Touted it too proudly in conversation with too many people? Committed the sin of hubris by broadcasting how small my tumor was, how noninvasive? Noninvasive! Hah! Why at this point in my life had my body betrayed me?

Talk about paradoxes and contradictions. I feel the same now as I've always felt except that there's an undetonated grenade in my chest. Having cancer has familiarized me with my body at the level of its cells, nodes, and genes while at the same time estranging me from my corporal Self. What else did my body have in store? The organism that stealthily produced this tumor could be, at this very moment, manufacturing many more. Until now, when something in its precincts went awry, my body had always alerted me by means of an ache, itch, rash, cramp, or swelling. Whether with shortness of breath, tennis elbow, indigestion, a knee click, or a sore throat, I could always count on it to inform me when something was amiss. Not long ago shock waves shot through my foot at the base of my fourth toe, making it impossible for me to hike without pain. I went to the podiatrist who removed a Morton's neuroma (an irritated nerve), my foot returned to normal, and I was back on the trails in eight weeks. That's how things used to work: my body sent me a distress signal, I went to the appropriate doctor, the problem got fixed. Not so with the tumor. My cancer didn't announce itself; it grew in hiding and had to be sought (by mammography) before it could be found.

In Judaism a "vain prayer" is one about which the outcome is already a fact even if you don't know it yet. For instance, if you're coming home from work and you see smoke rising from your street, you shouldn't pray that it's not your house burning (because if it is your house, it's already burning and your prayer will be in vain); you should pray for the strength to deal with whatever you find when you get home. Following suit, I resisted my inclination to spend the next eleven days praying for clean margins. Instead, I prayed that if cancer cells turn up in any of the eleven nodes that had been sent to the pathologist, I will be strong enough to do whatever I have to do to get rid of them.

Journal entry, October 31. "It's the day after my lumpectomy. I'm wearing a surgical bra and a drain from the incision where the nodes were removed. Fluids from the wound must be emptied morning and night. I'm feeling raw, compromised, vulnerable, and scared."

My relationship to my body changed after that. Not because of the scars (a scant two inches long and tucked in the fold under my arm) but because in some fundamental way I felt that my body had betrayed me. Over the years I'd come to know it so well—not just its warning signals but also its wonders, the heave and blush of an orgasm, the seismic transformations of puberty, the steel band of pelvic cramps during my prechildbirth periods, the film running backward during menopause.

The truth is, in 1965 I was better at reading my body's signals than my OB-GYN. Though I had never before been five months pregnant, I knew that something weird was going on, something beyond the normal arc of gestation. I had already outgrown all sizes of maternity clothes and was wearing muumuus.

"Either I'm having twins," I told the OB-GYN, "or I'm having an elephant."

He said something on the order of "What the hell do you know? I'm the M.D. with the stethoscope and I'm telling you I hear one heartbeat." In 1965 there was no ultrasound; there were only X-rays, and they could be dangerous. Still, I told the doctor I wanted to take the risk rather than have him (and me and Bert) blindsided by twins.

"No twins," he said. "One heartbeat." Nonetheless, probably to humor me, he sent me off to an X-ray lab. They took some pictures, gave me the films, and sent me back to the OB-GYN who would read them for me. In the cab back to the doctor's office, it occurred to me to try to read the films myself. True, I didn't have an M.D., but I took biology. How hard could it be to figure out which bones were which?

I carefully slid the large X-ray negative out of its envelope and pressed it against the back window of the taxi so the daylight would shine through. Two seconds later I found the ladder of my spine, the wings of my pelvic bones, and then—voila!—nesting in the center of my pelvis like an ostrich egg was a neat white circle: the baby's head! Thrilled, I traced the baby's spine up along the right side of my vertebrae where it met—Yikes!—another neat white circle, the head of my second baby, and stemming downward from the skull, that baby's spine. The two baby backbones, like arched bows, formed perfect parentheses on either side of my spine. Tears of excitement streaming down my cheeks, I charged into my OB-GYN's office, waving the films. "I was right! I'm carrying twins!" My body had told me something special was happening, but I was glad to have it verified in pictures. And indeed, a few months later I delivered two baby girls, who together tipped the scales at twelve and a half pounds.

That wasn't the first time my physical self issued trustworthy clues, only the most dramatic. Ordinarily, it simply produced a symptom and I interpreted what it meant. Two sneezes in a row? Harmless. Three or four sneezes in a row? I'd have a runny nose and sore throat by sundown. Itchy rash? Time to switch detergents. Cold sore? Insomnia? Sure signs that I'm distressed about something major. My body always registers emotional travail by popping out a skin eruption or not letting me sleep. Its early warning systems had served me well for seventy years only to be outwitted by the teeny tiny tumor. What happened to the mind-body connection? I wondered. Why didn't it tell me that my breast had been invaded by a foreign force? If it didn't know it had a tumor, what else doesn't it know? And if it *did* know but kept the tumor a secret, what else isn't it telling me?

I hate secrets, probably because my family of origin was stuffed with them. First there was the grandmother who committed bigamy before leaving Hungary, a scandal unmentioned until years after she died. (In rebellion against an arranged marriage, she'd jumped out the bedroom window on her wedding night and run off and married my grandfather without benefit of divorce.) Second, the aunt who told everyone that she was infertile rather than confess that she didn't want to have any children (an unthinkable choice in our traditional Jewish family). Third, a cousin who was never acknowledged to be, in the old parlance, "slow." Also the "bachelor uncle" who may have been gay; two uncles who died mysteriously (rumor had it at the hands of the Chicago mob), and an aunt on one side and an uncle on the other who were card-carrying Communists in the 1950s, when Senator Joe McCarthy was rounding up "Reds." Closer to the bone, I was thirteen before I found out my parents' secrets: both had been married before, and the grown woman I always thought was their child, just as I was their child, was actually my mother's daughter from her first marriage. What's more, I had another half-sister out there somewhere, a daughter my father had abandoned when his first marriage broke up. (I wouldn't meet that woman until a year later.) This heavy dose of deception may or may not explain why I became a writer, since writers are always trying to peel back the surface and get at the truth, but it certainly explains why I hate secrets and surprises. How long had my tumor been in hiding? How much damage had it done? What else might be happening inside me?

That I would get the disease seemed inevitable because it killed my mother, but I thought I'd know when it struck, see a change in my nipples, ridges in my nail beds, feel a lump or bump. I finally had to accept that my body had lost its telegraphic gifts. Maybe you've never expected much direct communication from your body, but I had trusted mine to tip me off if and when it got cancer. Reading its signals still works with three sneezes, a rash, or a cold sore, but obviously not with tumors. Its failure hit me hard. I've lost faith in my body.

The main difference between me pre- and postdiagnosis is not how I look or feel (which is no different from how I looked or felt BBC); it's what I know. I now know that life can turn on a dime because of a mammogram. I know the limits of the body as bellwether. Having outsourced its early warning system to doctors and diagnostic equipment, I know that machines, blood tests, and biopsies don't keep secrets and that each of us is only one MRI away from disaster. I know that advances in science and technology save lives—and I wish the CT-scan had been around to save my mother's. But even knowing this, I still miss the intimate, interactive relationship I once had with my organs. No doubt a woman is better off learning she's having twins from a sonogram rather than a hunch or a muumuu. And when it comes to a cancer diagnosis she should definitely look to the results of a biopsy rather than the early warning system of a twinge or sneeze. Still, I can't deny that by hiding the tumor, my body lost my trust. It changed from ally to stranger. I don't mean to complain, but I can't help noticing.

YOUR MONEY
OR YOUR HEALTH

Poverty Can Make You Sick
But Friendship Can Ameliorate Financial Woes

WHEN I TOLD MARILYN WISE I was writing a book entitled *How to Be a Friend to a Friend Who's Sick,* she said, "I hope you're going to include people like us."

By "us" she meant people who'd lost all their money and whose financial worries had literally made them sick. Most Americans with serious money troubles are products of systemic poverty or casualties of the economic downturn, mortgage and lending abuses, and soaring unemployment. The only redeeming thing about their ruination is that in most cases it unfolded gradually enough to give them time to adjust. But Marilyn and her husband, Sam (not their real names), a retired couple in their sixties, never saw the catastrophe coming. In one moment, on a single day, December 11, 2008, they learned from watching CNN that all their investments, including every penny of their retirement savings, had vanished into thin air. The collapse of Bernard Madoff's massive Ponzi scheme had totally wiped them out.

Media representations of Madoff's victims tend to make all of them sound like super-rich cry babies, but Marilyn and Samuel Wise were regular, middle-class folks. They didn't travel in Bernie's gilded circles or own homes near the Madoff's on Park Avenue, Montauk, or Palm Beach. Madoff had been managing the Wises' savings for years as a favor to Sam's father, who knew Madoff's father when both were young and struggling. Given that history, Sam trusted Bernie—who wouldn't?

Poverty isn't pancreatic cancer. Lots of people survive the loss of their jobs, homes, and savings, though the toll it takes on them is immeasurable and often permanent. For the Wises the toll was financial, physical, psychological, spiritual, emotional, and familial, and it's no exaggeration to say that, were it not for their friends, the two of them would add up to one quivering basket case.

HOW IT FEELS TO LOSE EVERYTHING

The instant evaporation of their savings didn't just bankrupt the Wises; it also unhinged them and made them doubt everything in life that once seemed secure. The shock of their loss threw them into a panic about the future. They had no idea how they would pay for their son's education or maintain their apartment, the only tangible asset they had left. In no time at all their worries literally made them sick.

Marilyn developed acid reflux. Her mouth was constantly parched. She lost a tooth that had never before given her trouble, couldn't sleep, felt shaky all the time, had trouble breathing, and couldn't concentrate. She became obsessively self-involved and terrified. Nothing she did could make her feel better or relieve what she called, "this crushing weight of sadness, this looming sense of dread."

Samuel, totally stunned at first, became overwhelmed with anxiety and fear that they wouldn't be able to pay their bills, they'd be forced to sell their apartment at the bottom of the market, and they wouldn't know where to go or what to do when the money from the sale ran out. Sam quickly lost his appetite and twenty pounds. He stopped playing his guitar, formerly his greatest leisure-time pleasure. For nearly a year he couldn't read a book or listen to music.

Psychological studies of Madoff's victims find a disproportionate number of them with similar health problems—ulcers and other gastrointestinal ills, high blood pressure, incapacitating anxieties, and clinical depression. One psychologist went so far as to identify among the Madoff cohort "a post-traumatic stress disorder of the sort experienced by Holocaust survivors and people who had been in wars."

About a year after the scam was exposed I interviewed the Wises about their ordeal and discovered that, though unlucky in their finances, they were supremely lucky in their friends.

Marilyn: "We became more dependent on our friends and much more nurtured by them than by our families. Families are complicated. Family problems worsen in a crisis. Our friends were amazingly loyal and helpful."

Sam: "I always knew how deeply I felt about my friends but not how deeply they felt about me. At first I was ashamed that Madoff duped us. I thought we would become pariahs to our friends. Instead, I felt only empathy from them. I watched them overcome their embarrassment on our behalf and their discomfort with our misery, and I saw how they tried to relate to us as normally as possible. I was grateful when one friend said, 'I hope you realize that what you and Marilyn are going through is everyone's greatest fear. Maybe that's why we're sometimes a little awkward around you.' That explained a lot.

"I talk openly about our situation to our close friends but I rarely tell a casual acquaintance what happened to us. It would only bring the elephant into the room.

Everyone wants to know our story, but it's annoying to have to explain it and be defensive and I don't enjoy going over the details. I feel like saying to people, 'Hey, it's my *circumstance*, it's not who I *am*.' My business card doesn't say Victim—or wouldn't say it if I *had* a business card."

Marilyn: "I told everyone we were Madoff victims right away because I was trying to get a job and I was networking like crazy and trying to make something happen that would bring in a little money. I felt my efforts could only be productive if all our friends knew how desperate we were. I followed up every lead they gave me. I sent out more than a thousand résumés. I worked as a temp and played an extra on TV. I felt okay asking my friends for help, and I know we never would have made it through those first few months without them."

Sam: "Before the Madoff debacle I used to volunteer as a fundraiser at our synagogue. When I told the community's leaders how bad things are with us, they insisted on paying me a salary for doing what I'd previously done for nothing. I don't earn much, but I know I'm lucky to have work at a time when there were no jobs to be had anywhere, especially for a guy in his sixties. It was a huge relief to have a little money coming in. Finally, I could read a book, do the crossword puzzle, become funny again. We started having friends for dinner. The menus are scaled way down of course, but we do it because it's important to us to give back to everyone who gave so much to us when we needed help so badly."

Marilyn: "I also think making dinner parties normalizes us. It's a symbol of our dignity."

Sam: "I'll say, 'Let's do lamb,' then we'll go to the store and see how expensive lamb is and we'll do chicken."

Marilyn: "Our friends always ask if they can bring a potluck dish. We always say no because we want to be the hosts for a change, but they always brings us two bottles of wine, not one."

Sam: "And they're always taking us out to eat. This makes me feel grateful but also uncomfortable because there's that awkward moment in restaurants when the bill comes and I have to worry about who pays the check and how much it is. At home we make dinner on a strict budget."

Marilyn: "Most of our friends know our situation isn't going to change. We're too old to start all over again. We're like a person with a chronic physical condition; we're not getting better. I sometimes have to clarify that fact to a new acquaintance to explain why we can't go somewhere or do something with them. Sometimes even our friends forget we're poor. They get confused because we basically look the same and our furniture looks the same and, with Sam's small salary, we've been able to hold onto our apartment. Only my closest friends know that I haven't bought a single piece of clothing since December 11, 2008."

Marilyn's feverish networking and job-hunting efforts yielded nothing, due, she says, to the fatal combination of ageism and the tight economy. Her next move was to try to parlay her longtime hobby, making patchwork quilts, into an income-producing business. Speaking of symbols, this one isn't lost on her either: she realizes she's piecing together leftover scraps while she and Samuel are piecing together the fragments of their shattered lives. And just as their friends have helped them in other ways, they're also helping Marilyn get her business off the ground by contributing beautiful fabrics, purchasing quilts for themselves, commissioning them as gifts, and lending their expertise when needed. One friend, a specialist at promotion and branding, helped her create a website so she could market her quilts to a wider audience. Another, a professional photographer, mentored her so she could take better pictures of the quilts for the website. The daughter of a friend taught her how to blog. And still another friend arranged for a boutique owner in the neighborhood to take a few of Marilyn's quilts on consignment and put them in his window display. All because she asked.

These days the Wises make ends meet with their monthly Social Security checks, his modest salary, and an occasional cash boost from the sale of one of her quilts, and they get help with their son's school bills from Marilyn's brother.

> *Sam:* "We sold our car and we live frugally. No eating out except at cheap ethnic places. No theater. No major cuts of meat. No new clothes, no good wine except when a friend brings it. No vacations. We buy milk at CVS because it's a dollar a gallon cheaper. We consider the price of everything before we buy. We miss being able to donate to the charities we care about because giving was important to us. But we're grateful that we haven't become a charity case ourselves."
>
> *Marilyn:* "I agree with him about charities. I never answer the phone when the caller ID says, 'Anonymous Caller' because it's usually a fundraising call. Once I picked up the receiver without looking and heard, 'Hello, may I speak to the person who handles your 401K or retirement plan.' I said, 'I'm sorry, he's in jail.' It was the first time I laughed in months."

I asked the couple if any of their friends had disappointed them.

> *Sam:* "I was hurt when I sensed people were thinking ill of my intelligence, as if I'd been naive to get myself into this fix. A couple of times I found myself having to say, 'I'm poor

but I'm not stupid.' But generally speaking I think we were lucky we lost everything during the economic downturn. Nowadays, almost everybody has money worries, so we don't feel so unique."

Marilyn: "I was disappointed with a friend who kept making excuses for why she couldn't come see me: she was tired, she was rushing someplace, she could only meet me between 10:20 and 11:15. Finally I told her, 'This conversation is making me uneasy so I'm going to hang up.' She's been e-mailing me ever since, but I haven't replied because I don't want to hear her defend herself. Being in crisis has given me permission to protect myself from pain in a way I didn't feel entitled to do before. But I'm no less sensitive to other people's problems just because I have so many of my own. I know we're not the only people in dire circumstances. Last week Sam and I were with a bunch of friends, and I realized that everyone in the room was dealing with something difficult. A 9/11 widow was still grieving. A couple was having problems with their daughter, who was transgendering to become their son. A friend had just buried his invalid wife after taking care of her for thirty years. Another friend was in the midst of a painful divorce. She told me, 'This experience is *so* horrible and terrible that I had better learn something from it.' Sam and I have learned a lot from what happened to us."

Sam: "I learned that as long as your children are okay and you're basically healthy and you have good friends, you can get through anything."

Marilyn: "I used to make a list of how things could be worse. Now I ask myself whose troubles would I want instead of ours; who would I trade places with? The answer is no one."

||||||||||||||||||||||||||||||||||||||||||||||||||||||||||||||||||||||||||||||||||||||||||||||||||||||||||||||||||||||||||||

SEVEN

DEALING WITH DEMENTIA—RELATING TO PEOPLE WHO HAVE IT AND PEOPLE TAKING CARE OF PEOPLE WHO HAVE IT

If They Lose Their Minds,
Must They Lose Their Friends?

WE KNOW A LOT ABOUT ALZHEIMER'S DISEASE (except how to cure it). We know it robs human beings of their memory, judgment, and dignity. We know its victims may wander off and become crazed, helpless, paranoid, hallucinatory, disoriented, and violent. We know the disease destroys their brains, obliterates their identities, tests the strength and patience of their caregivers, and depletes the financial resources of their families. What we don't know, and few experts seem to be studying, is the impact of dementia on friendship.

Consider this your demographic wake-up call: Alzheimer's strikes one in eight Americans over sixty-five, and as of January 1, 2011, the oldest members of the Baby Boom generation began turning sixty-five and crossing the Rubicon into senior status. (Boomers are people born between 1946 and 1964. They comprise 26 percent of the US total population.) From 2011 to 2030 *ten thousand Boomers per day* will turn sixty-five, dramatically altering the composition of the country and raising the likelihood that this dehumanizing disease will eventually affect you or someone you care about.

People who've watched a friend or relative slide into the abyss of dementia have been stunned by its ravages. Cary Riker, whose grandmother was its victim, says Alzheimer's was "worse than death." Cary witnessed "a proud, beautiful woman deteriorate into a state that can only be described as animalistic." To Anne Caldas, Alzheimer's is "a comatose state with eyes wide open . . . death on an installment plan." Anne describes watching "a kind and funny man become an agitated, angry, and afraid person with no connection to the world."

If your best friend has no idea that you were her maid of honor or college roommate, if she can't express her feelings or empathize with yours, if she's physically present and biologically functional but in all relational ways has ceased to exist, then what is left that can be called friendship? Is intimacy possible without memory, emotional reciprocity, a retrievable past? Can you "be friends" with a former coworker who shared your cubicle for five years if he now can't remember your name, the company that employed both of you, your shared history, or what you said two minutes ago? And if friendship is impossible, what, if any, are your obligations to such a person?

To better understand the challenges of dementia, this chapter will introduce you to one woman who is in the early stages of the disease; another who is the wife of a patient; a third woman, whose sister has Alzheimer's; and a man who ultimately felt he had to cut the cord with his friend.

KATHLEEN AND THE BEGINNING OF THE END

In response to a *New York Times* op-ed piece about dementia, fifty-three-year-old Kathleen Hart wrote a letter to the editor, saying, "It is easy to forget (no pun intended) about those of us with Alzheimer's because our suffering is 'invisible.' None of my neighbors sees me going to the hospital for any type of treatment, for example, not because there is nothing wrong with me, as they think, but because I have a disease for which no treatment is available.

"No one at the grocery store I go to sees me in a wheelchair or wearing a sling, which leads them to think I'm healthy, while, because of the deterioration of my brain, I'm having a hard time making a decision about what type of cereal to buy. In the later stages of the disease, I'll also be 'invisible,' because I'll be confined to a nursing home."

At this stage Kathleen is able to recognize the signs of creeping mental deterioration and her brain has a cognitive grasp of what's happening to her. Yet one can sense her reluctance to divulge the truth to her friends and neighbors, probably in an effort to cling to normalcy as long as possible. Normalcy means being able to choose a cereal at the grocery store and interact as one sentient human being with another. Kathleen knows that these ordinary acts soon will be beyond her capacity. Her friends will soon take notice of her more frequent memory lapses, maybe roll their eyes, maybe lose patience with her indecisiveness and spacey ways. For a while they'll probably chalk it up to her aging, but eventually they will realize, as Kathleen has for some time, what disease she has and where it's taking her. And then she will be "invisible."

Imagine the anguish of knowing that you are about to forever *not* know. What must it be like to stand on the brink of that spiraling, uncontrollable plunge into oblivion, that utter loss of the Self that imparts personhood to the body? If you were Kathleen, would you gather all your friends together and tell them you were leaving them, even though you'll still be there in the flesh? Would you want them to send you off with some final words? Shouldn't there be more overt acknowledgment of what's happening to such people, a moment of reckoning and remembrance of what was, maybe the creation of a ritual to ease a friend's journey across that liminal threshold?

Kathleen's poignant balancing act can't last, but right now she has one foot on terra firma and the other on a slippery ice floe being pulled out to sea by a powerful current. Soon she will float off, visible on the crest of a wave but gone for good. I know what I would want if I were her: while still able to cling to dry land, to think, to speak, and to listen, I would want to have two different get-togethers, one with my family and one with my friends, at which I could hear their perceptions of their life with me. I would want to luxuriate in their words while I can still understand them, savor my memories before they disappear, thank my family and friends while I still can for everything we've shared, and apologize in advance for the trouble I am about to cause and the burden I am about to become. Such a ritual would, I think, constitute a proper farewell. The problem is that I'm not sure how I would identity the exact point when I'm clearly losing it yet still sufficiently alert and aware enough to participate meaningfully in the gathering. I would probably deputize my husband or a close friend to make that determination and then organize the two events as fast as possible before many more of my brain cells wither and die.

SUSAN PLUM AND HER HUSBAND

When Fred was courting her many years ago, Susan told him she was worried about the two decades' difference in their ages. "What if you get some ghastly dementia?" she remembers asking him. "Don't worry about that," he'd said. "All the men in my family die of drink."

He neglected to mention that his relatives get dementia.

In his prime Fred Plum was a world-renowned clinician, the chairman of the neurology department at New York Hospital, the pioneering physician who taught other doctors how the brain works and who famously coined the term "persistent vegetative disorder." That a scientist of the mind was himself stricken with an Alzheimer's-like neurological disease seems a merciless though not uncommon irony (Susan says four of the seven patients on her husband's hospice floor are men who, like her husband, had been physicians).

Fred's decline was slow and agonizing. It was only when she could no longer keep him safe at home that Susan gave up caring for him and moved him to a dementia facility. After dropping him off she was devastated to return alone to their empty apartment. She watched President Obama's major speech on Afghanistan by herself. The full impact of Fred's condition hit her hard that night; throughout their marriage they had always relished discussing politics or reacting to news events together. That was over now, permanently, irrevocably over.

Susan credits her sanity during that period to her friends who kept reminding her that she didn't have to be so brave and under control. They wouldn't let her stay in the hospice seven nights a week, and they worked hard to keep her busy. "They're always asking me to go places and do things with them, and I usually accept their invitations, even though it bothers me to see the stacks of unread books grow higher and higher on my bedside table. Some nights I'd rather be home reading. But I don't want my friends to leave me alone."

Because she is so protective of her husband, Susan won't let his friends or colleagues visit. "I don't want them to have an enduring image of what Fred looks like now that he's so diminished. Advanced Alzheimer's patients look like they're dying of AIDS. I want to protect people's memory of him. Men especially are so competitive. His tennis partner understood why I didn't let him come."

When his condition worsened, the staff moved Fred to a different floor so he could have closer supervision. He was greatly agitated by the change. Susan says he sometimes doesn't recognize her, but when his nurse takes him back to the floor with the four doctors, he smiles. Even in the depths of aphasia, he seems to relish their companionship. "We all want to believe there's something there," she says wistfully.

The hospice told her Fred would probably die within a month after she brought him in. The day I interviewed her he had already been in hospice for *eight* months. He died two months later.

ELEANOR AND HER SISTER

Eleanor didn't need the label to know her sister had Alzheimer's. The signs had been accumulating for years before Trudy was officially diagnosed. At that point Eleanor had already assumed the responsibility of keeping an eye on Trudy because her erratic behavior had become a threat to her and a burden for her colleagues.

"Imagine being with someone twenty-four/seven who says the same thing over and over or follows you around like a dog," Eleanor says. "It's very isolating. My friends have had to rescue me. They had to figure out what I need, not just do things their way. A friend who has lived through the Alzheimer's nightmare with *her* sister gives me practical advice on coping with Trudy's demands, her insistent phone calls, her weird behavior. If I'm open to something this friend proposes, that's fine with her; if I'm not, she's okay with that too. She doesn't take it personally when I ignore her advice."

Eleanor's first challenge was to help her sister disengage from her professional commitments without wounding her dignity. Next Trudy had to be moved to an assisted-living facility. The only way Eleanor could accomplish this was through deceit by telling Trudy she'd lost the lease on her apartment. Hardest of all was the task of coordinating the myriad details involved in disassembling her sister's entire life.

Eleanor's friends have been with her through it all. "One of my local pals helped me to hang pictures and set up my sister's room in the new residence. A long-distance friend e-mails me the latest research data on dementia. My daughter Kelly has been terrific too. She helped me sort through Trudy's files, which was an emotionally trying process. We came upon papers that reminded us of who my sister *was*—her poems, her manuscripts—and I practically felt apart. But Kelly was fantastic. I would pick up something—like Trudy's divorce papers—and I'd be paralyzed, and Kelly was like a shark in the water. She'd say 'Okay Mom, that one goes into the 'To Be Dealt with Later Box'.' I couldn't have done any of this without Kelly."

Some time later, when I sent Eleanor her quotes to approve, she wrote back, "It's gotten so much worse that I feel like those were the good old days." Trudy had just gone into hospice. A week after that Eleanor e-mailed her friends: "My sister lost her long struggle against a relentless disease yesterday. You all know how hard she battled to remain her own vibrant self. But Alzheimer's Disease makes no allowance for the smart, fun and talented soul that she was. . . . You were her village and mine, and we are truly grateful for everything you did to make her life better these last years."

SEAN AND HIS FRIEND

||||||||||||||||||||||||||||||||||||||||||||||||

When Sean noticed Brendan becoming increasingly forgetful, his initial reaction was to ply his friend with jokes: "If you have short-term memory loss, press nine. If you have short-term memory loss, press nine. If you have short-term memory loss, press nine." Brendan roared at that one. Sean expected his friend to laugh even harder a few months later when, reacting to a Viagra ad, Sean kidded, "What good is a four-hour erection if you can't remember what to do with it?" But Brendan just sat there and stared blankly.

Sean's way of dealing with his friend's decline was simply to absent himself and refuse to witness it. He told everyone he'd stopped seeing Brendan because Brendan had become violent, but that wasn't the only reason. Sean stopped because he didn't want to confront his own future. "We were always so alike, so if it could happen to him, it could happen to me."

By cutting the cord with Brendan, Sean also severed his connection to Brendan's wife, who likewise was a friend of long standing. Sean said he had no choice but to abandon both of them. "I just couldn't see myself talking to her with my friend Brendan sitting there like a zombie. I'm sorry, but it would be too weird."

Abandonment is not an option for the family of a dementia patient. Caregiving, or, rather, caretaking is considered a birthright in most families, a covenantal commitment from womb to tomb, while among friends fealty is voluntary. Friendship comes with a mutual cancellation clause. If that sounds unduly harsh, in certain situations, ending it seems inevitable. When your friend's behavior negates the very definition of friendship, when she has no idea who you are or what you've been to each other, when he's more likely to lunge at your throat than hug you, the relationship, for all intents and purposes, is over.

I write those words reluctantly not only because abandonment strikes me as the coward's way out but also because when you retreat from an Alzheimer's patient, his or her caregiver suffers collateral damage. If you're contemplating retreat, I strongly encourage you to consider a holistic exit strategy. Abandon if you must, but don't disgrace the memory of the relationship you had with your friend by shirking your obligations to the person who sticks around to care for him or her. Talk to that person. Explain yourself. If she too was a friend of yours, find a place for her in your life. Your friend's spouse or partner should not be punished twice, once by losing her loved one to this invidious disease and again by losing her friends.

How to Make the Best of a Hopeless Situation

1) *Perform triage.* In the case of dementia, friendship has an expiration date. Unrequited devotion can be exhausting and time consuming. Each day contains a finite period of wakefulness, and the hours you devote to a vacant, unresponsive friend obviously are hours lost forever to your spouse,

children, colleagues, friends, neighbors, and yourself. To free up time for others, you may have to perform affiliative triage and take the energy-depleting relationship off life support. Otherwise, when tending to the moribund relationship, new casualties will fall in your wake.

The airlines have it right: "Always put on *your* oxygen mask before assisting a child or another passenger." In life as in flight, *you* must be able to breathe before you can be of use to anyone else.

2) *Don't quit cold turkey.* I've heard of frustrated, disheartened friends who dropped out of the dementia victim's life without warning. Other friends, like old soldiers, just fade away. Before you disappear, take time to explain your feelings and intentions to the person who is left with the patient's care. Then honor your obligation to your once-vibrant friend by providing that person with occasional relief.

3) *Care for the caregiver.* If you had a warm relationship with your friend's spouse or partner before your friend got dementia, don't drop her or him now. Remember that the caregiver's devotion is what makes it possible for you (and all your friend's other friends) to walk away. People who are on constant guard duty are usually desperate for time off, and you can help them get it. Treat them to dinner or a movie. Relieve them for a couple hours, and ask other friends to do the same. Or else pay for periodic coverage from a home health care professional and get those other friends to chip in as well.

4) *Keep friends company when they visit their stricken relative.* Eleanor, whose sister Trudy has lost everything to dementia,

suggests, "One thing that a friend can do when things get horrendous is come with you to visit your loved one. It is really helpful for them to see just how awful things are and to be a reality check. I've been lucky that way. Also a few of Trudy's friends continue to see her even in her completely gone state. And they let me know that and know how awful it is for them too. Somehow that matters."

5) *Preserve memories of the person's better days.* Don't let dementia's endgame eclipse your image of your friend in her or his prime. Watch old videos. Muse over photo albums and yearbooks. Reminisce with others who knew your friend and share your recollections of the good times you had together.

EIGHT

COMING THROUGH
FOR A FRIEND
AT THE END OF THE ROAD

Death and Dying,
Grief and Loss, Love and Candor
When It Counts Most

THE LAST LEG OF THE JOURNEY IS THE HARDEST. It's one thing for your friends to be confronting their own death and another for them to be grieving over the death of someone they love. The suffering of the dying person is about to end, but the suffering of the bereaved person has just begun. What both share, however, is a deep despair and a need for help, succor, and comfort.

Should you find yourself accompanying a friend on that final stretch of road, you'll be glad to have read the following testimonies from the spouses, children, parents, and friends who traveled that route before you. If your friend has already suffered a terrible loss, you can jump to the end of this chapter, where I've distilled Ten Commandments for Mourning with a Bereaved Friend.

THE LAST CONVERSATION

||||||||||||||||||||||||||||||||||||||||||||||||||

What if *you* know your friend is dying but you're not sure *they* know. Or they sort of know, but they haven't articulated it. Or *you* know *they* know, but you're not sure they want to talk about it. Or they want to talk about it, but you're not sure how to react when they do, or whether you should broach the subject yourself?

When I asked a friend how she felt about talking about death with a mutual friend who was dying, she said, "I'm afraid that conversation is way above my pay grade."

"I made up the rules as I went along," wrote Lynn Sherr, in her memoir, *Outside the Box.* "I have said goodbye, in one way or another, to my mother, my father, and my husband, all heartbreaking events at the end of terminal illnesses that wrenched more love and pain from deep down inside me than I ever thought existed." Of her husband, who died of lymphoma, Sherr says, "We never said goodbye, not formally, because our love needed no words and because it would have felt like rushing the inevitable."

Because no one told me she was dying, I never had an "exit conversation" with my mother, never got to say a proper good-bye or ask if she had a particular wisdom to impart, a secret to confess, a final wish. I was kept in the dark so that my schoolwork wouldn't suffer, and with the typical solipsism of a fifteen-year-old, I never challenged my father's or any other adult's account of her condition; I was too busy being a high school "coed," majoring in how to be popular, minoring in boys. My mom was sick—that much I knew—but I had neither the experience that might have informed my concern nor the inclination to assume the worst (my default stance in later years). At fifteen I believed that if you were under a doctor's care and took your medicine, you eventually got well. By the time my father broke the news that her condition was terminal, it was too late for conversation; she was too drugged to talk.

Decades later I remembered that missed opportunity when a good friend of mine, Geraldine Ferraro, was dying. Gerry was a confirmed optimist, a can-do person who refused to surrender hope when it was long past obvious that her cancer had won. Like her other friends, I didn't want to be the one to deflate her balloon. Nor did I want her to think I'd given up on her before she'd given up herself. At least that's how I justified not having had an honest conversation with her about her impending death, and I'm sure that was true to a point. However, I also realized I'd been avoiding that conversation because it was threatening to *me*. Given my recent diagnosis, I was in no hurry to talk about mortality.

One evening in December, assuming she was still in the hospital, I called her husband at home to ask him to convey my Christmas greetings. To my surprise, Gerry picked up the phone. I decided to waste no time on small talk; I was pretty sure this would be our last conversation. So I told her, flat out, how much I admired and loved her and what an incredible role model she'd been, not just since she'd been battling her illness but also through the thirty-odd years of our friendship. I recalled some of the highlights of our lives and those of our children—her three and my three—who'd known each other since they were kids and have stayed in touch all these years.

"That makes me very happy!" she said with more enthusiasm than I thought anyone that sick could muster. "You know, I have so many reasons to die happy, it's amazing!"

As usual, she accentuated the positive: "If this new medication works, I could last another five or six years—but I know I might not make it, so I've been planning my funeral service, the hymns I want, the speakers."

"What do the doctors say?" I asked.

"One was pretty direct. He said my time is getting close."

"How close?" (I hadn't planned to go there, but I'd resolved to be real so that's where I went.)

"I don't know and I wasn't about to grill him with my kids in the room. All I know is the chemo isn't working anymore and they're starting me on a new protocol to control the pain, which has been God-awful. Yesterday it throbbed in my heel of all things. Before that I had an infected lung, and before that, broken bones. Everything possible is being done medically. Meanwhile, I'm not dancing around the issue."

She said she'd been preparing her family for life without her, that she'd told her children which personal items she wanted each of them to have, and she'd "trained" her husband to cook for himself and posted a list of neighborhood restaurants whose managers were friendly to people dining alone. She'd also left instructions about where she wanted to be buried, what should be chiseled on her tombstone, and who should speak at her funeral. Then she did some reminiscing about our long friendship and the changes we had witnessed in our lives.

Her voice cracked. "I want you to know that it's okay with me if I die now. I've led a blessed life. I'm ready to go."

Thank God we were on the phone so she couldn't see the tears streaming down my cheeks. "What do you think about when you think about your own death?" I asked once I'd composed myself. It was the one thing I'd always wanted to know from people whose lives were ending, but I had never had the nerve to ask.

Gerry's laugh was as full throated as always. "You know me, Letty. I'm a good Catholic. I don't fear death because I believe in an afterlife, so that gives me an edge. I really believe I'm going to see Christ and my parents in heaven. That's what I'm thinking about now. I'm in pain but I'm also at peace."

That last conversation taught me the difference between talking about death as an abstract reality and talking about it with someone who's actually dying and knows it. It was both sorrowful *and* gratifying for me and, I hope, for Gerry. What gives me the *chutzpah* to say that? The comment she made just before we hung up: she said she wished she had the strength to call up all her friends and have the same talk with each of them. She said she wished she had more time to say good-bye.

If you sense that your terminally ill friend may want to say good-bye or sum up, I suggest you gently open the door to a last conversation and leave it up the patient to either close it or walk through.

READING THEIR SIGNALS

When Carrie realized that her husband was near death, she called her best friend, Stephanie, who lives three hundred miles away, and asked her to come keep her company. Stephanie was there by lunchtime the next day.

"She's an artist, so daily life is more flexible for her than for someone with a nine-to-five job," explained Carrie, "but she does have personal responsibilities, and she dropped everything to be with me and I loved her for it. Before I called her, though, I thought to myself, do I really want her hanging around? I mean, she's the type who steps in and takes charge. But she's also someone who knows how to read my signals, so she didn't hover over me. She was just here, sometimes on the phone continuing the business of her own life, sometimes reading, watching TV, sometimes shopping for groceries, cooking, and straightening up, all of which was helpful. She came to the hospital with me every day, and she was there with me the day my husband died."

Stephanie knew how to "be with" and when to "leave alone." This couldn't be said of some of Carrie's other friends, who hung around for days after the funeral—the one who came from overseas and was in no hurry to go back or the friends who so generously had brought food, helped plan the memorial service, and worked the phones and e-mail to spread the word but who overstayed beyond their usefulness. It's confusing when one feels caged or smothered by well-meaning friends whose goal is simply to offer help and attention.

"I got the impression that people expected me to be in a state of total devastation. Anyone who really knew me should have known that I wasn't going to fall apart. I tried to communicate that I was okay, that I appreciated everyone's thoughts and help, but I was doing fine. Maybe this has something to do with me being an only child, but I've never had a problem being by myself, so I was glad when the crowd finally retreated and people stopped calling me every minute. Friends ought to be sensitive to that. They should understand that sometimes what you need most is peace."

Ask and Act is a useful guideline when dealing with mourners, except when religious custom preempts everything and thus must dictate your behavior. If you're not sure about when and how to make a condolence call to a religious person, don't just show up when it's convenient for you. Ask someone close to the bereaved what's expected, when would be a good time to visit, and whether your friend is in any condition to see you. Don't take it personally if they say no. The mourner's world can be a morass of sorrow, logistical challenges, and familial complications. A visit may be the last thing your friend needs.

Last year my friend Kathleen Peratis flew to California to be at the bedside of her ninety-three-year-old mother who died several days later. Kathleen stayed on to handle the West Coast logistics but asked me to circulate the schedule for the New York *shiva* that would be held at her apartment the following Saturday and Sunday evening. (The Jewish tradition of the *shiva* refers to the first seven days of mourning, during which it is customary for friends to visit the home of the bereaved, bring food, and constitute a quorum so that the mourner can say *kaddish*, the memorial prayer.)

Kathleen returned to the city on Thursday night. Because my current mission in life is to get people to be honest about their needs and because I remember not wanting visitors but saying yes so as not to insult people, I e-mailed her on Friday morning to ask if she'd like company or would prefer to have the day to herself to unwind before the crowds came. I knew she had other friends and colleagues who hoped to visit, and I didn't want her to feel under pressure to take in more of us than she could handle. She e-mailed back that she'd already said yes to two friends, adding, "I think that is all I can manage today. But I love you for asking."

If it's impossible to ask the bereaved person what they want in a given situation, all you can do is to try to decode their signals. Fair warning: it's easy to read them wrong. Whether your friend is dying or grieving, your challenge is to figure out how to convey your own sadness without making it all about you. If no signals come through, my best advice is simply to treat your friends as you would want them to treat you if you were in their situation. (Hillel again.)

Ten Commandments for
Mourning with a Bereaved Friend

1) *Go to the funeral.* Yogi Berra famously said, "Always go to other people's funerals, otherwise they won't come to yours." Funny as it is, the line makes sense when applied to other people's *loved one's* funerals. Showing up at the memorial service for their mother or father is one of the most meaning-ful, memorable things you can do for a grieving friend. Get up at 7 A.M., schlep yourself to that church in Cranbury, New Jersey, or Podunk, Michigan, and just "be there."

2) *Express your sympathy briefly and simply.* Avoid soul-crushing clichés. Don't get florid. Just say something short and heartfelt. You can always fall back on "I'm so sorry for your loss" or "Please accept my condolences," which are classics not clichés. If you're on the receiving line after the funeral, move along. The time and place to share more exten-sive personal thoughts is when you visit your friend at home.

3) *Recall a positive attribute of your friend's loved one.* If you had a personal connection to the deceased, conjure a specific memory (e.g., "Your mom was kind to me when I lost my job"). If she was just an acquaintance, cite a detail, however small, to let your friend know their loved one was appreciated (e.g., "I always admired your mom's beautiful voice"). If you never met her, you can always say something like, "Those incredible eulogies made me wish I'd known her."

4) *Never say the following lines to the following categories of people:* To a friend whose parent has died: "Think of it this way, your dad won't become a burden." To a grieving spouse: "It was worse for my aunt; she was married way longer than you." Or, "There are other fish in the sea." Widowed after a long marriage, Jane Brody, the health writer, was grateful that "no one (not yet, at least) has said to me, 'Surely you'll meet someone else.' Nor has anyone offered to introduce me to a likely prospect. . . . When I complained about coming home to an empty house, however, I was not offended by the suggestion that perhaps I should get a dog. Thankfully, though, no one has said, 'I know how you feel— my dog died last year.'"

5) *Create a mourning ritual.* Bereaved friends who don't subscribe to a particular faith tradition might welcome your offer to create an alternative ritual—Bruce Feiler calls it a "secular shiva"—at which they can publicly honor their loved one. It could be an impromptu gathering or a more formal, scripted event. The idea is for friends to come together and remember the deceased and gather around the mourner. Among Bruce's suggestions: specify on the invitation that people of all faiths or no faith are welcome, order

in the food so no one has to cook, exclude traditional religious prayers so everyone feels comfortable, hold the event in a venue other than the mourner's home (to spare them preparation or clean-up), and allot plenty of time for the mourner to tell stories about his or her loved one.

6) *Never underestimate the impact of the written word.* Even more than the neighbors who offered to take out her garbage, lift heavy objects for her, and move her car for street cleaning, Jane Brody appreciated written condolence notes "that warmed my aching heart, made me smile, and told me more about Richard and how he affected others than I had realized even after forty-three years of marriage." Most of us tend to avoid focusing on the deceased for fear of saddening the mourner, but Jane loved it when friends "talked about the kind of person Richard was." She cherished people who "took time to recall how Richard had helped them" and said things "that while recognizing the pain of loss, reflected the value of a life well lived." Writing in *Good Housekeeping*, Elinor Lipman said she was amazed at the number of condolence cards and e-mails she received when her husband died. They weren't just from friends but also from casual acquaintances, such as the handyman she once hired to truck away an old treadmill, her son's buddy from Japan who remembered important advice her husband gave him, the wife of the man who plows her driveway, and the grocer who wrote to say he'd made a donation to her local food bank in her husband's memory. Elinor maintains that condolence notes needn't be timely. You can always say you "just heard" or "were too shaken by the news to write immediately." A message received long after the fact "doesn't open a wound but casts a new glow over a friendship."

7) *Help the mourner find or found a support group.* Misery doesn't always love company, but if you think your bereaved friend might benefit from a support group, don't just suggest they join one; check out existing groups in the area or help them organize one. Sam Feldman, whose wife, Gretchen, died in 2008, started a biweekly support group for widowers because he found he could only get solace among men who were in the same boat and willing to share the anguish of their loss. Most widows already have an intricate web of women friends who can support them emotionally after their husband's death, but research shows that most widowers tend to bottle up their sorrow and, as a result, suffer more mental distress, illness, disability, death, and suicide. If your friend is a widower, do him a favor and direct him to the National Widowers' Organization (http://www.nationalwidowers.org), which help men all over America establish support groups.

8) *Facilitate their memorializing.* In the first flush of loss, some people are too traumatized to recognize the emotional significance of the deceased's belongings, which is why precious letters, photos, mementos, artifacts, and other treasures so often get tossed or given away to family members who don't recognize their sentimental or historical value. I wish someone had facilitated my acquisition of some of my mother's belongings—for instance, her beautiful silver Hanukkah menorah, which ended up in non-relatives' hands. You can help your friend catalog, claim, or rescue such items before they're distributed or discarded.

9) *Don't offer your help unless you mean it.* Following protocol, people routinely say, "Don't hesitate to call on me" when *they* know they don't mean it and *you* know they don't mean it, and most of the time nothing happens. If you really

want to help a friend who's taking care of a sick loved one or who's grieving a loss, you have to make clear that you're not just saying it. Tell them to call on you for whatever they need and then say something like, "I really mean it. I want to help but I need you to tell me how." If you see something that needs doing, don't wait for them to tell you—just do it. Sometimes actions speak louder than offers. Once again, you can Ask and Act. Or Act and Ask. I can't stress this point enough except by capitalizing and repeating it.

10) *Let the silence be.* People who are never at a loss for words may be surprised by their speechlessness in the presence of grief. If you find yourself tongue-tied, don't fight it. An understanding silence beats fake sympathy any day of the week, and most mourners, even in the depths of their grief, can tell the difference.

Not long ago I paid a condolence call on Libby Fiance, whose husband, Sy, was an old friend and client of my husband's. We hadn't seen each other in many years, but the sight of her brought back memories of the two of them as a vibrant, fun-loving, young couple. I remembered how openly he adored her, how he crowed about what a great mom she was and how beautiful she was. One story leapt to mind: They were vacationing at a Caribbean resort. Libby got tired of losing at the slot machines one night and went to bed, leaving Sy at the gaming tables until heaven knows when. The next morning she woke up to dozens of hundred dollar bills taped to the dressing table mirror and the words, *I LOVE YOU!* scrawled in red lipstick on the glass.

I blinked away the image but felt a huge lump rise in my throat. For several seconds I couldn't speak. Finally, I murmured, "I'm sorry, Libby, I have no words."

"No words?!" she exclaimed. "Some writer!"

MEDITATIONS ON MY MORTALITY AND THE SHADOW OF LIFE

IN A PARTICULARLY LYRICAL PASSAGE in her book *Lost in Translation*, Eva Hoffman captures what it feels like to really wrap your brain around the fact that it's all going to end and you're going to die: "Suddenly time pierces me with its sadness. This moment will not last. With every step I take, a sliver of time vanishes. . . . How can this be, that this fullness, this moment which is perfectly abundant will be gone? How many moments do I have in life? I hear my own breathing: with every breath I am closer to death."

My mortality epiphany came not with the sound of my breath but with the beating of my heart. One night shortly after completing my radiation I was in bed on the cusp of sleep when my hand came to rest on my chest. Rather than stray to my scar, their usual destination, my fingers stayed put, arrested by the hammering of the heart beneath my palm. For the first time in my life, notwithstanding college biology, other people's heart attacks, and my familiarity with my own pulse after a workout, the thrum-thrum-thrum of my heart struck me as utterly and completely miraculous. That this organ had been pumping away on its own, day in and day out, for seventy years with no help or direction from me suddenly presented itself as an astonishing feat of human self-perpetuation. In that moment of marveling I knew—in the way that you finally take into yourself an immense fact of life that you've always accepted as true but never really absorbed—that some-day something would happen and my heart would stop.

Since then, whenever a "perfectly abundant" moment comes along, I unobtrusively press my palm to my heart and give myself over to the wonder of being alive and the privilege of experiencing that sensation or event or witnessing that sight or person, even as my valves and ventricles are pumping out the next batch of blood, and the next, and the next, each thump and thrum of this miraculous muscle taking me closer to the end.

This new hyperconsciousness of the workings of life's primal engine is, to my mind, one of the unexpected rewards of age and illness. It's not morbid; it's mindfulness raised to its nth degree, it's an up-close-and-personal confrontation with mortality, and I welcomed it. I'm not the first person to have discovered that facing death can make a person cherish life and treasure what she or he previously took for granted. But I may be the first person to point out that having had a serious illness and experienced a heightened awareness of one's mortality can change one's orientation to appliance service contracts, magazine subscriptions, roofing materials, and the lifespan of trees. Let me explain.

A week after my surgery our dishwasher broke down and I went to buy a new one. The salesman asked, as they always do, whether I wanted to purchase a five- or ten-year warranty. Mind you, I've bought dozens of appliances in my adult life (my husband always says of our marriage, "Lucky in love, unlucky in appliances"), and I've signed many a ten-year service contract without a thought. This time the question paralyzed me. Five years or ten? It felt like a life-and-death decision. P. C. Richard and Son's ten-year warranty offered the best deal, but, my new "accentuate the positive" philosophy aside, was it realistic to think I'd make it to eighty? Even seventy-five might be wishful thinking. At the point when I was standing in the appliance store, I had not yet received the pathologist's report on the eleven nodes nor had I begun my radiation. If I turned out to be "node positive," I would, according to statistical data, have a 55 percent chance of living for five years but only a 40 percent chance of living for ten years. I'd be damned if I was going to die with a couple years left on my warranty. I took the five-year deal and determined to survive, if only to prevent P. C. Richard and Son from profiting from my death.

An invitation to renew my *New Yorker* magazine subscription arrived one morning while I was in the grip of my mortality tremors. Condé Nast's best deal by far was a multiyear subscription. I checked the box beside the one-year option.

Recently our contractor said we needed a new roof and presented us with two choices that, thanks to an end-of-summer sale, cost the same: shingles guaranteed to last twenty years or those that "would last a lifetime." I had to laugh. *Whose lifetime?* I thought.

As for the growth rate of trees, that became an issue when we had persistent flooding in the wetlands around our house and an arborist advised us to plant "thirsty" flowers, bushes, and trees—vegetation known for voraciously sucking up water. He suggested elephant ears, river birch, white cedar. I asked about weeping willows. I'd heard they thrive with "wet feet," and I loved how their graceful drooping branches sway with the breeze. He tried hard to dissuade me on the grounds that weeping willows are messy, drop their leaves, and, worse yet, grow too quickly. "In a very few years they'll be huge," he warned. "They'll overwhelm everything."

"Weeping willows it is!" said I, thinking how nice it would be to enjoy them at their luxuriant best while I'm still alive.

My solipsistic attitude toward roofing materials and weeping willows—this willful disregard for what's good for the house or the earth beyond my own lifetime—happens not to jibe with my values or the Jewish teachings I grew up on. Those values are embodied in a famous Talmudic tale about a young man named Honi who, while walking along the road, saw an old man planting a carob tree.

"How long will it take for this tree to bear fruit?" Honi asked the elderly man.

"Seventy years," the man replied.

"And do you think you will live another seventy years and eat the fruit of this tree?" asked Honi.

"Perhaps not," the old man answered. "However, when I was born into this world, I found many carob trees planted by my parents and grandparents. Just as they planted trees for me, I am planting trees for my children and grandchildren so they will be able to eat of their fruits."

The impulse to plant something now to be reaped by future generations conforms to the stage of healthy personality development that the psychologist Erik Erikson called "generativity." Supposedly, our progress into this mindset, which typically kicks in during the middle phase of our lives (age forty to sixty-four) signifies that we've made a healthy transition from thinking about ourselves in the present to thinking about our legacy in a future we will never see. Most of the time, for instance, when it comes to environmental protection, I base my decisions on what's best for the world that my children and grandchildren will inherit. But in the case of the roof, its good condition twenty years or a lifetime from now seemed so remote as to be of no interest to me. And on the weeping willow issue, I showed clear signs of selfishness. I didn't care if it overran the landscape and made a mess for the next generation. I chose the fast-growing willow for my own immediate gratification.

The tension I feel between opting for immediate pleasure versus investing in the long term could be a function of age but to me it feels like a consequence of cancer. I make different choices now because I know I don't have forever. My best years aren't behind me; they're within me. They inform who I am, what I think, what I want to do next. And because mortality has brushed so close to my cheek, each day seems more precious, each happy moment more vivid, each pleasure more fully felt. Since being dubbed a "cancer survivor," the possibility of my own death is no longer distant and theoretical; it's with me all the time—not in a big, melodramatic way but like an almond stuck in the corner of my pocket. It doesn't get in the way, or stop me from doing what I want to do, but I know it's there. Contrary to my former propensity, I no longer behave as if I'm going to live forever. When my grandson Ethan, now a high school sophomore, talks about which college he might apply to, or my daughter Robin mentions that she and her husband, Ed, might want to live abroad in a few years, or my son, David, says his boys are outgrowing his apartment and they might have to move, I silently wonder if I'll be around to see it.

A few months ago, my daughter Abigail bought me an Emilio Pucci dress after I spoke longingly of the one I'd bought for a pittance in 1967 when Italy was chock-full of bargains. I adore the dress—how lightly it skims the body; its pale palette of pink, lemon, and beige; the memories it evokes of me and Bert traipsing around Rome as young marrieds. While luxuriating in my new dress and old reverie, a voice inside me says, "You may not be able to wear the dress often enough before you die to amortize what Abby paid for it." To which my practical voice replies, "That's okay. You can leave it to her in your will. Puccis never go out of style."

|||||||||||||||||||||||||||||

NOVEMBER 2012. More than three years have passed since the summer of my bliss. I still have much to be grateful for—enduring love, remarkable children, great friends, chamber music, fresh tomatoes, vodka straight from the freezer, funky restaurants, hiking in sun-dappled forests—but I'm in a new place now. I've been changed by my glimpse of where it all ends, probably sooner rather than later for those who, like me (and the dozens of people I interviewed), have been touched by illness and looked death in the eye. Ever since my "suspicious" mammogram turned out to be worthy of suspicion, the idea that "someday something's going to happen" sticks to me like my shadow—my actual shadow: the flat, black silhouette that contracts and lengthens before or behind me, now close to my heels, now stretching out along the sidewalk like spilled paint.

I tend to ignore my shadow, except when I'm with a child. I remember walking with my granddaughters, Molly and Maya, under a streetlight when they were very small and they suddenly started cavorting with their shadows. One formed a bird with her hands and fingers, the other crouched over until she looked like the headless horseman, then the two girls darted inside my shadow and disappeared. A few seconds later we poked out our limbs and wiggled them and turned ourselves into a six-armed Indian goddess. It occurs to me now that this is a metaphor for the mindfulness I carry with me every day. Yes, cancer made me face my mortality sooner than I would have liked, but it also showed me that joy can flourish within the shadow of death. I discovered that the upside of mortality tremors is a sweetened taste for life. Both exist for me in the present—the knowledge that Something's Going to Happen Someday and the immediacy and wonder of Life Right Now. I don't wish illness on my friends, but I would like to introduce them to the goddess within the shadow of death: the wonderful, wiggling, shadow of life.

‖‖‖

NINE

AS BAD AS IT GETS

Children Dying

IF THE RICHTER SCALE could measure human calamities, the loss of a child would register a ten. Excruciating as it is to read about dying children, the following testimonies—from three different women who lost their sons to illness, a friend of one of the women, and a playmate of one of the boys, as well as from parents of children who died suddenly from an accident or suicide—offer rare insights into the role friendship can play in mitigating the pain of this unbearable tragedy.

NANCY GOODMAN, MOTHER OF
JACOB FROMAN, AGE TEN

‖‖

"One Monday in February, he was diagnosed with brain cancer. Tuesday he had brain surgery, and twenty-three months later he was dead."

(Pediatric cancer is the second leading cause of death of children under fifteen, after accidents.)

"At the beginning of his treatment Jacob was scary to look at. He had significant physical and neurological impairment. He couldn't talk normally. He was anorexic, in a wheelchair, bald, and had a tube in his stomach. The first few times his school friends came over with their mothers, it was awkward. The kids would be edgy or they'd say they wanted to leave, but the next time they came they'd be fine. Or it might take two visits for them to get comfortable with Jacob in his newly impaired form.

"The children had to forge their own path, and I think they really tried hard to do that. They didn't ask Jacob questions about his illness; they mostly played video games with him. I'm sure their parents were thinking more about the implications and consequences of Jacob's illness than the kids were. I didn't give anyone explicit instructions on how to behave, but in our blog (www.caringbridge.org/visit/jacob froman) we would say how grateful we were when our friends brought their kids over. What they did when they were here mattered less than the fact that they kept coming back. Jacob loved spending time with kids his own age. He always wanted to be as normal as possible. If he got tired during a playdate, he would just fall asleep."

I asked Nancy how her friends responded to *her* needs.

"People behave very differently with someone whose child has a curable condition as opposed to someone whose child has a terminal illness. When you're in my category—the terminal and catastrophic category—your friends may feel uncomfortable reaching out, especially in the beginning. I had no emotional reserve, no energy to help them do it. People in my category don't have the bandwidth to take care of others.

"There's also a big difference in terms of how long friends stay involved. They're okay supporting a family when the child is in short-term treatment. The challenge comes when the family needs support forever, say for a chronic illness or for a child who is born disabled. I've watched friends of families with chronically and seriously ill children pull back or lose interest or get overwhelmed. Yet the families of these children never stop needing help."

Nancy said she saw very few of her friends when Jacob was sick. She didn't want to talk to anyone about their situation—it was too hard, it took too much effort to explain. All she wanted to do was take care of Jacob and research his illness. She wasn't working, she wasn't working out, she wasn't living a normal life, and she didn't sleep through the night for two years. Her world revolved around Jacob and the people who cared about him—his family, his longtime babysitter, staff members at the clinic where he was treated, the rabbi who gave the family personal pastoral care, and the principal of Jacob's school, who set the tone for how everyone there responded to him." The principal met with the teachers and brought in psychologists and trauma counselors and had a series of meetings with parents and children that were focused on getting everyone to understand what was happening. She established the school's positive approach and engaged response to Jacob's illness. We hired someone to take care of his physical needs, but she helped his teacher work out the amount of academic instruction and socializing he could handle. No one in his school knew it was terminal until the end.

"The P.E. coach encouraged the varsity basketball team to be very supportive and created ways for Jacob to participate in games. If you threw the ball to him in his wheelchair, you would get five points; a regular basket was only worth one point. Jacob viewed himself as the team mascot. He lived for opportunities to be ball boy or to talk with the players. The whole team came to his funeral. They all wore black ribbons for him after his death.

"Friendship in bereavement is completely different from friendship in the face of illness, and every piece of the dynamic is different if you're grieving the loss of a child as opposed to an elderly person whose death was expected. My friends did a great job rallying around me after Jacob died. Many of his friends wrote us beautiful letters. They put on bake sales and organized a book drive to raise money for my nonprofit, Kids v Cancer, which supports pediatric cancer research.

"We talk about Jacob all the time in our family, and I don't want our friends to avoid talking about him around us. People get upset when they call our younger son Jacob by mistake. It's not jarring to us. We like it. Sometimes we do it ourselves. I want people to feel comfortable remembering him.

"We recently had another baby, a little girl. I was touched by the outpouring of donations to Kids v Cancer and other expressions of support from friends who are so happy to see us doing well after losing Jacob."

Nancy's friendships may have taken a backseat while her son was sick, but she tended to them by keeping everyone informed, thanking those who brought their children for playdates, and recognizing how difficult the situation was for the families in their immediate orbit. She also made new friendships—with Jacob's doctor, the principal, the coach, the rabbi, and others who played meaningful roles in Jacob's life.

During his illness, she said, she didn't resent friends who continued to share their mundane worries about their own healthy children, and she never invalidated someone else's suffering because of her own.

Having talked to her at length, I'm sure she would call it pointless to measure one kind of hardship against another. However, for weeks after our interview my emotions were so torqued that I could barely listen to other people's problems. They sounded trivial compared to hers. If I had reacted that way after one afternoon's conversation, what, I wondered, must her close friends have felt after prolonged exposure to her ordeal? Did their empathy synapses short-circuit? Did they feel compassion fatigue? Did the scale of Nancy's worries change her friends' perception of their own? Did they understand that her retreat into her world wasn't a comment on their behavior but a symptom of her need to prioritize and devote all her energies to her son? Did any of them blunder badly? Those are some of the questions I put to my daughter Abigail—Nancy's friend and the person who had alerted me to Jacob's illness in the first place. Here is Abby's description of their relationship during that fraught period.

ABIGAIL POGREBIN,
NANCY GOODMAN'S FRIEND

lllllllllllllllllllllllllllllllllllllllllllllllllllllllll

"It was tricky because it was entirely up to her whether we got together. I felt that was the right balance, but I also felt bad about not being able to initiate our regular breakfast dates the way I used to. Still, I wanted her to know I wanted to see her, so I told her up front, 'Just know I'd like us to have breakfast together any time, but I'll leave it up to you when or if we do.'

"Nancy distanced herself from many of her friends because she was consumed with Jacob's care and didn't have the desire or energy to talk through his status over and over again with a lot of different people. She was just trying to keep him alive. When she wanted connection, she asked for it. I felt lucky I made the cut because I love being with her, but I knew not to push for more than she could give.

"I could talk about most normal things with her because she's a good listener. She made it okay for me to confide my work worries, for instance, and she gave me her usual smart advice. But I knew that for every waking moment and countless all-nighters, she was thinking about how to save her son, so it would have been the height of insensitivity if I'd complained about my mundane childrearing hurdles that I'm sure would have sounded like Nirvana compared to what she was facing.

"She rarely talked about how she was holding up—or collapsing—but almost entirely about her son's treatment protocol. I never got a sense from her that his situation was dire; it was all about the next new drug or strategy. When she talked about medication, it was like she was talking about hope. We both knew she was fighting terrible odds, but she never once broke down or went to the darkest place with me."

BENJAMIN SHAPIRO,
AGE THIRTEEN, JACOB'S FRIEND

IIIIIIIIIIIIIIIIIIIIIIIIIIIIIIIIIIIIIIIIIIIIIIIIIIIIIIIIIIIIIIIIII

"He was a year younger than me. We knew each other before, but we became close when our families vacationed together one summer and we spent every second together for about a week. At first I didn't really understand what was happening. I had this weird feeling that people only get cancer in the movies. Death seemed so extreme. My mind didn't go there, ever. I always thought he would be fine.

"Once he got really sick, I felt I wasn't myself with him because he was so fragile and not at all like he was during that vacation. His speech was stuttered. He had trouble walking. He wasn't the same person, and I didn't understand that. When I was with him I felt more like I was helping him, like I was his babysitter more than his friend. I never talked to him about his sickness. We played video games, Wii—that was the extent of it.

"One of the last times I saw him, a group of kids were playing whiffle ball on the lawn and Jacob's mom helped him out onto the field and he batted, and kept batting, until he finally hit the ball. All the kids were patient, no one pushed him, and we all cheered when he got a hit. But I'm sure he knew he wasn't actually *in* the game.

"I remember the day he died. I was eleven then; he was ten. I was in the sixth grade. My mom told me about it in the car on the way to school. I silently cried not just because he was a friend of mine but because it didn't make sense to me that someone who had been so normal and alive was now gone. I was confused by my feelings and by the fact of death. How could that happen to such a young kid? I deeply regret not talking to him more, not soaking up every second I had with him. I thought there might have been a way I could have done more, spent more time with him, given him more attention. But I kept thinking he was going to live and get back to normal. I thought his illness was like a hiccup in his life.

"When he died, I wanted people to know what a big issue this was, that cancer is an immediate crisis that has to be addressed."

Ben and his family found a way to address it. Upon leaving the luncheon following his bar mitzvah ceremonies, each guest was given a "party favor"—a small bag of malted milk balls attached to which was a card showing a smiling little boy with red hair and freckles, and this printed message:

In honor of my friend Jacob Froman, who lost his battle to brain cancer last year, my family has made a donation in your name to Kids v Cancer, an important organization created and run by Jacob's mom, Nancy Goodman. It will improve cancer research to help other kids with the same disease, so I hope you will honor Jacob by going to the website (kidsvcancer.org) or making your own donation to the cause. Jacob, I'll always miss you.
—Ben Shapiro

ESTHER ANN ASCH,
MOTHER OF JENNY, AGE NINE

||||||||||||||||||||||||||||||||||||||||||||||||||||||||||||||

"In a matter of hours, Jenny suffered an acute asthma attack, was rushed to the hospital, and during the tubing to help her breathe, suffered brain death and was put on life support. The doctors wouldn't let us pull the plug for three weeks. Some of my friends were extremely helpful during our ordeal. They had lots of things going on in their own lives, but they showed up at the hospital every day. One came down from Connecticut to sit with us. People brought us sandwiches. Three weeks is a very, very long journey when you know your child is going to die and you have a seven-year-old at home whom you have to take care of and protect. I was filled with rage and grief.

"My friends and I had many discussions about what kind of God would allow something like this to happen. I couldn't make sense of it—a child should never die before a parent. I was furious when people said Jenny's death was God's will. I don't accept this. To say that losing my little girl was something God willfully made happen—I just *don't* believe that.

"After she died some of our friends couldn't face us, probably because they had kids the same age. They reacted almost as if her death was catching. They didn't come to pay a condolence call, and in all the years since they've never said one word to me about Jenny, never even acknowledged her death. But her friends and classmates came every night, and they decided on their own to name the school's music room in her memory because she was very musical. They took up a collection and had a plaque made and created a ceremony for the presentation. That was the *best*."

DIANE SCHWEBEL FREEDMAN,
MOTHER OF ANNA JOY, AGE TWENTY-ONE MONTHS

"Anna was inside watching the movie *Mary Poppins* with our babysitter, Bernadette. At a certain point Bernadette went out the front door, where the bus from the day camp was to drop off our son, Sam. In that short time Anna wandered out back. The pool gate must have been defective. It popped open. A kiddie ball had blown into the pool. She must have gone in after it. When Bernadette came back and saw the baby was missing, she checked all over the house because all the doors were closed. Then she looked outside and saw Anna in the water.

"Anna was Medevacked out by helicopter. They worked on her for two hours before they gave up.

"Usually I was at home when the camp bus arrived, but that day my oldest and dearest friend, who was pregnant with her second child, told me the doctors had warned her she could go into premature labor, so I went over there to take care of her three-year-old. That's where I was when I got the call. My friend wanted to go to the hospital with me, but I wouldn't let her because I didn't want her to go into labor.

"I learned later that my next-door neighbor, Deirdre Cutler—a good friend but not my best friend at the time—heard Bernadette screaming and came over. I believe she was the one who called 911. She calmed Bernadette and took care of Sam for hours that day and evening while my husband, Perry, and I were at the hospital. When they officially told us Anna had died, I stayed with her while Perry went home to be with Sam. I don't know what Dierdre did that day, how she occupied him, or what she said specifically to calm him, but I know Sam was sleeping when Perry picked him up. For what she did for us, I couldn't thank Deirdre enough if I tried for the rest of my life. And she continued being amazing. For days after she just came and went and did whatever had to be done, and she always stayed behind the scenes and never wanted any acknowledgment. Besides all that, I felt a special connection to her because Anna was the same age as her son, and they played together often, so he was very affected by her death. Deirdre died a few years later—a terrible loss. She was so important to me.

"It's thirteen years since the accident, but it took a toll on my relationship with the friend I was helping out when the accident happened. She gave birth six days later to a daughter and made me the godmother, but we stopped seeing each other as much as we always had. It was unspoken, but her guilt was tremendous and lasted a long time. She didn't talk to me about it for many years, then finally, a few years ago, she did. She said she missed our friendship and wanted us to see each other more, which we have been doing. She knows it wasn't her fault and she knows I know it was no one's fault. But the fact is I wasn't here; I was there.

"In terms of other friends, it was weird to be aware that we were the source of gossip in our town. There was some misinformation in the local Westchester media—they said my babysitter left my kid alone at the pool as if she had been negligent.

"Otherwise, when it comes to friendship, I don't see a big difference between a child's dying from an accident or an illness. In both situations people really have no idea how to react. The death of a child is so against the order of things. It makes everyone uncomfortable. They want to do something to make it better. They can't, but they keep trying. One woman was so shocked by Anna's death that she interjected herself in my life more than she should have to the point where friends of mine said, 'You've known her less than a year—why is she always here?' Sometimes, less is better—not ignoring us but giving us space.

"I got pregnant within months of Anna's death because I was thirty-nine and Perry and I didn't want Sam to be an only child. Our twins, Rebecca and Jonathan, were born prematurely less than a year after Anna died. I went nuts when well-meaning people said, 'Oh, God sent you twins to replace your daughter.' Or made comparisons, like, 'You had this tragedy. I had mine.' One person said, 'Losing my dog was like losing a child.' I'm like, 'Nooooo . . . actually it *isn't*.'

"Most friends have a natural goodness and they want to help. But they say all kinds of things when they don't know what to say. I understand that; still, it's hard to hear. I sometimes wish they would just say, 'I don't know what to say,' and give me a hug.

"Someone told me, 'You gotta snap out of it after a year because if you're still depressed, people won't want to be around you.' It's like they'll only allow you so much time to feel really bad, then you're supposed to move on.

"On the other hand, some friends just knew how to deal with this awful thing. One of the preschool mothers had a maple tree planted in Anna's name. There was a dedication ceremony and a plaque and we were there. She did it for my son Sam. She did it so we could always go back and watch the tree grow, and we did do that for many years.

"Another friend, Bobby Begun, a special-ed teacher in New Rochelle, gave out a certificate each week in Anna's name to a student in his class who was kindest to the other students. When he retired he set

set up an annual $50 prize at the elementary school graduation called 'The Anna Joy Award.' I had other friends who did very thoughtful things as well, but that was something I will never forget.

"Among the lessons I wish I could impart to people in these types of situations is to let the bereaved person know you're there for them, but give them some space because while everyone else's lives go back to normal, the bereaved have to face and adjust to their new normal. It is a very long process, and the closest and most in-tune friends understand that. Others find this difficult, and those are the friendships that suffer. When I was the one who always had to make the effort, my relationship with that friend did not endure as well. But I had some great friends, and I made some new ones along the way who have given me strength through the tough times.

"The first few years, when I met new people and they asked how many kids I have, I used to say, 'I have four children but I only have the honor of raising three.' One day my sister said I made it sound like Children's Services took away one of my kids, so I stopped saying that. But no one really wants to hear I had four children and one died. So about seven years ago I started saying, 'I have three children.' Then I always look up to the sky and I say, 'I'm sorry.'"

SANDY SMITH,
MOTHER OF ANDREW, AGE EIGHT

"The two diagnoses came within days of each other: I had breast cancer and Andrew had a brain tumor. People couldn't believe it. Someone actually asked me if it was embarrassing. I mean what more could happen?"

Sandy, the wife of a pastor, said several people became very important in Andrew's life: his Sunday school teacher, with whom he grew very close; his physical therapist, who became part of the family (the last three days of his life she moved into Andrew's hospital room and never left); the teenaged son of one of the church families who used to come to the house once a week to play games with him; a National Guard recruiter who, after he heard about their situation through mutual friends, began to follow Andrew's page on Caring Bridge.org and traveled forty-five minutes several times a week to be with him, sing with him, pray with him, or distract him from his painful dressing changes.

"Kids were never negative or ugly toward him. One child asked him why his cheeks were so big, but by then we had taught him it was because of his medication so he could explain why. Our only negative experiences were with adults. A medical person at the hospital commented on how he looked 'so different.' She kept saying things like, 'You're so much more cheeky than the last time I saw you.' Finally, I followed her out and told her that my son is self-conscious about his appearance. She was very defensive, but I didn't let it go. I said, 'You really need to be careful about what you say.'

"Kids on steroids are obsessed with food; they're always hungry. My husband and I worked with Andrew to help him make wise food choices, and he tried hard to control himself, but on Easter Sunday we were at a buffet lunch and you know what it's like with all the food spread out. When he went to refill his plate, my husband overheard a woman say, 'How does anyone let their child get that fat?' I wanted to go up and tell her that for Andrew to even propel himself to the buffet table was a miracle because at that point he couldn't walk all that well. I wanted to tell her how my son used to look, what a beautiful little boy he was."

Unlike most parents in her situation, when the end came for Andrew, Sandy couldn't circle the wagons and control who had access to her and her family. She had no choice but to live her private anguish in the glass house of the church community.

"Normally it's the pastor who works with you and helps you move on. But my husband *is* the pastor and I'm the pastor's wife, so we don't do our grieving in church. That's not where we go for support. We feel we have to spare everyone.

"Some congregants are uncomfortable around us. They don't know what to do with us. They want us to move on so they can move beyond *their* suffering. In Christian circles you often hear people tell mourners they should 'move on', as if it's almost ungodly that they can't pull themselves together and get beyond their grief. We insist it's okay to grieve, but sometimes we feel this pressure, this need to explain ourselves. Someone left a quote for us on our CaringBridge blog: 'When your heart is open, healing will come.' They just don't get it! Our hearts are open. We still believe in God and we still believe God is good, but *we've lost a son!*"

About her frustration with people who constantly ask how she's doing, Sandy wrote on her blog: "There are times when these questions are perfectly legitimate and you know that they are coming from someone who truly wants to know the answer. But when the words are casually tossed my way as someone passes me in the hallway at church . . . I sometimes wonder, '*What do you want me to say?*' . . .

> "'*Well, I finished treatment for breast cancer in July 2008, had a two- to three-month reprieve before Andrew's brain tumor progressed and things got intense, eventually lived in the hospital with him for five months and two weeks, took him home and set up our own pediatric intensive care unit in the living room, enjoyed three good months before things began to deteriorate, and held him in my arms as he took his final breath on earth on December 4, 2009. I'm feeling fine. How about you?'*"

Since her son's death Sandy has counseled many parents of dying children as well as terminally ill adults. I asked how she splits her time when several people are in crisis at the same time.

"I think about what each individual needs from *me* personally. For instance, I know some people who are sick yet still putting one foot in front of the other, while one man is in hospice right now with stage IV cancer and his family needs me because they want to talk about funeral plans. I look at that as something that can't wait. I sense when someone is facing the biggest crisis—whether it's the day they find out that the tumor has grown or the day they *really* understand they're at the end of their lives. After someone dies you can be there for the family, but it's not the same kind of crisis as when a child is approaching the end of life and the family needs support. When they're about to experience this huge thing, it's comforting to have someone around who's been through it and knows what to expect."

Recently Sandy gave up a wedding in order to fly from her home in Michigan to Washington, D.C., to be with her friend Neely, whose little girl, Alexis, was dying. "I remember thinking, *Should I go? Shouldn't I go?* Neely and I met at the National Institutes of Health when Andrew was alive, and I have fond memories of her and me sitting in his room and talking, crying, and laughing until 2 A.M. I thought Neely would want me there. It wasn't enough for me to be texting her. I wanted to be sitting in the room with her. . . . She'd been there for me. She flew to Michigan for Andrew's funeral, and on the anniversary of his death, she called me even though Alexis was approaching the end of her life. *That's* a friend! Someone who sets aside their suffering long enough to comfort you."

Finally, Sandy mentioned the fear—shared by many bereaved parents—that their children will be forgotten by those who knew them. "Someone put together a video for a couple of local kids who were about to move to a foreign country to help them remember their experiences in our community. I knew that Andrew was present at every one of the events they showed in the video, but there were no pictures of him. It was as if he'd been erased. I understand that the filmmakers didn't want to hurt us and thought they were sparing us pain. But the fact that he was not included hurt us deeply."

Perhaps the fear that Andrew will be forgotten explains why, when anyone asks her how many children she has, Sandy answers, "Three. Two on earth, one in heaven."

"While we continue to adjust to our loss, we are intensely aware that the friends who supported us during the crisis have gone back to their lives. . . . They care, but time does not stand still. However, to a family missing the physical presence of a child, it can seem almost cruel that others are able to go on working and eating and sleeping as if nothing had changed."

KIM SPADY, MOTHER OF CALEB, AGE ELEVEN

Caleb died of cancer of the brain. Kim wrote this beautiful blog post about families who have lost a child gaining comfort from each other:

> We live in a world where it is as common for our boys to speak of spending a day in Heaven as it is to speak of spending an afternoon at the pool; Where tears flowing down momma's face while she cooks dinner is routine—nothing worth noting; Where we talk with other parents about our children's death just as vibrantly and vividly as we speak of their births; We share stories of funerals and memorials; We speak of clinical trials, medical procedures, disease progression, end of life care, dying, death, autopsies, the positives and negatives of donating our babies' brain tissue for research—all as if we were exchanging ideas for the next school fundraiser; We lament the difficulty of choosing gravestones. . . . We understand how important it is to be able to talk about the tiniest things—how those hands felt on daddy's cheek in the morning sun—how his sense of humor didn't die until his final breath was taken—how much she loved her baby brother. We can relate to how frustrating it is when a doctor writes your child off upon diagnosis; how heart-wrenching

it is when that child realizes the truth; how painful it is to watch him undergo his hundredth blood draw or fifteenth MRI, but what a blessing it is to still be fighting that long; And we can simply be together. We talk about the weather and our other children and our jobs and our lives. What a comfort that is, to be with others who are also holding those tiny shards of their heart in their hands, who recognize the valleys forged by the tears down our cheeks and who know the smiles we share are indeed reflections of genuine happiness that cannot diminish the pain in our souls.

Grieving is hard work. It is lonely work. I am thankful, though, that we don't have to do it alone.

SUICIDE

||||||||||||||||

The death of a child is always devastating and tragic whatever its cause, yet somehow losing a child to suicide seems to carry an added layer of heartbreak. For friends of the bereaved, it may call for you to draw upon a deeper well of sensitivity and caring. I took away both wisdom and anguish from the words of a father and two mothers whose young people took their own lives.

Bob Levey, Father of Greg, Age Thirty

"He died on February 18, 1991, immolated himself on the College Green in Amherst, Massachusetts, to protest the Iraq War. My wife, Ellen, and I were having breakfast. Two policemen came to the door to inform us. Ellen's uncle took care of the arrangements for the funeral and moving the body. We hastily called a memorial service, and a few days later there were thirty or more people in our house talking about Greg. I got nothing but support from my friends. They showed up on my doorstep for sympathetic hugs and quiet chatting. I believe that in dealing with loss, whatever its cause, showing up is the big deal.

People feel nervous about coming, but when they leave the visit I think they feel better. They shouldn't worry about feeling awkward or about what they're going to say. It's enough to just say, 'I know you're going through something awful. Tell me if there's anything I can do.' The short answer to what's the best thing to do is, 'Just show up!' It's not what you say or do or whether you bring a covered dish. Just make yourself present and don't be very curious. Don't ask, 'How do you feel?' Or, 'How's it going?' Ask, 'Do you want to go to lunch?'

"Because Greg's suicide was a news story, we got an enormous number of notes and letters which I still have in a sealed cardboard box. I never looked at them or responded. I wasn't interested in exchanging pleasantries, things like, 'Thanks for your note, life goes on, etcetera.'

"I have one memory that makes me cringe. Greg's death was a big deal to the peace groups in Amherst. They made a memorial ceremony to him on the spot where he died. That day a bunch of young people drove by and taunted the ceremony and said horrible obscenities about the person who died [to protest the war], who happened to be my son. The spot became a shrine, and people brought all kinds of stuff—stones placed in a circle, feathers, written messages, candles of all kinds, and eventually they gave everything to me in giant boxes. I kept the boxes upstairs for sixteen years before I threw them out.

"Losing my son was a life-changing event for me. It robbed me of any strong positive motivations in my life. It put me into a total catatonic state of inertia that has lingered off and on in my life. It doused my creativity to have lost him in this way. The pain is always just below the surface—a lingering sadness, almost as though it's a physical undergarment. It's probably unhealthy, but I've come to terms with that reality—it's my private situation. I talked it out in therapy for a while, but other than the shrink and Ellen and a few occasions with a good friend and a glass of wine, I haven't talked about the impact of Greg's death. I haven't cried in front of anyone but Ellen and Steve and Helen, dear friends with whom we vacation every year. If we'd get to talking about Greg, I'd get tearful. . . . For many years our friends, Frank and Pat, called me on February 18. Since Frank's sister died in a horrible car accident, he understood this kind of loss.

"When people I meet ask how many kids I have, I say I have a daughter . . . and I had a son but he killed himself when he was thirty. They always gasp. Some of them ask questions about the suicide, but most don't say anything beyond, 'Oh my God! I'm so sorry. I never knew that. I'm so sorry.' And that's fine.

"Years ago, at dinner, our friend Maureen made some reference to fire. She hadn't known how Greg took his life and she was deeply upset when her husband, who did know, told her about it on their drive home. She was full of abject apologies afterward, and I remember writing her a sympathetic note that there was nothing to be concerned about because I live with the memory of my son every day and she shouldn't think her accidental reference made any difference.

"One of the major functions of a parent is to brag about their children. When my friends talk about their kids, I can hear them without getting upset. I know my son could never get it together. His anger and fury at an unjust world undermined him. He was so obsessive about his political life that it obviously led to his death.

"I've been called upon twice since then to comfort someone who had a suicide in his family. It's hard. Once I was called by a friend whose son jumped in front of a train. I told him, 'This will change you forever, but your life will go on.' Less than a year later he killed himself.

"Another man whose teenage son committed suicide looked me up and wanted to talk about it. We went for a long walk and he wept, and I told him the same thing. 'You'll go on with your life. There will be normalcy around you, but it won't ever be completely normal for you.' I still, five or ten times a year, have a vivid dream about my son's fiery death and wake up in a sweat.

"Because it happened so long ago, the people around me don't have an ongoing sensitivity to it. They aren't thinking, 'Here's Bob, he's thinking about Greg.' For them, it's a nonevent. Everyone has their own list of troubles. I completely understand the world I live in. I don't take offense."

Carla Graubard, Mother of Teddy, Age Seventeen

After a week of illness and academic stress, Teddy Graubard, six-foot-one, a brilliant student whose many activities included the Math Olympiad, varsity football, and throwing discus for the track squad, cheated on a Latin test and was caught. On February 18, 2009, in an act that his mother calls an "impulsive suicide" (as opposed to one stemming from mental illness), he jumped to his death from the eleventh-floor window of his Manhattan private school. Carla offered this advice three years later:

"Don't be afraid to reach out—but also don't take it personally if you get a negative response. Or no response. Wait a bit and try again. No one will ever hold this against you. Don't be afraid to talk with your friend about their child; don't be afraid to ask what happened and why. Parents who experience the death of a child want to talk. And talk. And talk about their child's life and death. Acknowledge what happened, use the child's name, share memories and thoughts and stories. It is a great gift to the parents. It's not like this will remind the parents of their loss. They are thinking about it constantly anyway. . . . I am thinking about it constantly three years after Teddy died.

"If you want to help, be very specific. 'Please let me know if there's anything I can do,' is kind, but not especially helpful. Better to drop off a casserole or cookies. Ask, 'Would you like to come to dinner on Sunday night?' Or, 'We're going to see Movie XYZ Friday at 8. Do you want to join us?'

"Think about the person's surviving children. It meant the world to me and Clay [her younger son] when Teddy's football team asked

Clay to meet them in the park for a game. Or when a couple of Teddy's friends made dates with Clay to play video games or watch the Super Bowl with them.

"Finally, please don't say to us: 'Everything happens for a reason.' 'You're so strong. I could never be that strong.' 'God only gives you what you can handle.' 'Suicide is such a selfish act.'"

Judy Collins, Mother of Clark, Age Thirty-Three
Over cups of strong coffee in her sunny dining room, the legendary singer-author-activist Judy Collins, a friend of long standing, talked to me about her son.

"Clark had been sober for seven years when he had a relapse, a bad day; he was going through a divorce, he was depressed. On January 15, 1992, he got drunk, turned on the car engine and killed himself.

"My youngest brother, Denver, was the one who told me. He came to the house, put his arms around me and said, 'He's done it.' I knew what he meant. I went to pieces, I was barely breathing. But it shouldn't have been a shock. Before he got sober, Clark had tried to do it many times—his paternal grandfather died the same way; I attempted suicide when I was fourteen. Still suicide is *always* a shock.

"Most surprising were the silences from certain friends who couldn't stand to hear about it. They ignored phone calls, they didn't make phone calls. I'll always remember the ones who got it right.

"Joan Rivers [the stand-up comedian] called me immediately and said, 'There are no guilts in suicide. Guilt is playing God, guilt is imagining we're so powerful we could have stopped it. You didn't cause it. You couldn't have stopped it. You couldn't control it. You have to go right back to work. If you don't you won't heal.' Joan's husband had taken his own life, so she knew what she was talking about. I listened to her. I started singing right away, but my first job was to not kill myself. My second was to have a happy, joyous life. I'm glad I can work. One of the members of my suicide recovery group was Gloria Vanderbilt, whose son took his life before Clark took his. She told me, 'When I hear you sing, it's like both of our boys are alive.'

"Suicide is not the same as other kinds of deaths because when your child dies in an accident, the state and the church don't condemn you. With suicides they do. You have Saint Augustine breathing down your neck. I tell survivors, don't go to a religious fanatic if you want comfort. Don't ask to be buried in their cemetery. They make you feel, 'Oh, you should have done this or shouldn't have done that.' That condemnation doesn't happen if your loved one has a heart attack.

"The idea of guilt, and anyone who made me feel guilty, had to be eliminated from my life. I refuse to embed myself in trauma.

"Iris Bolton, who wrote *My Son ... My Son ...* about her son's suicide, said most books are all about the drama and the problem, not the solution. Her advice was, 'Don't let them shove drugs on you, because if you're not awake, you're not going to heal.'

"Mariette Hartley [the actress] lost her father to suicide. I bought her book, *Breaking the Silence*, when I came back from his funeral in Minnesota. When I went to California, we had some time together that was healing. Mariette shared her experiences with me. She helped a lot."

"It's hard for most survivors to tell the truth about their loss. The trick is to look back, but not to stare. Edwin Shneidman, the pioneer in suicide prevention, says most people who die leave a skeleton in *their* closet. The person who commits suicide leaves a skeleton in *your* closet. Besides the survivor being shattered, there's so much secrecy around it. When people hear how Clark died, their response—usually 'Ugggh! Oh my God!'—is all about fear. The social taboo around suicide has lessened but it's still there.

"When everyone at a dinner party is talking about their kids going to college or advancing in their careers, I don't volunteer my story unless someone says their kid has an addiction. Then I might raise it and try to help them. Just the other night someone who didn't know my experience asked about my son and I felt that awful bolt go through my body from my eyes to my toes. But I always tell the truth. I think it's important to get it all out. Instead of thinking, 'Why do I owe *you* the details of my tragedy?' I feel, 'I owe *everyone* the details. If I don't tell the truth, it demeans my reality.'

"I want to create change in the culture, to educate others and demystify suicide. I want to heal myself *and* heal the world. Whether it's two days, two months, or twenty years since it happened, you grieve your whole life. But I love talking about Clark. Always, after that first blow, like a hot steel rod, there is the wonder of having been with him for thirty-three years.

"What should people say to a survivor? They could say, 'Tell me about your loved one.' 'Can I come and cook a meal?' 'What can I do to help?' 'Can I just listen?' 'Would it help you to hear my story?' They could send over a book of poems about loss or suggest books to read. If they want to bring something, candles are always appropriate. My friends Susan and Ed Lick sent me a Jewish Yahrtzeit [memorial] candle that burns all day and all night. I was raised Methodist, I'm a Buddhist in practice, but that candle meant so much to me. As St. John said, sharing your own healing and what works for you spreads tolerance.

"I remember having tea at the old Stanhope Hotel with my friend Ellie Filbin, whose son also had committed suicide. She was very direct. She asked me, 'Did you love him?'

"I said, 'Yes!'

"'Did he love you?'

"'Absolutely!'

"She said, 'Well then, it's all right.'

"I think it was the poet Philip Levine who wrote, 'The only thing left is to love them.'"

Ten Rules for Friends
of a Bereaved Parent

1) *Stay the course.* Be prepared for a long siege of mourning, bottomless despair, unquenchable tears, dark moods, and a rage that seems to come from some fierce primal place. At times your grieving friend may be unrecognizable—cold, hostile, reclusive, erratic, inconsolable. Don't take it personally. Keep pumping out love and support. When they want quiet, keep still. When they want solitude, leave them alone. Do not feel rejected if they ask you to leave, but stay nearby or remain available unless they tell you to back off.

2) *Pay attention.* Try to intuit their needs. Notice the gradations of their grief—when they're most upset, what words or behaviors seem most consoling to them. Study what others do that makes them furrow their brow or recoil, which comments annoy them and which seem most calming. Observe how they respond when other people talk to them, touch them, try to comfort them, and let what you see sensitize you to their preferences and guide your own interactions.

3) *Be demonstrative.* If they're open to affection, don't be afraid to hug them, hold their hand, stroke them, rock them in your arms, or lie down beside them until they fall asleep. You might rub a man's temples or massage his shoulders. Brush a woman's hair, put your arms around her, or lace her fingers in yours.

4) *Don't rush their recovery.* Never say things like, "Isn't it time you reached closure?" "Maybe you should start trying to put this behind you." Or, "Life must go on." Let them advance through the stages of grief at their own pace.

5) *Don't try to distract them with trivial pursuits.* I know you want to help assuage the pain of this terrible loss, but a ball game, concert, or dinner isn't going to do the trick. Don't be insulted if they decline your invitations. They will let you know when they're ready to resume their normal activities, and even then, don't expect a lot of laughter.

6) *Remember their child.* Don't hide pictures in which the child appears and don't stop mentioning him or her by name. Most parents *want* to talk about their deceased son or daughter and are grateful to people who have specific memories to share. Remembering may reopen the parents' deepest wound, but if they thought their child was forgotten, they'd feel worse.

7) *Keep track of the calendar.* Expect certain dates to re-ignite their grief. The child's birthday, of course, and the anniversary of the day she or he died. Consider making a contribution to an appropriate charity in the child's memory on either of those dates. The first Thanksgiving without their child—the first Christmas, Hanukkah, Kwanza, New Year's Eve, Easter, Passover, Ramadan, Fourth of July, and Halloween—will be very difficult for them. Until the calendar completes its cycle, try to make yourself available, even if only by phone, should your

friend need your support on those emotionally charged dates.

8) *Don't try to drown your friend's sorrow.* The comforts of alcohol are, at best, temporary. The morning after a drunken binge the child will still be gone. Your friend will still feel bereft. But both of you will have a bitch of a hangover.

9) *Alert others to the situation.* Make sure *your* family, friends, boss, and coworkers are aware that you're deeply involved with a dear friend who has a terminally ill child or whose child has just died. It will explain why you haven't been yourself or why you've grown more upset, distracted, or depressed. Don't give anyone in your life a chance to misinterpret your behavior. Let them know your moodiness is not their fault. If the child is not a relative, they may not understand the intensity of the relationship and the genuineness of your sorrow, so you need to tell them exactly what's going on.

10) *Do not conflate one child with another.* Though they may go on to have other kids, the parents will never stop mourning and missing the one who died. The loss will leave a hole in their hearts that can never be filled. Don't make the mistake of assuming (or, God forbid, saying) that Tony has taken Tommy's place. Tony is a great kid, but he's not Tommy. Tommy was unique and irreplaceable.

THE BEST OF FRIENDS—
CASE HISTORIES TO
LEARN FROM AND LIVE BY

A Shout-Out for Those Who Got It Right

AS THE SINGER JEWEL APTLY PUT IT in an otherwise cornball lyric, "In the end, only kindness matters."

The anecdotal universe abounds in tales of people who acted kindly toward those who are sick or suffering: You've probably heard about the kids who shaved their heads in solidarity with a classmate who was undergoing chemotherapy, the competitors in the Special Olympics who saw a fellow runner take a tumble and turned back to help him complete the race, and the four-year-old who noticed his widowed neighbor weeping, ran over to the man, climbed on his lap, and nestled against his chest.

"What did you say to him?" the boy's mother asked when he returned home.

"Nothing," replied the child. "I just helped him cry."

What do these young people have in common? They translated empathy into action: they noticed someone else's distress and did something about it. This chapter will introduce you to people of all ages who prove the equation that kindness equals empathy plus action. I'll introduce you to a woman who gave a friend her kidney, a high school student who befriended a Holocaust survivor, a man who became a pillar of strength for a father whose son was born with a devastating disease, a woman who monitors her friend's condition by long-distance phone, a man on chemo and dialysis whose five friends swam relays with him—around Manhattan Island, a woman whose friend did something for her that made her feel that bald really *is* beautiful, a woman whose home hospitality made all the difference to a friend with cancer, someone who offered simple creature closeness to a postsurgery patient who was bloodied and miserable, a woman beset by multiple afflictions whose two closest friends always intuit exactly what she needs, and, finally, a sampling of ten support groups that prove the efficacy of collective caring.

As you read the following stories, ask yourself if you could perform similar acts of kindness for a friend of yours.

DONATE A KIDNEY

||||||||||||||||||||||||||||||||||||||

"I would die for you," " . . . fall on my sword for you," " . . . take a bullet," " . . . give you a kidney." Exaggeration and hyperbole are often used to describe one person's extreme devotion to another, but the line about the kidney happens to accurately describe what Virginia Postrel did for her friend Sally Satel. The two women are "kindred spirits" who've known each other for fifteen years. Because Virginia lives in Dallas and Sally in Washington, D.C., they rarely get together and mostly communicate by e-mail. Nevertheless, when Virginia heard that if Sally didn't get a kidney transplant soon, she'd be tethered to a dialysis machine three days a week, Virginia put herself in her friend's place and suffered along with her.

"For someone who prizes her independence and freedom of movement as much as Sally does, dialysis would have been a prison sentence," wrote Virginia in *Texas Monthly*. "I knew the chances of getting a cadaver kidney were low, although I didn't realize how truly miniscule: More than 66,000 Americans are on the waiting list for the 6,700 or so cadaver kidneys that are available each year. Just thinking about her situation made my heart race with empathetic panic."

Virginia's husband "wasn't thrilled with the idea of letting someone slice open his wife" and only came around when she made clear how determined she was to give Sally a kidney. The two women's blood types were compatible, but tests showed Virginia to be slightly anemic, so she had to eat iron-rich cereal for a week until her hemoglobin count met the minimum standard. She also had to make two trips from Dallas to D.C. for preliminary tests and meetings with the social worker, nephrologist, and surgeon before she was told all systems were Go. Virginia's operation to remove her right kidney was uneventful except for her violent reaction to the anesthesia, but Sally hemorrhaged badly and needed a second surgery to stop the bleeding. Happily, a few days later both were well enough to celebrate over hamburgers at Sally's apartment, and less than six weeks after that, with her new kidney functioning flawlessly, Sally was back at work.

"Usually, when someone is seriously ill, all you can do is lend moral support and maybe cook some meals or run a few errands," wrote Virginia. "Nothing you do will make that person well. But if you donate a kidney you can (with the help of a team of medical specialists) cure her. Who wouldn't want to do it?"

Want to? Sure. Actually go under the knife for anyone but a close family member? Not so fast. If organ donation is more of a self-sacrifice than you can imagine signing on for, here are some less invasive, more doable kindness options that worked well for others—the sick and suffering as well as those who care about them.

TAKING NOTICE, TAKING ACTION

Irene, a high school student, and Sarah, an elderly Jewish Holocaust survivor who suffers from crippling arthritis and sorrowful memories, first met when Sarah gave a talk at Irene's school. Afterward Irene went up to Sarah and told her that she too had been orphaned, not by losing her parents to Hitler's Final Solution, of course, but by their deaths in a hotel fire while they were away on vacation for their tenth wedding anniversary. Soon after that conversation Irene had to choose a "volunteer project" for her social studies class. She made a commitment to visit Sarah every Wednesday, to keep her company, do her grocery shopping, tidy up her small apartment, help her cook supper, and share the evening meal with her. Irene also had the idea of taping Sarah's recollections of her wartime experiences and sending the tapes to the Holocaust Museum in Washington.

One day Irene arrived to find Sarah bent over her legs, a bottle of nail polish clutched tightly in her fist, a grimace on her face. The old woman was trying to paint her toenails, but her arthritis made it too painful for her to reach her feet. By this time Irene knew all about the brutal degradation Sarah had suffered in the concentration camps. Recognizing that groomed nails were a symbol of Sarah's reclaimed feminine dignity, Irene added another ritual to her weekly visits: she gave Irene a manicure or pedicure.

AVAILABLE ANYTIME FOR ANYTHING

Alex Silver and his wife, Jamie, had genetic counseling, and Jamie received excellent obstetrical care, yet they knew almost immediately that something was terribly wrong with their newborn son, Jackson. The skin came off his heel when a nurse removed a tiny Band-Aid after performing the routine neonatal blood-sugar test. His mouth bled when he nursed. The edges of his diaper tore the skin off his stomach and thighs. By the time he was a few hours old, Jackson was covered in bandages.

It was very late when Alex capped the torment of those first few hours by calling his best friend, Bill Mack, who showed up right away and instantly made clear that he was "available for anything."

Alex remembers, "That whole night is a blur, but what sticks in my memory is Bill's pure love and support. He was in our hospital room when Jamie and I first heard the diagnosis—EB [Epidermolysis Bullosa, a disfiguring, chronically painful, life-threatening disease caused by an absence of the protein that keeps the layers of the skin together]. He didn't say anything and I didn't feel like talking, but he kept me company in the silence. He stayed in the hospital all night long, did it without being asked. He did it as if it was natural, and he never said anything about wanting to leave. It was an unspoken form of sup-port—his ability to express emotion while remaining in the background.

"Bill drove me back and forth to the hospital because I couldn't sleep for days and I wanted to be near my son. He was the person I called at all hours when I needed to speak my mind and say things like, 'This is surreal.' 'Nothing was supposed to go wrong.' 'We were told we were having a healthy baby.' 'Why did this happen to my child!?' 'Why would God do this to a baby!?' Bill was the person I could talk to about all that. He listened. He was selfless."

When I interviewed Alex, his son was three years old. The photo on Jackson's website (http://jgsf.org/about_jackson.html) showed an adorable brown-eyed boy sitting in the bathtub with bandages on his arms and a big smile on his face. "His skin still blisters or shears off from the simplest friction—playing, hugging, falling down, swallowing a hard cookie," says Alex. "We try to be preventative as best we can. He usually wears long sleeves and long pants, but you can still see the discolored skin on his face and neck. We have to wrap areas of his chest and feet with nonadhesive bandages. In severe cases kids can look like mummies, entirely wrapped. If there's a silver lining to any of this, it's that it brought out the best in people."

Clearly, the best of the best has come from his friend Bill, who continues to do whatever needs doing. "At first I felt horribly helpless," said Alex. "I'm in finance. I don't know anything about medicine." He quickly became active in an organization called DEBRA (Dystrophic Epidermolysis Bullosa Research Association of America) and learned about EB patient care and who's doing the most promising research. He discovered that EB affects only twenty to thirty thousand people in America, not a large enough market to make it attractive for the pharmaceutical companies to invest in research, so patients depend on the federal government and the generosity of private individuals and corporations to help find a cure. "When we started the Jackson Gabriel Silver Foundation to raise private funds, Bill did most of the legal work, all pro bono, and brought in an accountant willing to do the foundation's finances without charge."

Bill's important role in the life of Alex, Jamie, and Jackson proves that when trying to ease the burdens of a friend, it helps if you can fortify your empathy and kindness with some practical resources and all the professional help and expertise you can muster.

REACH OUT AND TOUCH SOMEONE

E-mail, though quick and efficient, doesn't always capture the tone or intensity of a friend's suffering. Sometimes you have to pick up the phone, as Emma did once a week for a year after her friend Lori's husband died. Despite the hefty long-distance charges, Emma called Lori every Tuesday morning, always prefacing their conversation with a "Good morning, sweetie. What are you up to?" She didn't call to conduct a profound colloquy on life and death but simply to keep tabs on

Lori and make sure she didn't become a recluse. Between the sound of her voice and the details she shared about her daily life, Lori's state of mind became clear to Emma, who was then able to gauge whether phone support was enough or whether it was time to hop on a plane and visit her friend in person.

GET IN THE SWIM

In May 2011 Richard Abramson, age sixty-seven, was diagnosed with multiple myeloma, the second-most common blood cancer. The disease, which is treatable but not curable, is in remission now, but he's still on chemo and, because his kidneys quit functioning, he's also on dialysis. None of that stopped Richard, a ranked competitive swimmer from the time he was seven years old, from wanting to keep swimming—or his friends from wanting to swim with him. In 2008 they had circled Manhattan, and the following year they swam across the English Channel in a relay. But that was Before. This is After. Yet on August 4, 2012, Richard and five of his buddies, ages thirty-four to sixty (none of them sick), divvied up the 28.8-mile river route around Manhattan and jumped in. A kayaker paddled beside each swimmer to keep him on course. Family members and friends observed the proceedings and enjoyed refreshments on a larger boat that chugged along at a safe distance. When it was Richard's turn to do one-sixth of the course, he swam 4.8 miles with his fans cheering him on.

"The bonding of our group is tremendous," he said of his ad hoc team, the NY Nadadores. But the story gets even better because it rippled out into the world. Having dedicated their swim to raising awareness and funds for research toward a cure for his disease, Richard and his friends sent out e-mails to their social networks with a link to a video of Richard swimming, and their outreach effort raked in $600,000 for Mt. Sinai Hospital's multiple myeloma research. Now they're making a movie about their team.

OFFER HOME HOSPITALITY

||||||||||||||||||||||||||||||||||||||||||||||||||||

Janet Dewart Bell, an African American who lives in Manhattan, chose to have her lumpectomy performed at Howard University Hospital in Washington by a world-renowned surgeon who was one of the first physicians to sound the alert about the high incidence of breast cancer in the black community. Rolling out the welcome mat was Janet's D.C.-based friend, P. J. Robinson, who invited Janet and her late husband, Derrick, as houseguests. When Janet flatlined on the operating table, her surgery had to be postponed and her stay extended, and P. J. became not just her host but also her nurse and a source of solace to Derrick, who was "shell-shocked" to see Janet stricken with the same disease that had claimed the life of his first wife. Janet says she felt buttressed by the support of her loving friend P. J., whose generous hospitality allowed her to recuperate in peace when she was at her most fragile and whose convenient location allowed her to attend her doctor's appointments without incurring airfare or hotel bills.

OFFER PHYSICAL COMFORT

||||||||||||||||||||||||||||||||||||||||||||||||||||

Esther Harper's anesthesia had worn off and she was recuperating miserably at home after having sinus surgery for a collapsed septum when her husband, who'd been taking care of their twins, felt himself coming down with bronchitis. "The minute I mentioned on the phone that he was sick and we might some need help with the children, Sam came running," said Esther of her friend Samantha. "She crawled in bed with me, even though I looked like Hannibal Lector, with my bloody nose and huge gauze pads tied from one ear to the other. She pulled up the covers and lay there holding me, gently stroking my head, and she kept saying, 'Don't worry, just rest. Don't worry, I'll take care of the kids. Don't worry, I'll bring over your favorite turkey chili.' I cried like a baby. She was like a mother to me. I'll never forget it."

MAKE BALD BEAUTIFUL

Debbie Green was diagnosed with non-Hodgkin's lymphoma in January 2010. Before she started chemotherapy she visited a clothing store where she saw a well-dressed woman, bald, wearing a baseball cap. Debbie looked away. Though she admired the woman for being out in the world, she felt "that very soon it would be me and no one would want to look at me either."

Her attitude changed when her friend Dr. David Kaminsky gave her a copy of *Turning Heads,* a book of pictures, many by famous photographers, of women of all ages who are undergoing treatment for cancer. All of them were bald—and beautiful. David's note said,

> Dear Debbie,
>
> As you move through chemo days, reflect on these gorgeous women whose lives were enhanced by the experience. Hair isn't the woman, it's an appendage with determination to prevail. It comes back. It will return to you like a devoted lover. In the meantime, you'll be as radiant and attractive as ever.
>
> Love, David K.

Debbie shared the book and note with her friend Stacy Jacob, who, similarly inspired by it, offered to do a photo shoot of Debbie—bald. The resulting pictures changed Debbie's feeling about herself so dramatically that the two women decided to create the "Turning Heads Project," whose goal is to photograph other women who have lost their hair as a result of cancer treatments and to interview them on video (http://turningheads project.org). Check out their website and you'll see that all are impeccably made up; wear gorgeous jewelry; and are bald, proud, and vibrant as they share their stories in a "poignant, straightforward way" in order to help others who are walking the same path.

"Cancer is a word, not a sentence," Debbie told me, a line I love. "We want people to understand that."

On the Turning Heads website Stacy writes about Debbie:

I had never seen her so beautiful as [she was] during that time. There were no bangs to hide her eyes and I saw how much they shined. When I looked at her, I saw so much more than I had ever noticed before. That baldness was a badge of honor. She was the same and yet different. Stronger. Wiser. I knew we had to capture this fleeting moment when Debbie was without hair. . . .

I dragged out my camera equipment and transformed my living room into a make-shift studio. [Debbie laughs, annotating for me that months before, Stacy had bought a lot of camera equipment that had been sitting in her closet unused until that day.] I made a fun, upbeat music mix to set the tone, gathered some props, and we did our own 'Supermodel' photo shoot. This was a time to be remembered. A time that you'd never choose for yourself or wish on a friend, but a time that came with many blessings as well. It brought us closer in our friendship, it gave us the ability to see beyond the external stuff like hair and into what really holds value for us and for our lives.

STAY THE COURSE THROUGH THICK AND THICKER

It's a miracle that Toby Perlman, wife of violinist Itzhak Perlman and mother of five, is still alive. Toby began life with an immature immune system and throughout her childhood and youth suffered chronic neck pain, inflammatory disease, toxic allergies, frequent infections, bronchitis, sinusitis, "and every other 'itis' known to medical science." As an adult she's had lung disease, shingles, pneumonia, four kinds of cancer (melanoma, uterine, abdominal, breast), and literally dozens of surgeries and hospitalizations. Yet she calls herself "the least hypochondriacal person you know. For me to lie down, I have to be falling down. I can fool anyone into thinking I'm better than I am." When one of her ailments flares up, Toby hides the problem from her family but not from her two best friends, Jenny and Martha.

With Jenny, a fellow cancer survivor, Toby has a profound, almost mystical, understanding. "We know what each other needs. We know how frightened each of us gets for the other when one of us is sick. Each time I get a bump or a rash, she tells me, 'You *know* it's cancer, Toby! You have to get it checked.' If she's in the hospital, she knows I have to be in the room with her. I won't be kept in the hall. She tells the doctors they have to let me in *or else*. And when she balks at going to her doctor, I tell her, 'You have to go, Jenny! It's not about you, it's about *me*. What will happen to me if you die? You have to stay alive for *me*.'"

Toby says it's an art to be a friend to a friend who's sick. "Everyone has good intentions. You want to say and do the right thing, but unless you really know someone well, you don't know what the right thing is. You think, 'I should call. Wait, maybe I shouldn't call.' You're coming from the right place but you really don't know what the person wants. In my case, Jenny and I know *everything* about each other, and one of the things she knows about me is that when I'm sick I don't want to talk to *anyone*."

Toby's other close friend, Martha, is similarly attuned to her. "After my worst cancer operation, Martha got on a plane and just appeared in my hospital room. I knew she needed to be there as much as I needed her to be there, and I knew I didn't have to talk to her either! She just came and stayed and she was perfect! She wasn't showing me what a good friend she was; she just *was*. She said things like, 'You want tea? Here's tea.' 'You don't want tea? Okay then, I'll see you later.' She didn't entertain me. She just let me be whatever I needed to be.

"Some people in my life can no longer empathize with me. They think I can't possibly be sick *again*; I must be making it up. But Jenny and Martha always take me seriously and treat me as I want to be treated. We know how to talk to each other, but we can also sit in a room and not say a word to each other. When I'm with them I feel totally comfortable and totally safe."

I think that's a perfect summary of the three strongest columns that support a friendship during illness:

1) *Know what to say and when to shut up.*
2) *Rest comfortably in each other's silences.*
3) *Make each other feel safe.*

EXPLORE OPPORTUNITIES FOR COLLECTIVE CARING

Hundreds of thousands of support groups for problems of every conceivable sort have sprung up all over the country—some hosted by hospitals, clinics, and rehab centers, and some initiated by patients or caregivers who recognize the need for a private space in which a number of similarly afflicted or comparably affected people can air their feelings, exchange pertinent information, and share tips on how to better cope with the situation they have in common. Before describing ten groups that work well for their participants, I should clarify that not all patients or caregivers are suited to the group model of sharing.

Marcia Seligson told me about a breast cancer support group in L.A. that turned out to be more depressing than comforting. She cautioned me that listening to women who are more frightened and pessimistic than I am or whose condition is more serious and threatening than mine might just give me new things to worry about, so I should think twice about joining such a group. After serious consideration I decided not to expose myself to women who were worse off than I am, not only for fear they'd give me negative ideas but because I knew I'd feel uncomfortable airing my relatively trivial concerns in the presence of patients with far greater burdens.

Susana Leval joined a support group sponsored by the hospital where she was being treated for breast cancer. In it she heard women talk about being angry at their bodies for getting cancer, hating their bodies after their surgeries and hating the men who left them after they had mastectomies or underwent chemo. Susana found the group helpful until she began taking on everyone else's problems and anxieties—not a useful enterprise for someone who was struggling with vulnerability herself. Ultimately she felt she had to stop talking about her illness or listening to anyone else talk about theirs. She just didn't want to go there anymore. She wanted to concentrate on getting back to normal.

Despite these few thumbs down, most people swear by the support groups that help them cope with the complexities of their own illness or the challenges of relating to or caring for a sick friend or loved one. Here are ten examples of "collective caring" at its best.

Alix Kates Shulman's Alzheimer's Support Group

For the last four years Alix and a dozen other spouses, partners, or caregivers of Alzheimer's patients have met every Monday morning for ninety minutes "to speak candidly of what is unspeakable in polite society or even among closest friends and family." They share advice on how to bathe, calm, and medicate their patients; keep them from wandering off; subdue their violent outbursts and wild hallucinations; and deal with their incontinence, "the mere mention of which spooks outsiders," said Alix in the *New York Times*. Because everyone in her group is in the same boat, they know that their anguish, rage, and frustration will be mirrored back to them and fully understood. Among the topics they have grappled with is "the disappearance of old friends, whose discomfort around our spouses keeps them away." Even after their Alzheimer's patient has died, caregivers, by now bereft of *their* friends as a result of their ordeal, have kept returning to the group for companionship and support.

The 150 Friends of Alexandra Bloom

In August 2009, when Alexandra learned she had breast cancer, her husband, Tom Nishioka, and three of his friends created a website to allow other pals of theirs to help them manage the challenges associated with her illness. According to the *New York Times*, "ten team captains" took charge of assigning various responsibilities to the 150 (!) people who signed on to the website—tasks like researching oncologists, looking into health insurance plans, marketing, cooking, or picking up Alexandra and Tom's twin daughters at their school. Among the volunteers were three "honorary grandmothers," each of whom visited the children once a week, brought treats, read to them, and spoiled them rotten. (It makes you wonder who got the biggest bang for the buck—the kids or the "grandmas.")

Colette's Helping Circle

Fifteen friends—fourteen women and one man—of this forty-two-year-old French American lawyer each committed to a day when they would accompany her to the hospital for her chemo treatments, hang with her in the waiting room, have a meal or snack with her afterward, then take her home. One of the volunteers created an online listserv that allowed each of the fifteen to sign up for their preferred days and swap dates or time slots when necessary.

At the end of her treatment regimen Colette hosted a buffet lunch to thank her helping circle. For a firsthand report, I interviewed one woman who was there:

"Most of us had never met each other before because we were from different parts of Colette's life—we were fellow parents from her children's school, colleagues from her law practice, the female half of the married couples she and her husband are friends with. It was quite an experience to put faces to all the e-mail addresses because we had been reporting to each other on this listserv, describing what we'd done on our day with Colette, and how she'd seemed, but we'd never met. At her buffet lunch we all sat down with our plates in our laps, and she surprised us by doing something extraordinary: without glancing at a note, she went around the room and gave a personal tribute to each of us that was so specific I was overwhelmed. She recounted in amazing detail how each of us had helped her. I found it so moving that she would choose to individualize her gratitude when it would have been so much easier to just call us all together and say, 'Thanks, guys, for what you did.' Instead, by focusing on each person separately, she allowed us to get to know one another and, in a funny way, to unite us through our devotion to her and our stories about the time we spent with her.

"When she first started going around the room, I have to admit I felt anxious. *What if I hadn't done as much for her as the others? Maybe I should have been more creative. How's this going to come out equal?* But she told a little gem of an anecdote about each of us, recalling this person's special kindness, that one's funny comment, something that happened on so-and-so's day with her. Then she gave each of us a small, framed needlepoint that said *Merci*—thank you in French—on the back of which was the person's name. Colette is the furthest thing from a gushy person, so this really was an incredible gesture. She showed us that giving is never a one-way street."

Bruce Feiler's "Council of Dads"

When Bruce found out he had bone cancer and needed nine months of chemo and a fifteen-hour surgery to reconstruct his leg, he nearly freaked out—not at the thought of his own ordeal but at the idea that he might disappear forever from his twin daughters' lives. To ensure that they would be surrounded by male guidance, he asked the six men who had most influenced his life to serve as part-time fathers to his girls and, if he died, help his wife care for them and transmit his legacy. (See *The Council of Dads: A Story of Family, Friendship and Learning How to Live.*) Bruce also appointed a "minister of information," whose job it was to disseminate news about his illness to everyone else and "be polite when I didn't have the energy or inclination to be." His siblings, together with his wife's siblings, organized "an online casserole club" so friends could buy dinners for the family through a meal service. The twins' grandparents rotated in and out. Bruce's high school classmates made a video of their reunion to enable him to see what he missed. I'm glad to report that Bruce is alive and flourishing, but neither he nor anyone else involved in his support system will ever forget the life lessons they learned when he was in extremis.

The Meditation Farewell for Joan Berkley

At 4 P.M. on Sunday August 26, 2012, forty friends of a dying woman gathered in Mission Hills, Kansas, for a meditative session, during which a facilitator guided them to shut their eyes and envision her surrounded by bubbles of any shape or color, and to fix the image in their minds and hearts so they could conjure it in the future and recall Joan and that day. According to SuEllen Fried, who was there, "Joan knew this was the last time she would see most of us, so she took the opportunity to talk to us about how her final journey had brought greater depth in her friendships, and she urged us to not wait for the approach of death to deepen our relationships but to do it now." Joan died not long after that day, but her friends still have their beautiful bubble images to remember her by.

The Thirty Friends of Esther Broner

Only days after she lost her husband to Parkinson's disease, Esther, who had neglected her health while taking care of Bob, entered the hospital for quadruple bypass surgery. As if widowhood and heart surgery weren't enough of a kick in the head, she contracted an acute lung disease that, over the course of an agonizing year, sent her in and out of intensive care, rehab, and a nursing home. Through it all she was never alone. Besides her four children, one of whom, Nahama, lived nearby, Esther had the enthusiastic support of about thirty devoted friends, myself among them. All of us were kept informed of her condition via frequent updates from her gatekeepers—mostly by Nahama, the daughter, but also by Marcia Freedman, an old friend—who sent us e-mails about what help was needed, told us when Esther was or wasn't strong enough to receive visitors, and held chaos in check by coordinating everyone's visits so Esther would not be overwhelmed by too many people (or scones, casseroles, or tangerines) at one time.

A few days before our friend was to be discharged from the nursing home, Barbara and Nan paid for a cleaning service to descend on Esther's apartment and clean it from floor to ceiling. Nahama and her brother Adam painted the walls and straightened up her belongings so she could to return to a fresh, orderly environment with few reminders of the anguish of her husband's final days. Marcia and Gil unpacked her many cartons of books. Systems were put in place: Esther wore a little gizmo around her neck that, if pressed, sounded an alarm in an emergency terminal; Nahama, Barbara, Anita, and Gil were on the med-alert. Barbara brought soup most days. Anita, a pro at navigating municipal agencies, guided Nahama to the appropriate social services, like Citymeals on Wheels, and also brought books and soup on Sunday nights. I helped secure a loan from the Authors Guild so that Esther, a published writer, could buy office equipment and get back to work on her latest project, a play. Gena, Sue, Vivian, and Lilly organized weekly potluck dinners—dubbed "PMs for E. M." because Esther's writing name was E. M. Broner. This allowed her to look forward to a couple hours of lively conversation with different constellations of friends who brought homemade specialties, cheese, falafel, hummus, cookies, and wine. Gloria, Carol, and Linsey established a biweekly writing workshop/feminist collective that they called, "The Marilyn French Society" in honor of the late writer who had been one of Esther's dearest friends and a member of her "coven."

This all-embracing web of support had a huge impact not only on Esther's well-being but also on all her friends, who appreciated the chance to help her in a meaningful way and to cement their individual relationships with her by spending designated private time with her. The only negative in this marvel of collective caring was its mildly unsettling effect on those of the thirty participants who had no family nearby and nothing like Esther's vast network of friends. These women couldn't help wondering who was going to take care of *them* when they become infirm.

Good question and one that all of us should be asking ourselves. Few people possess Esther's remarkable gift for friendship or her talent to inspire devotion from the community that rallied around her at the end. In friendship, as in life, we sow what we reap. Now, while you're still healthy, consider establishing a support group of mutual friends and have everyone pledge to swing into action when one of your group becomes ill or incapacitated.

(P.S. Besides Nahama and her husband, sixteen friends of Esther chipped in to cover the costs of her funeral.)

The Friends of Jim Club

A recent *Dear Abby* column featured a letter from a man whose friend, Jim, was a stroke victim. It said Jim was being cared for by his wife, who had confided to the letter writer how disappointed and hurt she'd been that none of Jim's friends had ever followed through on their offers of assistance. The wife's complaint had inspired the letter writer to organize the Friends of Jim Club, a bunch of guys who each spend two hours a month with their stricken friend. The wife, who had been holding down a full-time job, taking care of Jim, and also doing all the cooking and household chores, now has the FOJ Club supplying her with back-up troops. Different friends visit Jim regularly on different days while his wife is able to book a haircut in advance, make a lunch date with a friend, or just take a nap. Two hours a month isn't too much to ask of anyone. If you know a convalescent or caregiver who needs that kind of support right now, why not send around an e-mail blast and launch your Friends of _____ Club today?

Kimberly Allison's Gurus

Kim appointed a number of her friends, whom she calls "gurus," to help her cope with the effects of her cancer ordeal—a double mastectomy, six months of chemo, debilitating meds, and exhausting radiation. One friend served as her cancer-health guru, another chose her music, still another counseled her on postcancer fashion and makeup, and one was in charge of her nutrition and exercise. Kim also arranged for friends of her parents to check on *them* regularly, which eliminated the stress she might otherwise have felt about *their* well-being. When you organize a gaggle of gurus for your sick friend, don't forget to consider your own special competencies.

Margy Hirsch's Rosh Hodesh Group

In some Jewish communities women meet in small groups on the first day of each month of the Hebrew calendar to share personal stories, study sacred texts, discuss religious or philosophical issues, and perform or create life-cycle ceremonies or holiday rituals. As soon as Margy's Rosh Hodesh group heard that she was scheduled to have a bilateral mastectomy, they decided to create a healing ceremony for her that featured songs, poetry, and prayers honoring Margy's special spiritual affinity for water as a source of life and her origins on the High Plains of Kansas. The women lit candles, meditated together, made a circle around Margy as they touched her arms or shoulders, sang *Mi She-bairach* (the traditional Jewish prayer for healing), and ended with a vegetarian meal. Like Colette's friends, members of Margy's group signed up for a chemo day, but instead of taking her to her treatments, on their assigned day they each brought dinner to her family. As described in *Lilith* magazine, the efforts of Margy's Rosh Hodesh group "decreased her fear [and] helped her know that no matter what happened with her cancer, she wasn't going to be alone."

Pat Koch Thaler's "Village"

Nine years ago Pat made a full recovery from kidney cancer only to be diagnosed in May 2012 with a rare lung tumor that required surgery, chemo, and radiation. Today there's a list of thirteen names and phone numbers near Pat's phone headed, "It Takes a Village." They are her friends at Cedar Crest, a retirement community of fifteen hundred residents, who've promised to give Pat whatever help she needs. Members of her "village" have brought Pat dinner when she was too tired to go to the community restaurant, picked up groceries for her when she was too weak to shop, left goodies on her doorstop, and called to check on her. One day when she was feeling woozy, they took turns sitting with her for hours at a time. The list also shows six names under the heading, "Available for driving." One of those six friends recently drove Pat to the ER when she suffered an atrial fibrillation and stayed with her until she was released. Eight months after her surgery Pat e-mailed me to say, "I am slowly recovering my strength, and my friends are still driving me around."

The Fab Five

For a decade or so five friends who live in different cities have been part of an intense (and intensely entertaining) discussion group that, in a burst of midlife self-congratulation, dubbed itself The Fab Five. I'm one of them. Our members keep in touch by e-mail throughout the year, but our primary purpose is to come together at two weekend retreats—one in winter, one in summer—to discuss in depth every aspect of our lives: personal and family issues, health problems, work hurdles, short-term worries and long-term goals, as well as events transpiring in the larger world. We have served as each other's steam valves and sounding boards during benchmark moments typical of "women of a certain age." During these years two of our members retired from high-profile careers and had to decide what to do with the rest of their lives, two have fought cancer, a third had a serious heart problem and an ailing husband. Two of us rode the emotional roller coaster of our children's divorces. One has watched a sibling descend into Alzheimer's. Others of us have dealt with the struggles of a troubled grandchild and several aging relatives.

When the cancer she'd been battling for years finally made her too sick to travel, one of our members missed three weekend retreats in a row, but we brought her into our circle each Saturday morning by having her participate in our discussions via a speakerphone set up on the coffee table. For about a half an hour, or as long as her strength held up, she chimed in on every subject, as her bleak medical prognosis, though alarming to us, not having dulled her spirit or destroyed her inveterate optimism.

The following year, sensing a serious regression in her condition, four of us broke with our customary semiannual schedule and went to visit our sick friend in April. By then we hadn't seen her in more than eighteen months. Though mentally lucid, perfectly coiffed, and brimming with her customary vim and vinegar, the physical change in her was unnerving. She'd become an invalid—fragile, stooped, swollen from steroids, and leaning on a walker. Her bony arms and legs bore black-and-blue splotches that attested to her many fractures, intravenous punctures, and pressure bruises. She and I had always been the same height, five-foot-four; we used to laugh about being two shrimps among three giraffes. This time, however, when I went to hug her, even I had to bend over, as if stooping to say good-bye to a child. We four visitors managed to hold our smiles until the elevator door closed behind us. Then one of us burst into tears and we all fell apart.

That June our friend was on the speakerphone just long enough to report on her deteriorating condition. The pain in her back, pelvis, and legs was excruciating. The drugs that once worked were no longer effective. She was about to embark on yet another experimental treatment protocol, her last best hope. Awed by her intrepid fortitude, we cheered her on.

When I called her a few weeks later she sounded awful. "Please tell the others I can't do it anymore," she said. "Can't talk. Can't do e-mail. It's not just you guys; it's everyone. Sometimes the pain's so intense, I want to die."

At our December retreat the voice on the speakerphone was her daughter's. "Morphine drip," she said. "Palliative care. Just trying to make her comfortable."

Three months later the Fab Five became the Fab Four. With time, we know, another will fall by the wayside, then another and another, until only one of us is left standing. Meanwhile, we remain old friends who cherish our semiannual weekends secure in the knowledge that as long as we last, we'll face our individual setbacks together.

||||||||||||||||||||||||

IT'S A CLICHÉ TO CLAIM that one has learned a lot from cancer. Then again, a cliché by any other name is just a fact told once too often. This much I know I owe to my illness: it taught me the blessings of silence despite my natural instinct to fill empty air. It taught me to fly reconnaissance before bombarding someone with help. It taught me to pay very close attention to sick people's signals—that there's a time when they want special attention and a time when the kindest thing you can do is to confer upon them the honor of the ordinary and treat them like anyone else. It taught me to Ask and Act when I'm with a sick friend and to clearly convey what I need when I'm the patient. Above all, it taught me the importance of telling each other the truth.

Here's hoping you and your friends will do the same.

ACKNOWLEDGMENTS

AS MY DEDICATION PAGE SUGGESTS, I'm deeply grateful to all those (named and pseudonymous) who were willing to confide in me about two of the most intimate aspects of any person's life: relationships and illness. This book would be much the poorer without their stories.

It might not exist at all if not for the efforts of my masterful agent, David Kuhn, and his inspired editorial guidance.

I also owe an immense debt of gratitude to my writer daughters, Abigail and Robin, each of whom read the manuscript not once but twice and whose comments, suggestions, additions (and deletions) improved this book immeasurably at key stages of its development.

In Lisa Kaufman, I have found the ideal editor—a woman of refined intelligence and sophisticated literary sensibilities who gently steered the book into its final port.

Appreciation to Phyllis Wender for her friendship over more than five decades but especially for her selfless devotion, kindness and understanding during these last few years.

And, as always, thanks to my husband Bert for his unconditional love and for never complaining about the hours I spend at my computer.

APPENDIX: RESOURCES

|||||||||||||||||||||||||||||||||||||||||||||||||||||||||||||||||||||||||||||||||||||||||||||||||||||||||||||||

RECOMMENDED READING: NONFICTION

||||||||||||||||||||||||||||||||||||||||||||||||||||||||||||||||

The Etiquette of Illness: What To Say When You Can't Find the Words by Susan Halpern (Bloomsbury, 2004). Anecdotes, advice, and insights by a psychotherapist who herself has survived lymphoma. Seven helpful chapters include "Acts of Kindness" and "Talking to Children About Illness and Death."

Passages in Caregiving: Turning Chaos into Confidence by Gail Sheehy (Harper Paperback, 2011). Inspired by her many years of caring for her husband, Clay Felker, the legendary editor of *New York* magazine, Sheehy, author of the best-seller *Passages*, has produced a comprehensive handbook packed with solid advice and practical strategies.

Share the Care: How to Organize a Group to Care for Someone Who Is Seriously Ill by Cappy Capossella and Sheila Warnock (order at www.share thecare.org). A step-by-step guide to creating a nurturing, effective support group of friends and relatives who want to be helpful to someone who is ill, disabled, or dying. The book is based on the personal experiences of the two authors and ten other women who united to take care of a terminally ill friend. Although most were strangers to one another, they functioned as a well-oiled care-giving collective for more than three years and evolved a system that you and your friends can easily replicate.

Do Good: 201 Ways to Lend a Hand by Marcy Silverman and Cindy Sacks (Andrews McMeel Publishing, 2009). One or two sentences per page. Common-sense ideas ranging from "Send a care package: Florida oranges" to "Find what's broken and fix it." One of the authors was moved to produce this little paperback after her husband was diagnosed with Lou Gehrig's disease.

The End of Your Life Book Club by Will Schwalbe (Knopf, 2012). A memoir of Schwalbe's wide-ranging, super-smart conversations with his dying mother, Mary

Anne, about literature, which led to conversations about everything else—courage, human rights, faith, devotion, gratitude, and love. Let it inspire you to create your own two-person book club with a sick friend.

Help Me Live: 20 Things People with Cancer Want You to Know by Lori Hope (Celestial Arts, Revised, 2011). A lung cancer survivor writes intimately about her druthers and that of other patients. Each chapter title is a direct quote related to its subject matter—for instance, "I need to laugh—or just forget about cancer for a while!" And "I want compassion, not pity."

The Council of Dads: A Story of Family, Friendship and Learning How to Live by Bruce Feiler (Harper Perennial, 2010). The author of the best-seller *Walking the Bible* describes his grueling medical struggles and how a group of remarkable men came through in meaningful ways for him, his wife, and twin daughters.

All Gone—A Memoir of My Mother's Dementia. With Refreshments by Alex Witchel (Riverhead Books, 2012). A candid, wrenching, often funny account of how a vibrant, dynamic woman began "disappearing in plain sight" and how her daughter coped with depression, isolation, and despair, often by cooking family recipes.

My Breast by Joyce Wadler (Pocket Books, 1997). An upbeat but fiercely honest memoir of the author's bout with breast cancer and its impact on her life.

RECOMMENDED READING: FICTION

|||||||||||||||||||||||||||||||||||||||||||||||||||||||||||||||||||||||||

Talk Before Sleep by Elizabeth Berg (Ballantine Paperback, 2006). This luminous novel should be required reading for anyone who knows someone who's seriously ill or dying. In lyrical, often hilarious scenes Berg shows what happens when Ruth gets a rabid form of cancer and her dear friend, Ann, along with three other lovable, idiosyncratic pals, helps her face the end with dignity, humor, and strength.

Crossing to Safety by Wallace Stegner (Modern Library paperback, 2002). A beautifully written story about the enduring friendship of two couples over the course of their long, full lives, including when illness and death challenge their relationships.

ONLINE RESOURCES

||||||||||||||||||||||||||||||||||||||

CaringBridge. An excellent online tool for networking, information, and communication between and among friends of the patient (www.caringbridge.org).

CarePages. Referrals, discussion forums, and free patient blogs connect friends and family during a health challenge (www.CarePages.com).

Share the Care. Offers step-by-step instructions to help you organize a nurturing group of supportive friends and other partners who are committed to caring for someone who is terminally ill; chronically ill; disabled; ill with cancer, AIDS, ALS, or Alzheimer's; recuperating from a serious injury; or elderly and in need of assistance. Trains health care professionals and faith-based and community agencies on how to "create a unique caregiver 'family' from friends, relatives, neighbors, co-workers and acquaintances." Provides educational materials useful to health professionals and clergy members to help them help caregivers who often feel isolated and overwhelmed by the illness of a friend or family member (http://www .sharethecare.org).

Diva Living with AIDS. Rae Lewis Thornton, a motivational speaker and writer, chronicles her experiences with full-blown AIDS on her blog (www.raelewisthorn ton.com).

Funny You Don't Look Sick: An Autobiography of Illness. This documentary film by and about Susan Abod shows what it's like to live with Chronic Fatigue Syndrome and multiple chemical sensitivities and thus can help you become a better friend to those similarly afflicted (http://susanabod.com/funny-you -dont-look-sick-an-autobiography-of-an-illness/).

Get free stuff. Wigs, hats, make-up, housecleaning, transportation, and more at www.breastcancerfreebies.com.

27 Ways to Comfort a Sick Friend. (http://cms.carepages.com/CarePages/en /ArticlesTips/HelpfulTips/BetterYou/comfort_sick_friend.html).

A Sampling of Illness Blog Posts at WikiHow that are neither authoritative nor substantive but occasionally contain a useful tip or two (www.WikiHow .com). For instance:

- http://www.wikihow.com/Help-a-Really-Sick-Friend-or-Relative
- http://www.wikihow.com/Make-a-Care-Package-for-a-Sick
  -Friend%22
- http://www.wikihow.com/Hang-Out-with-a-Sick-Friend

RESOURCES TO HELP YOU SUPPORT
A DEPRESSED OR SUICIDAL FRIEND

I can't vouch for their reliability, but here are a few sites you might check out:

- http://www.mayoclinic.com/health/depression/MH00016
- http://www.psychologytoday.com/blog/embracing-the-dark
  -side/200905/how-help-depressed-friend-and-when-stop-trying
  -part-1
- http://www.psychologytoday.com/blog/embracing-the-dark
  -side/200906/how-help-depressed-friend-and-when-stop-trying
  -part-2
- http://www.helpguide.org/mental/suicide_prevention.htm
- http://depression.about.com/cs/suicideprevent/a/suicidal.htm
- http://www.wikihow.com/Help-a-Friend-with-Depression
- The national suicide hotline is 800-273-TALK (8255)

RESOURCES TO HELP FRIENDS WHO ARE GRIEVING

How to Bring Food to Grieving Friends. Nine panels of solid, practical advice (http://www.beliefnet.com/Love-Family/Recipes/2008/09/How-to-Bring-Food-to
-Grieving-Friends.aspx).

Ambiguous Loss: Learning to Live with Unresolved Grief, by Pauline Boss (Harvard University Press, 2000). Strategies to cushion the pain and help friends come to terms with their grief over a divorce, miscarriage, mysterious disappearances, the trauma of war, a soldier missing in action, a loved one lost to Alzheimer's, and other situations in which there is no emotional closure.

The National Widowers' Organization. Provides a virtual toolkit for men coping with the loss of a loved one and a place where men can meet others going through the same transition (http://www.nationalwidowers.org/).

Sanity and Grace: A Journey of Suicide, Survival and Strength, by Judy Collins (Jeremy P. Tarcher/Penguin Books, 2003). The renowned singer/songwriter chronicles her journey from pain to peace of mind in the aftermath of her son's suicide and offers healing advice and heartfelt comfort to those who have experienced a loved one's untimely loss.

21 Ways to Help a Grieving Friend. A concise summary of the basics (http://www.beliefnet.com/Inspiration/2010/05/21-Ways-to-Help-a-Grieving-Friend.aspx).

RESOURCES TO HELP YOU HELP FRIENDS WHO ARE CAREGIVERS

You'd Better Not Die Or I'll Kill You: A Caregiver's Survival Guide to Keeping You in Good Health and Spirits by Jane Heller (Chronicle Books, 2012). Fulfills the promise of its subtitle.

The Alzheimer's Association website hosts blogs, a message center, updates on research and information for caregivers (http://www.alz.org).

The Well Spouse Association is an advocacy organization that serves the needs of people caring for a chronically ill and/or disabled spouse/partner (http://www.wellspouse.org/).

Loving Someone Who Has Dementia: How To Find Hope While Coping With Stress and Grief, by Pauline Boss (Jossey-Bass, 2011). Helps you understand the caregiver experience and guides you toward more sensitive, less enervating ways of tending to the dementia patient and those who take care of them.

The Caregiving Wife's Handbook: Caring for Your Seriously Ill Husband, Caring for Yourself, by Diana Denholm (Hunter House 2012). Lists fifty dos and don'ts to help make the task easier and less taxing. Major quibble: a better title would be *The Caregiver's Handbook.* Addressing this advice to women as if only wives take care of husbands and not vice versa?

The Care Organizer. This workbook will help caregivers keep track of emergency numbers, insurance information, daily medications, notes on doctor visits, tests, medical equipment, contact information for physicians and caregivers, and medical appointments. Includes an activities calendar and plastic pockets for receipts, bills, and business cards. (www.dana-farberfriendsplace.org/careorganizer.html)

FUNNY VIDEOS

IIIIIIIIIIIIIIIIIIIIIIIIIIIIII

The Laryngospasms. Sick people are capable of enjoying sick humor, especially when the joke's on *their* disease or on the surgical procedures, tests, and treatments we all love to hate. My pick for Best of Show in this genre is the music video sung to the tune of "Breaking Up Is Hard to Do," in which five real anesthesiologists, dressed in scrubs, belt out, "Waking Up Is Hard to Do." The group, which calls itself The Laryngospasms, harmonizes like the Four Freshmen while serenading a fake patient in what appears to be a real operating room. I've logged onto this video more than a dozen times, and it still has me grinning (nottotallyrad.blogspot.com/2009/11/waking-up-is-hard-to-do.html).

Bowser and Blue. You won't be able to keep a straight face while watching this Canadian comedy team, try to keep a straight face while crooning their "Ode to Proctologists." Who knew colonoscopy could be a laughing matter? (youtube.com/watch?v=_NOw2rORwSc). Sample stanza:

> *We praise the colorectal surgeon,*
> *Misunderstood and much maligned,*
> *Slaving away in the heart of darkness,*
> *Working where the sun don't shine.*

Stephen Lynch's "Gynecologist." Worth watching for lyrics like, "Next on my agenda/checking your pudenda" (youtube.com/watch?v=AeTfPcF7PtE).

CANCER HUMOR

||||||||||||||||||||||||||||||||

Because cancer was my disease *du jour* (and the most common affliction among my contemporaries), I gravitated to websites that hit that particular nail on the head. Here are a few of them:

"A Malignant Melanoma Walks into a Bar . . ." Features a brief video of comedian Nick Ross doing a number on his Hodgkin's lymphoma. When he invites his cancer to join him on stage, it turns out to be a bearded guy in a bathrobe (newsweek.com/2009/07/28/a-malignant-melanoma-walks-into-a-bar.html).

"Cancertainment." (planetcancer.org) Includes games, comics, videos, music, shows, poems, jokes, and riddles. Sample: One of the top ten reasons to date a cancer patient? *Recreational drugs are paid for by insurance.* One of the top ten pick-up lines for cancer patients? *Is that a chemo pump in your pocket or are you just happy to see me?* One of the top ten signs you've joined a cheap HMO? *Annual breast exams are conducted at Hooters.* Ouch!

I'm Too Young for This! Cancer Foundation. Lists free stuff, social networking activities, adventure retreats, chat rooms, forums, blogs, camping excursions, fertility advocacy, peer counseling, scholarships, financial aid, and where people under forty can find the best happy hours (www.stupidcancer.com).

Illness Blogs. If your sick friend isn't the type to be fazed by raw candor and ribald language, turn them on to some of the cool blogs written by young patients:

- **"What's Up Your Butt?"** by Megan (who has stage III colon cancer) (shortcolon.blogspot.com)

- **"I Am Not an Asshole. Surgically Speaking,"** by Becca (colon cancer) (thecolonchronicles.blogspot.com)

- **"My Blood Hates Me,"** by Matt (leukemia) (hatefulblood. blogspot.com)

- **"I've Still Got Both My Nuts: The Superman Cancer-slayer,"** by Benjamin Rubenstein (Ewing's sarcoma and bone marrow cancer, both before he turned twenty-one (www.cancerslayerblog.com)

- *"Making Cancer My Bitch"* by Ryan (Hodgkin's lymphoma) (igotthe cancer.blogspot.com)

- *"Cancer is Hilarious"* by Kaylin, includes a link to the online cancer comic book *Terminally Illin'* (cancerisnotfunny.blogspot.com)

- *"The Stupid Cancer Show,"* an Internet radio program, is co-hosted by young adult survivors Matthew Zachary and Lisa Bernhard every Monday night (blogtalkradio.com/stupidcancershow)

OTHER RESOURCES MENTIONED IN THIS BOOK

Words with Friends. Great game to play with a sick friend. Available on Facebook, Android, or http://www.zyngawithfriends.com/wp/category/blog/.

Portable metal ramp for handicap access: www.portable-wheelchair-ramps.com/Wheelchair_Ramps/signature_suitcase_ramps.aspx.

Alice B. Toklas's "haschich fudge." Recipe for a unique (albeit illegal) edible gift for friends suffering intolerable pain or loss of appetite due to extreme nausea or side effects of their treatments (www.subrosa.arbre.us/SubRosaBrownies.html).

Turning Heads Project. Dedicated to enhancing self-image, boosting confidence, and changing perceptions of what it means to lose your hair as a result of chemotherapy. Provides free professional photo shoots, including makeup and styling as well as access to an online community for anyone who has lost his or her hair as a result of cancer treatments (http://turningheadsproject.org).

Finding the Right Words. Article by Elinor Lipman (*Good Housekeeping,* December 2010).

INDEX

Nadine Markova

LETTY COTTIN POGREBIN is an award-winning journalist, widely published opinion writer, acclaimed public speaker, admired political activist, and author of several nonfiction bestsellers, including *Growing Up Free, Getting Over Getting Older,* and *Deborah, Golda, and Me.* Her last book was a novel, *Three Daughters.* She lives in New York.

PublicAffairs is a publishing house founded in 1997. It is a tribute to the standards, values, and flair of three persons who have served as mentors to countless reporters, writers, editors, and book people of all kinds, including me.

I. F. Stone, proprietor of *I. F. Stone's Weekly*, combined a commitment to the First Amendment with entrepreneurial zeal and reporting skill and became one of the great independent journalists in American history. At the age of eighty, Izzy published *The Trial of Socrates*, which was a national bestseller. He wrote the book after he taught himself ancient Greek.

Benjamin C. Bradlee was for nearly thirty years the charismatic editorial leader of *The Washington Post*. It was Ben who gave the *Post* the range and courage to pursue such historic issues as Watergate. He supported his reporters with a tenacity that made them fearless and it is no accident that so many became authors of influential, best-selling books.

Robert L. Bernstein, the chief executive of Random House for more than a quarter century, guided one of the nation's premier publishing houses. Bob was personally responsible for many books of political dissent and argument that challenged tyranny around the globe. He is also the founder and longtime chair of Human Rights Watch, one of the most respected human rights organizations in the world.

·　　·　　·

For fifty years, the banner of Public Affairs Press was carried by its owner Morris B. Schnapper, who published Gandhi, Nasser, Toynbee, Truman, and about 1,500 other authors. In 1983, Schnapper was described by *The Washington Post* as "a redoubtable gadfly." His legacy will endure in the books to come.

Peter Osnos, *Founder and Editor-at-Large*